INTRODUCTION

For years I struggled to believe in my worth, my capabilities, my strength. And on many occasions I failed to meet the test. Because I didn't understand the source of all strength and goodness, I turned to men first and then to alcohol and drugs. I expected to find my security but found instead an even deeper level of despair. And then, seven years ago, I found Al-Anon which nudged open the door to a new way of life. A year later I found A.A. and the door swung wide.

The program has given me roots where none existed before. It has given me courage to dare to do that which I shuddered before in years gone by. It has given me a sense of belonging to the human race. I no longer feel that I'm outside of the fish bowl looking in.

And the additional and very fortunate gift which has accompanied my program involvement is friendship with women. For years I had been leery of women, assuming they were after my boyfriends, husband and lovers. I was always quite certain that women were not to be trusted. Coming together with women in meetings, hearing how much alike we all are, eased my anxieties. But more importantly, it offered me the opportunity to love women as sisters, as equal travelers on our parallel spiritual journeys.

From so many women these last few years I've received "just the message I needed at the time." The more I've learned to turn in a woman's direction as she speaks, the greater my desire has grown to "hear" what women in all walks of life, all experiences, all times in history have said. Thus, it seemed only fitting when I wrote this book to let the wise words of many women, close at hand and far away, some recovering, some still suffering, some free from any particular struggles but who struggled nonetheless, set the tone for a book that speaks to us all. I've taken the liberty to quote from women who represent the full spectrum of womanhood, believing that much spoken by any one of us is sacred, meaning-ful and necessary to the fuller development of at least one person someplace in time.

I wrote the meditations to complement the quote chosen for each day. So often I've needed to hear "the right message" in order to move forward when inside I was all a jitter—something to center on which could invite the Spirit within to take charge for me. I hope these meditations may bridge whatever gap exists, on any one day in your life, between you and your Spirit. Their sole intent is to make life easier for you; to give you hope when all seems lost. Please accept each day's meditation as an offering of my hand to you. I've learned that when we travel together, nothing is too great for us to bear. And each day can be a new beginning.

I want to offer my thanks to all women for making this book possible. The efforts of the women all around me to live, to survive, to succeed, gave me strength to push ahead one day at a time.

I offer a special thanks to a woman friend and excellent editor who smoothed the rough spots so these words could touch your life in a more certain way. To my family, friends and spouse I say thanks for being patient when my writing took precedence over all else. My need was great to write a book that I believed was needed by my sister travelers on this journey we share.

January

JANUARY 1

We don't always understand the ways of Almighty God—the crosses
sent us, the sacrifices demanded . . . But we accept with faith and resignation
the holy will with no looking back, and we are at peace.
—Anonymous

Acceptance of our past, acceptance of the conditions presently in our lives that we cannot change, brings relief. It brings the peacefulness we so often, so frantically, seek.

We can put the past behind us. Each day is a new beginning. And each day of abstinence offers us the chance to look ahead with hope. A power greater than ourselves helped us to find this program. That power is ever with us. When we fear facing new situations, or when familiar situations turn sour, we can look to that power for help in saying what needs to be said and for doing what needs to be done. Our higher power is as close as our breath. Conscious awareness of its presence strengthens us, moment by moment.

The past is gone. Today is full of possibilities.
With each breath I will be aware of the strength at hand.

MY THOUGHTS FOR THE DAY

I believe that true identity is found . . . in creative activity springing from within. It is found, paradoxically, when one loses oneself. Woman can best refind herself by losing herself in some kind of creative activity of her own.
—ANNE MORROW LINDBERGH

Creative activity might mean bird watching, tennis, quilting, cooking, painting, writing. Creative activity immerses us fully in the here and now, and at the same time it frees us. We become one with the activity and are nourished by it. We grow as the activity grows. We learn who we are in the very process of *not thinking about* who we are.

Spirituality and creativity are akin. There is an exhilaration rooted deep within us that is a lifeline to God. Creative activity releases the exhilaration, and the energy goes through us and out to others. We find ourselves and our higher power through the loss of our self-conscious selves while creating—a picture, a sentence, a special meal.

Creativity is a given. It is another dimension of the spiritual presence guiding us all. I'll get out of its way today.

M Y   T H O U G H T S   F O R   T H E   D A Y

....

....

....

....

....

....

....

....

....

J A N U A R Y   3

Like an old gold-panning prospector, you must resign yourself
to digging up a lot of sand from which you will later
patiently wash out a few minute particles of gold ore.
—DOROTHY BRYANT

Sometimes we feel buried in sand, blocked, clogged, unable to move. Then we must remember that we are not alone. Help is at hand, if only we will ask for it. If we invoke our higher power, our source of spiritual strength can help us to believe that there is gold somewhere in all this sand, and that the sand itself is useful.

No one and no thing is good all the time. Let us remember that if we expect nothing but gold, we are distorting life, getting in our own way. We don't want to falsify the texture of our lives; the homespun quality helps us to appreciate the gold when it appears.

I will find some gold among the sand, today.

M Y   T H O U G H T S   ❧   F O R   T H E   D A Y

....

....

....

....

....

....

....

....

....

JANUARY 4

*Once I knew that I wanted to be an artist, I had made myself into one. I did not
understand that wanting doesn't always lead to action. Many of the women had
been raised without the sense that they could mold and shape their own lives,
and so, wanting to be an artist (but without the ability to realize their wants)
was, for some of them, only an idle fantasy, like wanting to go to the moon.*
—JUDY CHICAGO

There are probably not many of us, in this recovery program, who grappled with life as
straight on as Judy Chicago did. It is likely we didn't understand that we could mold and
shape our lives. How lucky we are to be learning that now with the help of the Twelve Steps
and one another. Each day we are confronted with many opportunities to make responsible
choices, reasonable decisions. These choices and decisions are the molders, the shapers, of
who we are becoming. Our identity as women is strengthened each time we thoughtfully
make a choice. The action we take through making each choice gives our identity more substance—our wholeness as women is guaranteed through these choices.

*Many opportunities to make choices will arise today.
I can be thoughtful and make choices that will lead to my greater wholeness.*

MY THOUGHTS FOR THE DAY

....

....

....

....

....

....

....

J A N U A R Y   5

Instead of concentrating on why we can't do a thing, we would be
wise to change our "Yes, but . . ." attitude to a more positive one.
Saying "yes" means I really do want to change my life for the better.
—LIANE CORDES

We truly can do these things that are our "hearts' pure desires." However, most of us look at the whole task and feel overwhelmed. We need, instead, to look at the task's many parts. One part at a time, one day at a time, we can accomplish any goal we set for ourselves. I know a recovering woman who wrote a 300-page dissertation, the final achievement to obtain her Ph.D. When asked at a meeting how she ever did it, her reply was, "One word at a time." That's wonderful advice. No matter how many goals were missed or plans dashed when we were still using, now that we are recovering, each of us can do whatever is in our hearts—if we do it little by little, not all at once, today.

Today, I will do one small task that will contribute
toward the achievement of a life goal.

M Y   T H O U G H T S   *❀*   F O R   T H E   D A Y

....

....

....

....

....

....

....

....

J A N U A R Y   6

There are as many ways to live and grow as there are people.
Our own ways are the only ways that should matter to us.
—EVELYN MANDEL

Wanting to control other people, to make them live as we'd have them live, makes the attainment of serenity impossible. And serenity is the goal we are seeking in this recovery program, in this life.

We are each powerless over others, which relieves us of a great burden. Controlling our own behavior is a big enough job. Learning to behave responsibly takes practice. Most of us in this recovery program have behaved irresponsibly for much of our lives. Emotional immaturity is slow to depart, but every responsible action we take gives us the courage for another—and then another. Our own fulfillment is the by-product of the accumulation of our own responsible actions. Others' actions need not concern us.

Today, I will weigh my behavior carefully.
Responsible behavior builds gladness of heart.

M Y   T H O U G H T S   F O R   T H E   D A Y

JANUARY 7

The greatest gift we can give one another is
rapt attention to one another's existence.
—SUE ATCHLEY EBAUGH

We all want to matter to others. Very often in the past—and sometimes in the present—our behavior has screamed for the attention we seek from others. Perhaps, instead of trying to get attention, we ought to give it. The program tells us we have to give it away in order to keep it. Wisdom of the ages also dictates that in life there are no accidents. Those people close to us and those just passing through our lives have reason to be there. Giving attention to another's humanity is our calling.

I will fully attend to another person I have occasion to be with today.
She will matter to me, and my attention will matter to her.

MY THOUGHTS FOR THE DAY

JANUARY 8

*When people make changes in their lives in a certain area, they may start by
changing the way they talk about that subject, how they act about it, their
attitude toward it, or an underlying decision concerning it.*
—JEAN ILLSLEY CLARKE

Acting "as if" is powerful. It leads the way to a changed attitude, a changed woman. If
we are self-conscious in crowds and fearful about meeting new people and yet act poised
and extend our hands in friendship, we'll not only behave in a new way, but feel good about
it, too. Each act we take in this way brings us closer to the woman we are behaving like. Each
positive change we make builds our self-esteem. Realizing that through our own actions we
are becoming the kind of women we admire gives us the strength, in fact, encourages the
excitement in us that's needed to keep changing. Making positive changes in our lives is the
stuff that comprises self-esteem. Each gain makes the next one easier to attempt.

*I will accept an opportunity today to act "as if"
I can handle a situation I used to run from.*

MY   THOUGHTS   FOR   THE   DAY

....

....

....

....

....

....

....

....

JANUARY 9

The Chinese say that water is the most powerful element, because it is perfectly nonresistant. It can wear away a rock and sweep all before it.
—FLORENCE SCOVEL SHINN

Nonresistance, ironically, may be a posture we struggle with. Nonresistance means surrendering the ego absolutely. For many of us, the ego, particularly disguised as false pride, spurred us on to struggle after struggle. "Can't they see I'm right?" we moaned, and our resistance only created more of itself. Conversely, flowing with life, "bubbling" with the ripples, giving up our ego, releases from us an energy that heals the situation—that smooths the negative vibrations in our path. Peace comes to us. We will find serenity each time we willingly humble ourselves.

Resistance is more familiar. Nonresistance means growth and peace.
I'll try for serenity today.

M Y   T H O U G H T S   F O R   T H E   D A Y

....

....

....

....

....

....

....

....

....

*A complete revaluation takes place in your physical and
mental being when you've laughed and had some fun.*
—CATHERINE PONDER

Norman Cousins, in his book *Anatomy of an Illness*, describes how he cured his fatal illness with laughter. Laughter recharges our entire being; every cell is activated. We come alive, and full vitality restores us physically and emotionally. Many of us need both emotional and physical healing, but perhaps we've overlooked the times to laugh because we've been caught in a negative posture.

Unfortunately, negativity becomes habitual for many of us. However, it's never too late to turn our lives around, to laugh instead of complain. Choosing to see the bright side of life, to laugh at our mistakes, lessens our pain, emotional and physical. Laughter encourages wellness. It is habit-forming and, better yet, contagious. Bringing laughter to others can heal them as well.

We all want health and happiness in ourselves and others, and we can find it by creating it. The best prescription for whatever ails us may well be a good laugh.

Today I'll seek out those chances to dispense a little medicine.

M Y   T H O U G H T S   FOR   T H E   D A Y

J A N · U A R Y   1 1

*Fear is only an illusion. It is the illusion that creates the feeling of
separateness—the false sense of isolation that exists only in your imagination.*
—JERALDINE SAUNDERS

We are one. We are connected, interdependent parts of the whole. We are not separate from each other except in the mind, in our false understanding of reality. As we come to understand our connectedness, our need for one another to complete the whole of creation, our fears will die.

It is often said we learn who we really are by closely observing our behavior toward the people in our lives. We meet ourselves in those others. They are our reflections. They are, perhaps, parts we ourselves have not yet learned to love. The program's message is to trust, to have faith; our higher power is in control. We are faced with no person, no situation too big to handle if we trust the program, if we remember the connections among us all.

*I will look around today at others, with knowledge of our oneness.
Fearing not, I will smile upon the wholeness of life.*

M Y   T H O U G H T S   FOR   T H E   D A Y

....

....

....

....

....

....

....

....

JANUARY 12

It isn't sufficient to seek wholeness through men,
it never was and it never will be for any woman, married or single.
—PATRICIA O'BRIEN

Most of us were encouraged from childhood on to "find a husband." The message, often subtle, was nonetheless there. And many of us did marry. However, no relationship carries a lifetime guarantee. Pinning our hopes on another person keeps us dependent; it keeps us in a "holding pattern." It keeps us from making those choices tailored to who we are and who we want to be.

Our recovery as women is closely aligned with our growth in decision making, our choosing responsible behavior and activities, our personal achievement. We do, each of us, need to discover our own wholeness. We need to celebrate our personhood. We need to cheer one another on as women recovering from an addictive past, as worthwhile women in full measure.

I will respect my wholeness today. I will help another woman nurture hers.

MY THOUGHTS 🌿 FOR THE DAY

....

....

....

....

....

....

....

....

J A N U A R Y   1 3

I want, by understanding myself, to understand others. I want to be all that
I am capable of becoming . . . This all sounds very strenuous and serious.
But now that I have wrestled with it, it's no longer so.
I feel happy—deep down. All is well.
—KATHERINE MANSFIELD

All is well. In the midst of turmoil, let us remember, all is well; in the midst of the pain of self-awareness, all is well. The struggle of the turmoil, the pain that accompanies the lessons of self-awareness, are preparing us for becoming all we are meant to become. We each have a special gift to offer in this life. We will come to understand those gifts and be able to give them as we grow with the pain of self-understanding. All is well. Deep down happiness ripples; it's rippling to the surface of our lives.

My lesson for today is understanding, of myself and others.
Happiness is the grade I earn each day of my "becoming."

M Y   T H O U G H T S   F O R   T H E   D A Y

....

....

....

....

....

....

....

....

JANUARY 14

*In a culture where approval/disapproval has become the predominant
regulator of effort and position, and often the substitute for love,
our personal freedoms are dissipated.*
—VIOLA SPOLIN

Wanting others to approve our efforts, our appearance, our aspirations and behavior is perfectly normal, certainly not unhealthy. However, needing the approval in order to proceed with our lives is.

In early childhood we are taught to obey others and to please them. We confuse love with approval, and we begin to march to someone else's drum. Then we get even more approval. But soon we get out of step with ourselves; we neglect our personal needs and become puppets.

Giving away our power to the whims of others weakens our Spirit. Personal freedom means choosing our own behavior; it means acting rather than reacting. It also means allowing ourselves the full adventure of living, of meeting each moment wholly, of responding in a pure, spontaneous, personally honest manner. Only then can we give to life what is ours to give.

Each of us has a unique part to play in the drama of life. And we need to rely on our higher power for our cues, not on those whose approval we think we need. When we turn within for guidance, all the approval we could hope for will be ours.

*I will be free today. I will let no one control my actions. I will let God give
the only approval that counts. Aligning my will with God's will guarantees it.*

MY THOUGHTS 🌿 FOR THE DAY

....

....

....

....

....

JANUARY 15

Everything is so dangerous that nothing is really very frightening.
—GERTRUDE STEIN

Life is full of dangers and risks and challenges. We can choose to meet them fearfully or in a spirit of welcome. To choose fear, to say, "I won't take that risk because I might lose," is to prevent ourselves from ever winning. If we welcome the danger, the risk, or the challenge, we acknowledge that life is made up of losses as well as victories, of gains as well as pain.

Life holds the dangers as well as the rewards. We choose how we will act. Sometimes we may feel trapped in a cycle of fearfulness. If we examine our own part, will we find that we are neglecting to take a balanced view? Perhaps, through a fear of losing, we are missing many chances for satisfaction.

I will remember: I have the power to choose what
my attitude will be toward this day's offerings.

MY THOUGHTS ❧ FOR THE DAY

JANUARY 16

I feel we have picked each other from the crowd as fellow-travelers, for neither of us is to the other's personality the end-all and the be-all.
—JOANNA FIELD

We must look around at the people in our lives today, and know that we have something special to offer each of them, and they to us. We do travel separate paths together. We may need to learn tolerance; perhaps a friend's behavior pushes us to be more tolerant. Impatience may be our nemesis, and everywhere we turn are long lines and traffic jams. Our experiences with others aren't chance. Fellow travelers are carefully selected by the inner self, the spiritual guide who understands our needs in this life.

We are both the teachers and the pupils. We need both our friends and those we may label our enemies for what they can help us learn.

I will carefully look about me today with gladness at the travelers I've selected to learn from.

MY THOUGHTS ❦ FOR THE DAY

....

....

....

....

....

....

....

....

She lacks confidence, she craves admiration insatiably. She lives on the
reflections of herself in the eyes of others. She does not dare to be herself.
—ANAÏS NIN

How aptly these words describe the woman so many of us were. Many activities were not attempted, courses weren't taken, conversations weren't initiated because we lacked confidence. The pain, the constant search for acceptance and love in the eyes and behavior of others, still haunts us. But those days are past. We are daring to be ourselves, one day at a time.

Confidence still wavers on occasion, and we may need assurance that we're lovable. Gratefully, we can look to one another for the additional boost we may need to face the day. Being there for one another, knowing that we understand each other's fears as women, offers the strength to go ahead that we may lack today or tomorrow.

Today a woman may need me to dare to be herself. I will be there.

M Y   T H O U G H T S   F O R   T H E   D A Y

JANUARY 18

*We are born in innocence. Corruption comes later. The first fear is a
corruption, the first reaching for a something that defies us. The first
nuance of difference, the first need to feel better than the different one,
more loved, stronger, richer, more blessed—these are corruptions.*
—LAURA Z. HOBSON

We are corrupted. To be human is to be corrupted. Our corruptions interfere with our happiness at the very time we are seeking happiness. When we think if only we were prettier, smarter, had a better job, then we'd be happy, we are giving in to corruptions. And these corruptions stifle our growth. We are each who we need to be. We have a supporting role in one another's lives. We can teach and learn from one another.

Recovery is choosing to help ourselves and one another to be as we are; to quit making comparisons; to understand our equality as women; to celebrate our differences, knowing they give intensity to life's colors for us all.

I can celebrate our special and different gifts today. My heart will be lightened.

MY THOUGHTS FOR THE DAY

....

....

....

....

....

....

....

....

JANUARY 19

The especial genius of women, I believe to be electrical in movement,
intuitive in function, spiritual in tendency.
—MARGARET FULLER

We are women, and we are moving, together and alone. We are moving into new images of ourselves. There is a healing power that comes from moving, from sharing one's ideas and changing one's self. And it is by trusting ourselves and trusting others that we bring harmony, thoughtfulness, and courage to all our actions.

Life holds many possibilities, and we are able to realize them when we risk changing ourselves through taking action. Those of us struggling to recover are taking action; we are changing ourselves. And as we listen to and support one another, we encourage the necessary changes in our sisters. As one is healed, we are all healed.

Today holds a special promise for me. I can be in harmony. I can share with others.
My courage will strengthen others, and others will strengthen me.

MY THOUGHTS ✿ FOR THE DAY

....

....

....

....

....

....

....

....

....

JANUARY 20

*The pain of leaving those you grow to love is only the
prelude to understanding yourself and others.*
—SHIRLEY MACLAINE

Life is a process of letting go, letting go of conditions we can't control, letting go of people—watching them move out of our lives, letting go of times, places, experiences. Leaving behind anyone or anyplace we have loved may sadden us, but it also provides us opportunities for growth we hadn't imagined. These experiences push us beyond our former selves to deeper understandings of ourselves and of others.

So often those experiences that sadden us, that trigger pain, are the best lessons life is able to offer. Experiencing the pain, surviving the pain that wrenches us emotionally, stretches us to new heights. Life is enriched by the pain. Our experiences with all other persons thereafter are deeper. Instead of dreading the ending of a time, the departure of a loved one, we must try to appreciate what we have gained already and know that life is fuller for it.

Today will bring both good-byes and hellos. I can meet both with gladness.

MY THOUGHTS FOR THE DAY

JANUARY 21

Too many activities, and people, and things. Too many worthy activities, valuable things, and interesting people. For it is not merely the trivial which clutters our lives but the important as well.
—ANNE MORROW LINDBERGH

We need interaction with others, and we need activities. We have many gifts to offer those who cross our paths, and we need the many gifts they have to offer us. But we soon have little to share, to give to others, if we neglect the special times, the empty spaces needed for nurturing the soul.

Some time away from people, activities, and things, some time away to commune with God, to seek guidance, to seek security in the fullest sense, will prepare us to better give our gifts to others. That time alone will also ready us to accept others' gifts to us.

It is true we find God's message in others. But the time alone with God lowers the barriers that too often prevent us from hearing another of God's messages as expressed through the friends and even foes who cross our paths.

My gift to myself is some time alone. I deserve that gift today and every day.

MY THOUGHTS FOR THE DAY

....

....

....

....

....

....

....

....

....

JANUARY 22

One cannot have wisdom without living life.
—DOROTHY MCCALL

Living life means responding, wholly, to our joys and our pitfalls. It means not avoiding the experiences or activities that we fear we can't handle. Only through our survival of them do we come to know who we really are; we come to understand the strength available to us at every moment. And that is wisdom.

When we approach life tentatively, we reap only a portion of its gifts. It's like watching a movie in black and white that's supposed to be in Technicolor. Our lives are in color, but we must have courage to let the colors emerge, to feel them, absorb them, be changed by them. Within our depths, we find our true selves. The complexities of life teach us wisdom. And becoming wise eases the many pitfalls in our path.

Living life is much more than just being alive.
I can choose to jump in with both feet. Wisdom awaits me in the depths.

MY THOUGHTS FOR THE DAY

....

....

....

....

....

....

....

....

JANUARY 23

She had trouble defining herself independently of her husband, tried to talk to him about it, but he said nonsense, he had no trouble defining her at all.
—CYNTHIA PROPPER SETON

To recover means to learn who we are, independent of friends, children, parents, or intimate partners. It means knowing how we want to spend our time, what books we like to read, what hobbies interest us, what our favorite foods are. It means understanding self-direction. It means charting a daily personal course and staying on it. It means defining our responsibilities and carrying them out.

Having an independent identity does not preclude depending on others for certain needs. Perhaps we revel in massage—both getting and giving. Maybe we share the expenses of a household or the responsibilities of raising children. Depending on others to meet their responsibilities does not negate our independent identity; it strengthens it. We choose where and when to be dependent. Healthy dependency complements healthy independence.

Recovery is giving me options. Each day gives me new opportunities.

MY THOUGHTS FOR THE DAY

....

....

....

....

....

....

....

....

JANUARY 24

I look in the mirror through the eyes of the child that was me.
—JUDY COLLINS

The child within each of us is fragile, but very much alive, and she interprets our experiences before we are even conscious of them. It is our child who may fear new places, unfamiliar people, strange situations. Our child needs nurturing, the kind she may not have received in the past. We can take her hand, coax her along, let her know she won't be abandoned. No new place, unfamiliar person, or strange situation need overwhelm her.

It's quite amazing the strength that comes to us when we nurture ourselves, when we acknowledge the scared child within and hold her, making her secure. We face nothing alone. Together, we can face anything.

I will take care of my child today and won't abandon her to face,
alone, any of the experiences the day may bring.

MY THOUGHTS FOR THE DAY

....

....

....

....

....

....

....

....

....

....

JANUARY 25

*The time of discipline began. Each of us the pupil of whichever
one of us could best teach what each of us needed to learn.*
—MARIA ISABEL BARRENO

When the pupil is ready, the teacher appears." Life's lessons often come unexpectedly. They come, nevertheless, and they come according to a time frame that is Divine. As we grow emotionally and spiritually, we are readied for further lessons for which teachers will appear. Perhaps the teacher will be a loving relationship, a difficult loss, or a truant child. The time of learning is seldom free from pain and questioning. But from these experiences and what they can teach us, we are ready to learn. As we are ready, they come.

We all enjoy the easy times when the sailing is smooth, when all is well, when we are feeling no pain. And these periods serve a purpose. They shore us up for the lessons which carry us to a stronger recovery, to a stronger sense of ourselves. To understand that all is well, throughout the learning process, is the basic lesson we need to learn. All is well. The teacher is the guide up the next rung of the ladder.

Let me be grateful for my lessons today and know that all is well.

MY THOUGHTS ❀ FOR THE DAY

....

....

....

....

....

....

....

....

JANUARY 26

You've got to get up every morning with a smile on your face,
And show the world all the love in your heart.
Then people gonna treat you better.
You're gonna find, yes, you will,
That you're beautiful as you feel.
—CAROLE KING

Act "as if." There's magic in behaving the way we want to be, even though we don't yet feel it. The behavior seems to lead the way. The attitude, the mental state, follows.

Many days we may not get up with love in our hearts for our family, our friends, our co-workers. We may, in fact, want them to show their love for us first. But if we reach out, give love unconditionally, focus on another's needs, love will return tenfold. And the act of loving them will lift our own spirits. We will know love; we will feel love for ourselves and the many other persons close to us.

The attitude we cultivate, whether one of love or selfishness, inferiority or superiority, will determine how the events of our lives affect us. The principle is so simple. If we meet life with love, with a smile, we'll find love and something to smile about.

My attitude will make this day what it becomes.
Meeting it head-on, with love, will assure me of a lovely day.

M Y   T H O U G H T S   *   F O R   T H E   D A Y

....

....

....

....

....

....

....

JANUARY 27

Surviving meant being born over and over.
—ERICA JONG

We have decided to live. And each day we make the decision anew. Each time we call a friend, work a Step, or go to a meeting, we are renewing our contract with life. We are being reborn. Before coming to this program we died, emotionally and spiritually, many times. Some of us nearly died physically. But here we are, starting a new day, looking for guidance from one another. We are the survivors. And survival is there for the taking.

We will have days when we struggle with our decision to live. We will want to throw in the towel. We will want to give in or give up. But we've learned from one another about choices. And the choice to survive, knowing we never have to do it alone, gets easier with time.

I am one of the survivors. Today is my day for celebration.

MY THOUGHTS FOR THE DAY

JANUARY 28

*I think self-awareness is probably the most important
thing towards being a champion.*
—BILLIE JEAN KING

Champions are made. How lucky we are to have the Steps to guide us to become champions. The program promises us self-awareness, but we have to put forth the effort. And the process isn't always easy. We have liabilities, all of us, and it's generally easier to see them than our assets. Self-awareness is recognizing both. To become a champion, whether as an athlete, a homemaker, a teacher, a secretary, or an attorney, is to maximize the assets and minimize the liabilities, but to accept the existence of both. The program that we share offers us daily opportunities to know ourselves, to help other women know themselves, and to strengthen our assets along the way. We can feel our assets growing, and it feels good. We can see our liabilities diminish, and it feels good. The program offers us a championship.

*I can strengthen my assets, first by knowing them, and then by
emphasizing them repeatedly. I'll focus on one today.*

MY THOUGHTS ❧ FOR THE DAY

....

....

....

....

....

....

....

....

....

JANUARY 29

"I can't help it" . . . that's what we all say when
we don't want to exert ourselves.
—Eva Lathbury

Irresponsible behavior is not unfamiliar to us. Passivity is equally familiar. In the past, excusing ourselves of all responsibility prevented us from being blamed. We have learned that it also prevented us from feeling worthy, from fulfilling our potential, from feeling the excitement that comes with achievement.

Our fear of failure helped us to be irresponsible. We may still fear failure, but the program offers us an antidote. We can't fail if we have turned our lives over to our higher power. We will be shown the way to proceed. Our fellow travelers have messages for us that will smooth our path.

I have chosen recovery. I have already said, "I can help it."
I will celebrate that I am taking responsibility for my life today.

MY THOUGHTS FOR THE DAY

JANUARY 30

Fortunately [psycho]analysis is not the only way to resolve inner conflicts.
Life itself still remains a very effective therapist.
—KAREN HORNEY

The passage of time, coupled with an openness to the messages gleaned from our conversations with others, can provide answers we need for the way out of painful situations. Life is ebb and flow, peaks and valleys, struggles and sweet times. What we fail to realize, all too often, is that the struggles make possible the times that are sweet.

Our conflicts are our special lessons in life. We can learn to flow with them, move through them, trust their value to us as growing, changing women. How good it feels to have found security with one another and that power greater than ourselves who can, when we are willing, show us the path to resolution.

Life will never be free of conflict—nor should it be. Our lessons move us to higher planes of awareness. We can experience the joy hidden within the conflict. We can help one another remember that the sweetness of a moment is tied to the pain of a former, forgotten moment.

All events, all experiences, are connected. The path I travel, alone and with others,
is bringing me brighter days. I will trust my path. It's right for me.

MY THOUGHTS FOR THE DAY

JANUARY 31

Woman must not accept; she must challenge. She must not be awed by that which has been built up around her; she must reverence that woman in her which struggles for expression.
—MARGARET SANGER

Our desire to grow, to make a place for ourselves in the world of our friends, to know that we have counted in the lives of others, is healthy and necessary to our existence as whole women. The inner urging to move ahead, to try a new approach to an old problem, to go after a new job, to learn a new skill, is evidence of God's eternal Spirit within.

Our meaning in this life is found through following the guidance that beckons us toward these new horizons, perhaps new friends, even new locations. We can trust the urge. We can reverence the urge. It will not lead us astray, provided we do not try to lead it. We each have a special gift to express in this life among those to whom we've been led.

For years, many of us quelled the inner urge out of fear; but, fortunately, it didn't desert us. To be human is to have a constant desire to be more than we are. The fears still come, but as we move through them, with the support of other women, other friends, the program gives us the thrill of achievement. We know there is meaning in our existence.

The need to grow, to change, to affect the world around us is part of God's plan for each of us. I will trust the urge; I will let it guide my steps.

MY THOUGHTS FOR THE DAY

....

....

....

....

....

....

....

February

FEBRUARY 1

*You were there when I needed you. You stood above all of the others
with your strength and you guided me. To each of you I offer
my being, my love and all that I am.*
—DEIDRA SARAULT

Each of us is guided while we act as guides to one another, throughout the day, throughout our lives. We are interdependent. Everywhere we look, someone is learning from us and we from her. We often know not what we give, when we give it. And we seldom realize the value of what we're receiving at the time we accept it.

Resistance to what another person is offering us may be our natural response. But the passage of time highlights the value of the experience. We can look for the comforters in our lives. They are there offering us strength and hope enough to see us through any difficulty.

We need both the rough times and the soft shoulders of a friend. They contribute equally to the designs our lives are weaving. The rough times press us to pray, to reach out to others for solace. And our pain gives others the chance to heal our wounds. We are all healers offering strength. And we all need healing.

One of the greatest gifts of my recovery is giving and receiving strength.

M Y   T H O U G H T S ❀ F O R   T H E   D A Y

....

....

....

....

....

....

....

....

FEBRUARY 2

What most of us want is to be heard, to communicate.
—DORY PREVIN

Our personhood is denied; the self we are presenting to the world is negated each time we speak, yet go unheard. "The greatest gift we can give one another is rapt attention." If we want attention, we must also give it. That means letting go of all extraneous thoughts when we're in conversation with someone. We cannot expect to get from others what we are unable or unwilling to give.

Being heard and hearing another person is more than just listening. It's letting ourselves be touched, in an intimate way, by the other's words. We don't want judgment, or shame, or to be discounted when we share who we are with another. We want to know that we have been intimately heard. And when we have a chance to hear another, we listen intently for the words meant for us, words that will stretch our womanhood and bring us closer to our inner selves as well.

The beauty of hearing each other is that it helps us to hear ourselves. We know better who we are when we listen to one another. Every conversation offers us a chance to be real, to help another person be real.

Rapt attention is my greatest gift. If I want to receive it, I must give it.

M Y   T H O U G H T S   F O R   T H E   D A Y

When we begin to take our failures nonseriously, it means we are ceasing to be afraid of them. It is of immense importance to learn to laugh at ourselves.
—KATHERINE MANSFIELD

Perfectionism and its control over our lives stands seriously in the way of our growth and well-being, emotionally, spiritually, and even physically. Life's lessons come through failures probably more than successes. Through our failures we learn humility. We learn to look to others for help and guidance. We learn how to let others fail, too. We fail because we are human.

When we no longer fear failure, we are free to attempt greater feats. We dare to learn more, and life is fuller for it—not just our own lives, but the lives that we touch.

Laughter over our mistakes eases the risk of trying again. Laughter keeps us young, and the lighthearted find more pleasure in each day.

I will fail at something I try today. I can laugh about it, though.
My laughter will open the way to another try.

M Y   T H O U G H T S   F O R   T H E   D A Y

....

....

....

....

....

....

....

....

....

FEBRUARY 4

Genius is the talent for seeing things straight. It is seeing things in a
straight line without any bend or break or aberration of sight,
seeing them as they are, without any warping of vision.
—MAUDE ADAMS

We are learning, each day of our abstinence, to see more clearly what lies before us. Less and less are we hampered by our own selfish needs, distorting that which we face. We all have within us the talent for seeing things as they really are. But it is a process that takes practice, a process of turning within to the untapped talent which is one of the gifts of a spiritual life.

We are spiritual entities, one and all. And the genius to see as God sees is ours for the asking. This program is paving our way. Each day it becomes easier to live an honest life. Each day we trust more the people we encounter. And each day we take greater risks being our true selves.

The need to distort that which we see ahead lessens as we begin reaping the benefits of the honest, caring, spirit-filled life. Our unhealthy egos stood in our way in the past. And they can get in the way even now, if we forget to look ahead with the eyes of our inner genius.

My path today is straight, clean, and love-filled, if I choose to follow my genius.

MY THOUGHTS 🌺 FOR THE DAY

....

....

....

....

....

....

....

FEBRUARY 5

Don't compromise yourself. You are all you've got.
—JANIS JOPLIN

When we don't know who we are, it's easy to compromise ourselves. When we don't know where we stand on an issue, it's easy to be swayed by a forceful voice. Values may be cloudy in our minds, or we may not be aware of them at all. It's then that we are vulnerable to the persuasion of another. In this Twelve Step program, we are offered the way to know ourselves. We are supported in our efforts, and we realize we have friends who don't want us to compromise ourselves—who value our struggle to know and to be true to ourselves.

One of recovery's greatest gifts is discovering we can make decisions that represent us, our inner selves, and those decisions please us. We all are familiar with the tiny tug of shame that locates itself in our solar plexus. When we "go along," when we give in on a personally important issue, we pay a consequence. We lose a bit of ourselves. Over the years we've lost many bits. We have a choice, however.

I will have a chance, soon, to act according to my wishes. I will take it.

MY THOUGHTS ❧ FOR THE DAY

....

....

....

....

....

....

....

F E B R U A R Y   6

I believe that a sign of maturity is accepting deferred gratification.
—PEGGY CAHN

It's okay to want to feel good all the time. Happiness is something we all deserve. However, there are often preparatory steps we need to take, a number of which will not bring joy, before we arrive at a place of sustained happiness.

The level of our pain at any particular moment has prompted us to seek short-term highs. And with each attempt at a quick "fix," we will be reminded that, just as with our many former attempts, the high is very short-term.

Long-term happiness is not the by-product of short-term gratification. We don't have to *earn* happiness, exactly, but we do have to discover where it's found. How fortunate we are to have the program guiding our search. We will find happiness when we learn to get quiet and listen to our inner selves. We will find happiness when we focus less on our personal problems and more on the needs of others.

Many of us will need to redefine what happiness is. Understanding our value and necessity to our circle of acquaintances will bring us happiness, a happiness that will sustain us. Gratitude for our friends, our growing health, and our abstinence also sustain us. Sincerely touching the soul of someone else can tap the well of happiness within each of us.

I will find happiness. Searching within myself.
I will patiently, trustingly share myself with others.

M Y   T H O U G H T S   FOR   T H E   D A Y

....

....

....

....

....

....

FEBRUARY 7

However confused the scene of our life appears, however torn we may be who
now do face that scene, it can be faced, and we can go on to be whole.
—MURIEL RUKEYSER

We can expect to feel fear, even dread at some points in our lives. We will always have situations that, for a time at least, seem more than we can bear. But the clouds will lift. We are never given more than we can handle, and with each passing day we become more at ease with ourselves and all that life gives us. We are learning that "this too shall pass." Our confidence grows as our spiritual program gains strength.

Our ties to one another and our ties to the program make us whole. When we reflect on who we were and how far we've come, we will see that problems we drank over in days gone by are handled today and often with ease. The joy we share is that no problem is too great to be faced any longer. And no situation will ever have to be faced alone, unless we reject God's help.

I will be grateful for my growth toward wholeness and the opportunities I face
today. They are bringing me into harmony with the Divine plan for my life.

MY THOUGHTS ❧ FOR THE DAY

....

....

....

....

....

....

....

....

FEBRUARY 8

Reaction isn't action—that is, it isn't truly creative.
—ELIZABETH JANEWAY

We must learn how to act rather than react. Unfortunately, we've had lots of training at reacting. And we're all such good imitators. We are a society of reactors. We let the good or the bad behavior of another person determine our own behavior as a matter of course. But the opportunities are unlimited for us to responsibly choose our behavior, independent of all others in our life.

Change is ours, if we want it. A scowl from a spouse need not make us feel rejected. Criticism at work doesn't have to ruin our day. An inconsiderate bus driver might still be politely thanked. And when we decide for ourselves just how we want to act and follow through, self-esteem soars.

If we are put down, it may momentarily create self-doubt; but when we quickly reassure ourselves that all is well and respond with respect, we grow. A sense of well-being rushes through our bodies.

Being in command of our own feelings and our own actions prevents that free-floating anxiety from grasping us. We are who we choose to be. And new adventures await us.

The opportunities to react will be many today. But each time I can pause,
determine the action I'd feel better about, and take it.
My emotional health gets a booster shot each time I make a responsible choice.

MY THOUGHTS FOR THE DAY

....

....

....

....

....

....

We have seen too much defeatism, too much pessimism, too much of a negative approach. The answer is simple: if you want something very badly, you can achieve it. It may take patience, very hard work, a real struggle, and a long time; but it can be . . . faith is a prerequisite of any undertaking. . . .
—MARGO JONES

How many dreams have we let die? How many projects did we start, only to leave them unfinished? How many times have we promised ourselves, "This time will be different," but then didn't work to make it so? Negativity breeds more negativity. Fortunately, its opposite does likewise. Our attitude will carry us a long way. And a positive attitude will make all things possible.

We are meant for good living. But we must seek it out and be open to its invitation, be willing to put forth the necessary effort. Our dreams are our invitations to move forward, to strive for a further goal. And having faith in our ability to achieve our dreams will make easier the necessary steps.

We have been blessed with dreams, all of us. They are gifts meant to stretch our capabilities.

I can trust my dreams and aspirations. They are mine, alone, and special to me. Achievement is possible; faith and a positive attitude will ease my efforts.

M Y   T H O U G H T S   F O R   T H E   D A Y

FEBRUARY 10

God knows no distance.
—CHARLESZETTA WADDLES

As close as our breath is the strength we need to carry us through any troubled time. But our memory often fails us. We try, alone, to solve our problems, to determine the proper course of action. And we stumble. In time we will turn, automatically, to that power available. And whatever our need, it will be met.

Relying on God, however we understand God's presence, is foreign to many of us. We were encouraged from early childhood to be self-reliant. Even when we desperately needed another's help, we feared asking for it. When confidence wavered, as it so often did, we hid the fear— sometimes with alcohol, sometimes with pills. Sometimes we simply hid at home. Our fears never fully abated.

Finding out, as we all have found, that we have never needed to fear anything, that God was never distant, takes time to sink in. Slowly and with practice it will become natural to turn within, to be God-reliant rather than self-reliant.

Whatever our needs today, God is the answer.

There is nothing to fear. At last, I have come to know God.
All roads will be made smooth.

MY THOUGHTS ❧ FOR THE DAY

....

....

....

....

....

....

....

FEBRUARY 11

It's odd that you can get so anesthetized by your own pain or your own prob-
lem that you don't quite fully share the hell of someone close to you.
—LADY BIRD JOHNSON

Preoccupation with self can be the bane of our existence. It prevents all but the narrowest perspective on any problem. It cuts off any guidance from our higher power that may be offered through a friend. It blocks whatever truths are trying to gain our attention. The paradox is that whatever our pain, it is lessened by turning our attention elsewhere, to another's pain or joy.

When we open our minds to fresh input from others, insights emerge. We need the messages others are trying to give us. Nothing that is said in a loving spirit is empty of meaning for our lives.

We might consider that every conversation we have is a conversation with our Creator. What we need to know, for our own growth, is guaranteed to be revealed in our many conversations with others. But we can't hear another's thoughts until we let go of our own.

Full attention to the persons sent to me will offer me exactly
what I need, today. My inner guide has beckoned them.
I can be alert, expect solutions, and celebrate the wonder of it all.

MY THOUGHTS FOR THE DAY

FEBRUARY 12

There are no new truths, but only truths that have not been recognized by those who have perceived them without noticing.
—MARY MCCARTHY

We understand today ideas we couldn't grasp yesterday. We are conscious this year of details of our past that we may have glossed over at the time. Our blinders are slowly giving way, readying us for the truths we couldn't absorb before.

"When the student is ready, the teacher appears." And the teacher comes bearing truths that we need to assimilate into our growing bank of knowledge. The truths we may be given today, or any day, won't always make us happy immediately. We may learn that a job is no longer right for us. Or that a relationship has reached an end. And the impending changes create unrest. But in the grand scheme of our lives, the changes wrought by these truths are good and will contribute in time to our happiness.

Let's celebrate the truths as they come and trust the outcome to God. We are traveling a very special road. The way is rocky. The bends limit our vision, but we will be given all the direction we need.

The truths I receive today will guide my steps. I shall move in peace.

M Y   T H O U G H T S   ❦   F O R   T H E   D A Y

....

....

....

....

....

....

....

....

FEBRUARY 13

I have sacrificed everything in my life that I consider precious in order to advance the political career of my husband.
—PAT NIXON

Putting another person's needs first is what most of us were trained to do when growing up. We were seldom encouraged to embark on an individual course, and years of taking a back seat taught us that our hopes mattered little.

Now, for some of us, the future looks like a blank wall. It is time to carve out a plan for ourselves, yet how do we decide where we want to go? And how do we get there? The program says, "Live one day at a time." Our friends say, "Take one step at a time."

We have chosen to do something about the circumstances we found ourselves in, or we wouldn't be reading these words. We can stop for a moment and reflect on the many changes thus far. We are already on our way. We have taken a number of necessary steps. What an exciting adventure we have embarked upon! And we will be helped all along the way.

We can trust our inner yearnings, the ones we may have stifled in times past. We can realize our hearts' pure desires, if we seek guidance.

My time has come. I can mold my future. I will take each day, each experience, and let it draw me to the next important step.

MY THOUGHTS ❀ FOR THE DAY

....

....

....

....

....

....

....

FEBRUARY 14

Friendship of a kind that cannot easily be reversed tomorrow must have its roots in common interests and shared beliefs.
—BARBARA W. TUCHMAN

The gift of friendship has been extended to each of us sharing this program. Our interest is common: we want to stay abstinent. And we share the belief that a power greater than ourselves can restore us to sanity. We trust our commitment to one another here. We are learning to live the program's principles in all our affairs.

In years gone by, friendships were often missing from our lives. We had a friend, here and there, certainly, but could she really be trusted—with our secrets, with our spouse? An overriding fear and one not without reason. It's likely that we, too, failed to be good friends. Friendship, anytime, means risking vulnerability. It means making a decision to be trustworthy. And it means not backing away from either, anytime.

Friendships so enrich our lives; they complete us. The experiences shared among friends give us all an edge on living. It is no accident that we have been drawn here together. What we have will help another.

I must be willing to give away my intimate self to my sisters in trust. My strength as a recovering woman will increase as my ties of friendship increase.

MY THOUGHTS FOR THE DAY

....

....

....

....

....

....

....

FEBRUARY 15

*Fortuitous circumstances constitute the moulds
that shape the majority of human lives.*
—AUGUSTA EVANS

Being in the right place at the right time is how we generally explain our good fortune or the good fortune of a friend. But it's to our advantage to understand how we managed to be in the right place at just the right moment.

We have probably heard many times at meetings that God's timetable is not necessarily the same as our timetable. That events will happen as scheduled to fit a picture bigger than the picture encompassed by our egos. And frequently our patience wears thin because we aren't privy to God's timetable. But we can trust, today and always, that doors open on time. Opportunities are offered when we are ready for them. Nary a moment passes that doesn't invite us to both give and receive a special message—a particular lesson. We are always in God's care, and every circumstance of our lives is helping to mold the women we are meant to be.

*I will take a long look at where I am today and be grateful for my place.
It's right for me, now, and is preparing me for the adventure ahead.*

MY THOUGHTS ❀ FOR THE DAY

....

....

....

....

....

....

....

....

FEBRUARY 16

Within our dreams and aspirations we find our opportunities.
—SUE ATCHLEY EBAUGH

Our dreams beckon us to new heights. All that we may need is the courage to move toward them, taking the necessary steps to realize those dreams. Trusting that we will be shown the steps, one at a time, patiently waiting for the right step and right time is all we need to do, today.

Our dreams, when they are for the good of ourselves and others, are invitations from God to spread our wings, to attempt new heights. Those dreams are part of the destiny designed for us. They are not happenstance. Our gifts are unique. Our contributions are ours alone. Our dreams reflect the contributions we are called on to make in this life.

Our opportunities for fulfillment are varied and not always recognized as for our good. Again and again we need to turn to God, be patient, and trust that we are being called to offer something very special to those around us. No one of us has escaped a special plan. And every one of us is inspired in particular ways, with particular talents. Our recovery is clearing the way for us to burst forth with our talents.

I will be grateful for all that I am, for all that I have. And I will remember,
what I give today to friends around me is mine only to give.

MY THOUGHTS FOR THE DAY

....

....

....

....

....

....

....

FEBRUARY 17

One can never pay in gratitude; one can only pay "in kind"
somewhere else in life.
—ANNE MORROW LINDBERGH

Life is a series of payments. The common expression "What goes around, comes around" is a truth that governs each of our lives. As women and as members of the human family, we have received untold "payments" from others. On occasion, the payment may not have been one we'd have chosen for ourselves. It takes the distance of time to realize that our payments are meant for our good. And we can share the goodness; in fact, we need to share the goodness with one another. If we give to another the joy given to us, if we give to another the understanding given to us, if we give to another the friendship given to us, we will be ready to receive more in kind.

You and I meet today to make payments. I will receive yours gladly.

M Y   T H O U G H T S   F O R   T H E   D A Y

....

....

....

....

....

....

....

....

....

FEBRUARY 18

To keep your character intact you cannot stoop to filthy acts.
It makes it easier to stoop the next time.
—KATHARINE HEPBURN

Behaving the way we believe God wants us to behave sounds so easy on the surface. We don't willingly hurt others, do we? Or do we? . . . When did we last secretly burn with jealousy over another's good fortune or good looks? Has there been a time, recently, when we sulked for lack of attention . . . or perhaps picked a fight?

We can simplify life from this moment forth. There is only one path to walk, one decision to make, in every instance, and all our burdens will be lifted, all our anxiety released. We can decide to act in good faith. We can be silent a moment with ourselves and let our inner guide direct our behavior, our words, our thoughts.

Each of us knows, when we dare to let our spiritual nature reign, the right act in every case. Letting God choose our acts will ease our lives. No more obsessive confusion. No more regrets. No more immobility due to fear of wrong moves.

Freedom is guaranteed when I depend on God to direct my behavior.
Life's burdens are lifted.
I will go forth today, doing God's will, and my Spirit will be light.

MY THOUGHTS ❧ FOR THE DAY

No trumpets sound when the important decisions of our life are made.
Destiny is made known silently.
—AGNES DeMILLE

The day ahead offers us choices of many kinds—some big ones, many that will affect other persons close to us, a few that will have profound effects on our destiny. But no choice, no decision we make, will be wrong. A particular decision may lead us slightly astray. Down a dead-end path perhaps—but we can always turn back and choose again.

We are seldom aware of the gravity of a particular choice at the time of making it. Only hindsight reveals the wisdom of an important choice. Nevertheless, no choice is without importance in the overall picture of our lives. And at the same time, no choice is all-powerful regarding our destiny. We are offered chances again and again for making the right choices, the ones that will most contribute to the bigger plan for our lives.

I need not worry about today's opportunities for decision making.
I will listen to those around me. I will seek guidance in the
messages coming to me. I will make the choices I need to, today.

M Y   T H O U G H T S   FOR   T H E   D A Y

....

....

....

....

....

....

....

....

FEBRUARY 20

You must do the thing you think you cannot do.
—ELEANOR ROOSEVELT

How can we ever do that which seems impossible? Taking a class, quitting a job, leaving a destructive relationship behind, asking for help; none of these can we do alone or with ease. All of these we can handle when we rely on the help offered by the program, the help of one another, the help promised by our higher power. Tackling with God's help that which seems impossible, reduces it to manageable size. It also deflates the power our fears have given it.

That which we fear grows in proportion to our obsession with it. The more we fear a thing, the bigger it becomes, which in turn increases our fear. How lucky we are that God awaits our call for the strength, the companionship that is guaranteed us! We are in partnership, all the way, every day, if we'd only recognize it. We can move toward and through anything. And the added benefit is that we come to trust our partnership. We soon know that all situations can be met. All experiences can be survived. Avoidance is no longer our technique for survival.

A deep breath invites the inner strength to move through me. I will feel the exhilaration of God's power. And I will know the excitement of growth and peace.

MY THOUGHTS ❀ FOR THE DAY

....

....

....

....

....

....

....

FEBRUARY 21

We can never go back again, that much is certain.
—DAPHNE DuMAURIER

Yesterday is gone, but its experiences will be reflected in those of today. We learned from both the good and the bad situations of yesterday. Where we travel today, likewise, will influence our direction tomorrow. We can't do over what has gone before, but we can positively incorporate all that life is offering us from this moment forth.

We are moving toward greater understanding of life's mysteries with each experience. As today unfolds, we can be moved by the adventures. What we experience is ours alone and will contribute to the unfolding of our special destiny. We move forward, only forward. The doors behind us are closed forever.

Facing what comes to us, with strength, is a gift from this program we share. Letting go of the yesterdays and the last years is another gift offered by this program. And trust that what we face along with what we let go will weave the pattern of our rightful unfolding—that is the ultimate gift given to us by this program.

I need never go back again. I am spared that. My destiny lies in the future.
And I can be certain it will bring me all that I desire, and more.

MY THOUGHTS FOR THE DAY

....

....

....

....

....

....

....

....

FEBRUARY 22

Toleration is the greatest gift of the mind.
—HELEN KELLER

Facing conditions we would like to change, letting go of people we wish were different, takes growth, patience, tolerance. We're so easily enticed into thinking we'd be happier, "If only he'd change," or "If I had a better job," or "If the kids would settle down." Yet we carry the seed of happiness within us every moment. Learning tolerance for all conditions will nurture that seed.

Intolerance, impatience, depression—in fact, any negative attitude—is habit-forming. Many of us in this recovery program continue to struggle with the habits we've formed. Bad habits must be replaced with new, good habits. We can develop a new behavior, one that pleases us, like smiling at every stranger in a checkout line. We can repeat it in every line. It becomes a habit and a good one.

Toleration of others opens many doors, for them and for us. It nurtures the soul, ours and theirs. It breeds happiness. Those of us sharing these Steps are truly blessed. We're learning about love, how to give it and how to receive it.

There are so many eyes I'll look into today that don't know love. I will give some away with unconditional tolerance. It's a gift—to myself and others.

MY THOUGHTS ❧ FOR THE DAY

....

....

....

....

....

....

....

F E B R U A R Y   2 3

I want to dance always, to be good and not evil, and when it is all over
not to have the feeling that I might have done better.
—RUTH ST. DENIS

Our wants in life may be simple, or they may be complex. They may yet be confused in our minds, but the clarity will come if we're patient. God has a way of giving us an "inner tug" when a certain direction beckons. Our responsibility is to follow that tug and trust it, fully. Too often we look back on our lives with regret. What is done, is done. We learned lessons from those mistakes. Every day is a new beginning. And we can close every day with no regrets when we have followed our consciences, that "inner tug" that beckons.

The opportunities will come today. Opportunities to be good or evil. Opportunities for making choices over which we will feel good or full of regret at the day's close. Many of our choices will bring us closer to the satisfaction, the contentment with life, that we all search for as women, as human beings. We need not fear coming to life's close, wishing we had done more or better. Living each day in good conscience, waiting for the tug and following it, will ensure a life well lived.

My ego can block out the tug, if I let it. Or I can trust.

M Y   T H O U G H T S   ❦   F O R   T H E   D A Y

FEBRUARY 24

The beauty of the world has two edges, one of laughter,
one of anguish, cutting the heart asunder.
—VIRGINIA WOOLF

Anguish is undoubtedly more familiar to us than is the beauty of laughter. We feel anguish over our failings; we feel anguish over our losses; we feel anguish over the attempts to succeed that beckon to us.

Anguish comes of fear. And we so hope to avoid it. However, it seasons us as women; it enriches us even while it momentarily diminishes us. It is a major contributor to the sum and substance of our lives. The anguish we experience prepares us to help others face their own particular anguish.

Our laughter, too, must be savored and shared. And laughter builds more laughter. Laughter lends a perspective to our anguish. Life is made richer, fuller, by the ebb and flow, the laughter and the anguish in concert.

If only we could remember, when the anguish is present, that it is making our Spirits whole. That it, along with laughter, is a healer of the soul. That it lifts our load at the same time that it burdens us. That it prepares us to better receive life's other gifts.

I can help another face anguish. It brings us together. It softens me.
And it makes way for the laughter soon to come.

MY THOUGHTS FOR THE DAY

....

....

....

....

....

....

....

FEBRUARY 25

You need only claim the events of your life to make yourself yours.
—FLORIDA SCOTT-MAXWELL

The search is on. Everyone, everywhere, asks the question at some time, "Who am I?" Women like ourselves are fortunate to have this program. It shows us the way to self-discovery. It directs our steps to the celebration of self that is a gift of recovery. The events of our past may plague us. But they did contribute to the fullness we feel today. And for them, for their involvement in who we've become, we can be grateful.

Claiming ourselves, the good and the bad, is healing. It's taking responsibility—for where we were and where we're going. Claiming ourselves makes us the active participants in our lives. The choices are many and varied. Not actively participating in life is also a choice. Passivity may have been our dominant choice in years gone by. But now, today, we are choosing recovery. We are choosing action that is healing, and wholeness is the result.

Making myself mine will exhilarate me. It will give me hope.
It will prepare me for anything to come. I will know a new joy.

MY THOUGHTS ❀ FOR THE DAY

Happiness is a byproduct of an effort to make someone else happy.
—GRETTA BROOKER PALMER

We have striven for happiness, generally in self-centered ways. We expected others to favor us with their attention, for example. Or we waited for invitations or gifts. We have probably tried to buy happiness with the purchase of a new dress or shoes. Fleeting moments of happiness were gained, that's all. And soon we were discontent once again. And the search was begun anew.

But things have changed for some of us. We are learning, maybe slowly, how to find a more permanent happiness. And we know the happiness that comes from "getting" is elusive. *Giving* to others, giving attention, sharing hope, sharing our own stories, listening to theirs, is the key to finding the happiness for which we've searched so long. We must get outside of ourselves and focus on another's joy or sorrow. Only then do we get a clear perspective on who we are and the necessary role we play in the lives of others who need our attention and who have a message we also need to hear.

The creative power stirring in me needs recognition. Looking deeply into another
person, listening intently to the stirring will elicit joy. I will feel in touch with
my own creative power, a lasting thrill, not a fleeting moment of happiness.

M Y   T H O U G H T S   ❧   F O R   T H E   D A Y

....

....

....

....

....

....

....

Being alone and feeling vulnerable. Like two separate themes, these two parts of myself unite in my being and sow the seeds of my longing for unconditional love.
—MARY CASEY

How easily we slip into self-doubt, fearing we're incapable or unlovable, perhaps both. How common for us to look into the faces of our friends and lovers in search of affirmation and love.

Our alienation from ourselves, from one another, from God's Spirit which exists everywhere causes our discontent. It is our discontent. When souls touch, love is born, love of self and love of the other. Our aloneness exists when we create barriers that keep us separate from our friends, our family. Only we can reach over or around the barriers to offer love, to receive love.

Recovery offers us the tools for loving, but we must dare to pick them up. Listening to others and sharing ourselves begins the process of loving. Risking to offer love before receiving it will free us from the continual search for love in the faces of others.

I won't wait to be loved today. I will love someone else, fully. I won't doubt that I, too, am loved. I will feel it. I will find unconditional love.

M Y   T H O U G H T S   F O R   T H E   D A Y

FEBRUARY 28

The weariest night, the longest day, sooner or later must perforce come to an end.
—BARONESS ORCZY

The difficult spells in our lives come to an end. And no matter the depth of our disturbance, we will survive. We forget that the depths teach us how to better appreciate the heights.

Sorrow heightens joy. Depression heightens laughter. We wouldn't know the joys and laughter were it not for the sorrows. In them we learn to be patient, waiting for the wisdom which will light our way. In them we learn to listen for the guidance that beckons us forth.

We must reflect on the troubling experiences we've passed through of late. They made us wiser; they gave us strength. They changed us, moving us ever closer to the women, whole and happy, we desire to be.

Difficulties often precede enlightenment. They pull us inward, perhaps push us to search for our connectedness to God, a connectedness that is at home in our hearts. The paradox is that these painful periods strengthen our oneness with the Spirit.

If the day looks bleak, I will accept it as a hand reaching toward me,
to pull me forward, to secure my place in the spiritual family.

MY   THOUGHTS   FOR   THE   DAY

....

....

....

....

....

....

....

....

F E B R U A R Y   2 9

. . . I was taught that the way of progress is neither swift nor easy.
—MARIE CURIE

We are looking for progress, not perfection; however, we sometimes get lost or confused between the two. Expecting ourselves to be perfect at something we are only now learning is a familiar affliction. As we accept our humanness, we'll allow the mistakes that are a normal part of the process of living and learning—a process we call progress.

Our need to be perfect will lessen with time. And we can help ourselves break the old habits. Perfection and self-worth are not symbiotic, except in our minds. And it's a symbiosis that has done us a grave injustice. Breaking the old thought patterns takes a commitment. We must first decide and believe that we are worthwhile, simply because we are. There is only one of us; we have a particular gift to offer this world. And our being is perfect as is. Affirming this, repeatedly, is our beginning. But with this, too, progress will be slow; perfection need only be worked for, not achieved.

The patterns I am weaving with my life are complex, full of intricate detail and knots. I need to go slow, taking only one stitch at a time. With hindsight I will see that whatever the progress, it was the perfect fit to the overall design.

M Y   T H O U G H T S   FOR   T H E   D A Y

March

MARCH 1

Each experience we have plays its part in the total picture of our lives. The steps we have taken, the path we travel today, and our direction tomorrow are not by chance. There is a pattern. We each have a destiny. We may have veered off the path in the past, and we may veer off it again. But we'll be guided back, and our paths intersect. None of us is traveling alone. We have each other and the creative force that is at the helm.

When we look around us and reflect on how our lives are influenced by the persons close to us, we become aware that our presence affects their lives as well. Most of us could never have predicted the events that have influenced us. Nor can we anticipate what the future may hold. We can be certain, however, that we are safe; a power greater than ourselves is orchestrating our affairs.

There were times we feared we'd never survive an experience. Perhaps we still struggle with fears about new experiences. But every experience adds a necessary thread to the pattern our life is weaving. We have the gift of reflection. We can understand, today, the importance of particular events of the past. Next month, next year, we'll understand today.

I shall enjoy the richness of today. My life is weaving an intricate,
necessary pattern that is uniquely mine.

MY THOUGHTS FOR THE DAY

*Everyone has talent. What is rare is the courage to follow
the talent to the dark place where it leads.*
—ERICA JONG

There was a time when we didn't believe we had any talents. We couldn't imagine we had any purpose or any gift to give to the world. But it's true: We all have talents, many of them. If we each haven't yet discovered ours, we soon will. With time and the Steps and friends, we will be encouraged to recognize them, to celebrate them, to cultivate them, to dare to give them away.

Utilizing our talents fully, which is part of life's bigger plan, may lead us to new jobs, new friends, to places presently unknown. The prospect of new horizons may excite us. It may also elicit dread. We can trust that, just as we are given no problems too big to handle, we are given no talents too great to develop. The strength to move ahead will always be available if we have faith. And the program offers us faith.

*I will look for my talents today. I will also look for talents in my friends.
I can celebrate them, and soon the way to use them will become clear.*

M Y   T H O U G H T S   *❀*   F O R   T H E   D A Y

....

....

....

....

....

....

....

....

Most kids hear what you say; some kids do what you say;
but all kids do what you do.
—KATHLEEN CASEY THEISEN

We are role models for many people: our children, our co-workers, other women in the program. Step Twelve encourages us to set good examples for anyone who might be looking on. Living a principled life takes practice, and progress, not perfection, is hoped for.

Abstinence has offered us a new set of tools for shaping our behavior. No longer must we regret what we did yesterday or last week. We are learning to monitor our actions, but even more importantly, we are defining our values. They, in turn, influence what we say and do.

Thoughtful responses to the situations we encounter require conscious attention to those events. We need reminding, perhaps, that our behavior is continuously telling others who we are, what we value, and how we view the people close to us. All of us, consciously or otherwise, imitate behavior patterns of persons we admire. Unfortunately, we sometimes mimic unfavorable behavior, too.

There are those casting their attention our way. The opportunity to model favorable behavior awaits us.

People will follow my lead. I shall walk softly, humbly and lovingly.

M Y   T H O U G H T S   &   F O R   T H E   D A Y

....

....

....

....

....

....

....

MARCH 4

It is good to have an end to journey towards;
but it is the journey that matters, in the end.
—URSULA K. LEGUIN

Goals give direction to our lives. We need to know who we are and where we want to go. But the trip itself, the steps we travel, offer us daily satisfaction moment by moment—fulfillment, if we'd but realize it. Too often we keep our sights on the goal's completion, rather than the process—the day-to-day living that makes the completion possible.

How often do we think, "When I finish college, I'll feel stronger." Or, "After the divorce is final, I can get back to work." Or even, "When I land that promotion, my troubles are over." Life will begin "when"—or so it seems in our minds. And when this attitude controls our thinking, we pass up our opportunity to live, altogether.

Looking back on goals already completed in our lives, what so quickly follows the end of a job well done is a letdown. And how sad that the hours, the days, the weeks, maybe even the months we toiled are gone, with little sense of all they could have meant.

I will not forget that every moment of every day I can be
God-centered and joyous. The goal I'm striving toward will carry
with it a special gift; it will offer the growing person within me
an extra thrill, if I've attended to the journey as much as its end.

MY THOUGHTS FOR THE DAY

MARCH 5

Loving, like prayer, is a power as well as a process. It's curative. It is creative.
—ZONA GALE

The expression of love softens us and the ones we love. It opens a channel between us. It invites an intimate response that closes the distance.

It feels good to express love, whether through a smile, a touch, or a prayer. It heightens our sense of being alive. Acknowledging another's presence means that we, too, are acknowledged. Each of us is familiar with feeling forgotten, unnoticed, or taken for granted, and recognition assures us all that we haven't been overlooked.

Knowing we are loved may be the key to our doing the things we fear. Love supports us to charge ahead, and we can support others to charge ahead. We know that if we fail, we have someone to turn to.

Love heals. It strengthens, making us courageous both when we receive it and when we give it. Knowing we are loved makes our existence special. It affirms that we count in another's life. We need to honor our friends by assuring them of their specialness, too.

I need others. I need to strengthen my supports, my connections to others for the security, even success, of each of us. I can express my love today, and assure my loved ones that they are needed. Then, they and I will surge ahead with new life.

MY THOUGHTS ✿ FOR THE DAY

....

....

....

....

....

....

....

MARCH 6

Life is made up of desires that seem big and vital one minute, and little and absurd the next. I guess we get what's best for us in the end.
—ALICE CALDWELL RICE

It is often said that we will be granted our heart's "pure desires." When we have many unmet desires, maybe we should be grateful. Wants that are ultimately not for our good can open the way to many unneeded and painful experiences.

How often we sit, wishing for a better job, a more loving relationship, a different weather forecast. How seldom we take positive advantage of what is at hand, not realizing that whatever *is*, right now, is the ticket to the next act in the drama of our lives.

We have before us a very limited picture. We cannot possibly know just what we need to travel the distance that's in store for us. Our desires, when they are pure, will carry us to the right destination. They are inspired. But the desires that are motivated by our selfish egos will lead us astray. Many times in the past we did not give up those desires. And the painful memories linger.

Desiring God's will is my most fruitful desire. It's also what is best for me; thus, what I need. All things are working for good when I let my higher power determine my desires.

MY THOUGHTS FOR THE DAY

MARCH 7

Parents can only give good advice or put them on the right paths, but the final forming of a person's character lies in their own hands.
—ANNE FRANK

We must take responsibility for ourselves, for who we become, for how we live each day. The temptation to blame others may be ever present. And much of our past adds up to wasted days or years perhaps, because we did blame someone else for the unhappiness in our lives.

We may have blamed our own parents for not loving us enough. We may have labeled our husbands the villains. Other people did affect us. That's true. However, we chose, you and I, to let them control us, overwhelm us, shame us. We always had other options, but we didn't choose them.

Today is a new day. Recovery has opened up our options. We are learning who we are and how we want to live our lives. How exhilarating to know that you and I can take today and put our own special flavor in it. We can meet our personal needs. We can, with anticipation, chart our course. The days of passivity are over, if we choose to move ahead with this day.

I will look to this day. Every day is a new beginning.

MY THOUGHTS FOR THE DAY

....

....

....

....

....

....

....

....

MARCH 8

To create is to boggle the mind and alter the mood. Once the urge has surged,
it maintains its own momentum. We may go along for the ride,
but when we attempt to steer the course, the momentum dies.
—SUE ATCHLEY EBAUGH

A sense of spiritual well-being warms us when we are selfless, when we step away from our obsessing egos, when we let our pure, unfettered desires direct our thoughts and our steps. Our egos may be keeping us caged in old behavior, old fears. Egos struggle for self-preservation; unfortunately, it's our old, unhealthy self the ego is preserving.

The Steps make it possible for us to unload our baggage from earlier days, baggage that intrudes on our perceptions of today's events. The Steps clear the path so we can move responsibly forward.

Living creatively is living in the thick of the flow, trusting the flow, spontaneously moving with the flow, not controlling the flow. We are Spirit-full when we let ourselves roll forward, resisting not, doubting not. And our greatest contributions will be discovered when our ego takes a rest.

My creativity awaits my discovery.
It's there. I will release it from the clutches of my ego.

MY THOUGHTS FOR THE DAY

....

....

....

....

....

....

....

MARCH 9

I want to get you excited about who you are, what you are, what you have, and what can still be for you. I want to inspire you to see that you can go far beyond where you are right now.
—VIRGINIA SATIR

Deciding to recover was our first step. That decision meant we did want to go beyond where we were. We did want something better for ourselves. And at times, in fleeting moments, we have been excited about who we are and our prospects for a better life.

The excitement and the inspiration come and go; they are seldom stationary. We can actively create the excitement and the inspiration. We need not wait for them to come to us. That's one of the choices we have as human beings, as women.

Passively waiting for "the good life" is past behavior. Each day, this day, we can set our sights on reaching a goal—we can take a step, or two, toward that goal. Progress is there for the making—achievement is there for the taking.

Whatever our hearts' pure desires, we can move toward that goal. We are what we need to be. We have what we need to move ahead.

Today, I will let my excitement for life's possibilities spur me on.

MY THOUGHTS ❀ FOR THE DAY

....

....

....

....

....

....

....

....

It is healthier to see the good points of others than to analyze our own bad ones.
—FRANCOISE SAGAN

Looking for the good in others is good for one's soul. Self-respect, self-love grows each time we openly acknowledge another's admirable qualities. Comparisons we make of ourselves with others, focusing on how we fail to measure up (another woman is prettier, thinner, more intelligent, has a better sense of humor, attracts people, and on and on) is a common experience. And we come away from the comparison feeling generally inadequate and unloving toward the other woman.

It is a spiritual truth that our love for and praise of others will improve our own self-image. It will rub off on us, so to speak. An improved self-image diminishes whatever bad qualities one has imagined.

Praise softens. Criticism hardens. We can become all that we want to become. We can draw the love of others to us as we more willingly offer love and praise. We have an opportunity to help one another as we help ourselves grow in the self-love that is so necessary to the successful living of each day.

I will see the good points in others today. And I will give praise.

M Y   T H O U G H T S   F O R   T H E   D A Y

....

....

....

....

....

....

....

....

MARCH 11

The influence of a beautiful, helpful, hopeful character is contagious, and may revolutionize a whole town.
—ELEANOR H. PORTER

We have met certain people who inspired laughter, hope, or changes in us, or those close to us. We look forward to seeing them. We leave their presence believing in ourselves, aware that we can tackle whatever problems had us immobilized. That special gift to inspire is ours for the taking, too. The inspiration comes from God.

We can look to God for the strength we need. It will come. We can look also to God for direction, for the steps we need to take today. And then wait. Those persons who inspire us have developed a secure connection to their God. And it's their connection that comes through them to inspire us.

We can take some time today, before the demands overwhelm us, to weave our connection to our higher power. When that contact is secure, we won't have to await inspiration from another person to forge ahead with our plans. The inspiration will live within us, and it will beckon us onward. Our way will be illuminated.

I shall meditate upon this. Conscious contact with God is only a prayer away. My life will be brightened. My burdens will be lifted. My hopes will become realities, whenever I look to God for the gift of inspiration.

MY THOUGHTS FOR THE DAY

MARCH 12

Love is not getting, but giving. It is sacrifice. And sacrifice is glorious!
—JOANNA FIELD

How easily we mistake attention for love. Even more easily, we trick ourselves into thinking our ability to control someone signifies love—especially theirs for us. But love is something far different from either attention or control. Far different.

Love frees others from our grasp—and lets them return on their own. Love is placing another's personal needs above our own, without regret. Love is selfless, yet it exhilarates the self. Giving love softens our edges, completes us, and connects us to the people with whom we are fulfilling our destinies.

Wanting love is a normal human desire, not one we should deny. And we shall receive love, the less our emphasis is on getting it, the more on giving it. We invite love when we freely and honestly give it. Another invitation for love comes from loving ourselves; self-hatred, which trapped many of us for years, hampers us no longer.

Love inspires—ourselves and those we give it to. It brightens our way, lessens our burdens, makes possible our rightful unfolding.

I won't look for love today. I will just give it. It will bless me tenfold.

MY THOUGHTS ❦ FOR THE DAY

....

....

....

....

....

....

....

....

MARCH 13

People need joy. Quite as much as clothing. Some of them need it far more.
—MARGARET COLLIER GRAHAM

Life is not without pain and travail. They are necessary to new awareness which prompts growth. And the gift of growth is joy. Pain and joy are thus intertwined. It is possible to feel only the burden of pain and not the exhilaration of joy, however.

Before seeking help to change our lives, many of us were heavily burdened by pain. But we were unable to open ourselves to the knowledge made possible by that pain. We were on a treadmill, accumulating painful experiences at every step, unable to capture the joy that was ever present.

We can have hope. Joy does await each of us today. We must open our eyes to it, just as we must open our hearts to one another. We must be willing to peel away the layers of pain to expose the core, the seedling of joy. And we need joy in our lives, just as surely as we need rest and a good diet. We need the light heart that joy fosters for a better perspective on the many experiences we'll face today, and every day.

Recovery has given me this new option. It guarantees me that every burden will be lightened. The knowledge that joy is inherent, within every experience, is mine, now and forever.

MY THOUGHTS ❀ FOR THE DAY

....

....

....

....

....

....

....

The child is an almost universal symbol for the soul's transformation.
The child is whole, not yet divided . . . when we would heal the mind . . .
we ask this child to speak to us.
—SUSAN GRIFFIN

Was there ever a time when we did not feel divided from ourselves? Occasionally we get a glimpse of what such spiritual wholeness would be like, but most of the time we struggle with feelings of conflict, unevenness, a divided heart. Perhaps "the child" is a metaphor for a spiritual guide, like our own higher power, that can help us in our journey toward self-acceptance.

"I may not be perfect, but parts of me are excellent," writes author Ashleigh Brilliant. If we can be happy with this proud, funny boast then perhaps we can stop berating ourselves for our imperfections. If we dwell on our own contradictory impulses, we give them too much importance, too much power.

Let me trust to my glimpses of harmony and wholeness
and be grateful for the richness of my spirit.

M Y   T H O U G H T S   FOR   T H E   D A Y

MARCH 15

Flattery is so necessary to all of us that we flatter one another just to be flattered in return.

—MARJORIE BOWEN

We are all deserving of unconditional love and acceptance. And all the people in our lives, past and present, deserve our unconditional love and acceptance, too. However, it's doubtful that we either feel it all of the time from others or give it away.

It's human of us to find fault—to have expectations that are too high. But for this we pay a price. Instead of experiencing our lives serenely, contentedly, flowing with what is, we often criticize, judge, and feel generally disgruntled throughout the day. What a waste! We do have another choice, fortunately. We can let go and let God, and live and let live. Also we can recall, today and every day, that we are all special individuals in this world who are loved, fully, by our Creator.

The greatest contribution we can make to the lives of others is to be affirming. We can let our spouse, children, and friends know we care about them. That we love and accept them. The love that we also long for will come back to us. We thrill at being affirmed. And we will thrill at affirming.

It feels good to help another feel appreciated.
Love and acceptance are my lifeline, from God around us all.

MY THOUGHTS FOR THE DAY

True intimacy with another human being can only be experienced when you
have found true peace within yourself.
—ANGELA L. WOZNIAK

Intimacy means disclosure—full expression of ourselves to another person. Nothing held back. All bared. There are risks, of course: rejection, criticism, perhaps ridicule. But the comfort we feel within is directly proportional to the peace we've come to know.

Each day we commit ourselves to recovery, we find a little more peace. Each conversation we have with our higher power brings us a little more security. Each time we turn our full attention to another person's needs, we feel our own burdens lightened.

Peace comes in stages. As we continue to accept our powerlessness, the depth of our peace increases. Turning more often to a power greater than ourselves eases our resistance to whatever condition prevails. Forgiving ourselves and others, daily, heightens our appreciation of all life and enhances our humility. Therein lies peace.

We each are a necessary part of the creative spirit prevailing in this world. The details of our lives are well in hand. We can be at peace. Who we are is who we need to be.

Intimacy lets me help someone else also live a full and peace-filled life.
I will reach out to someone today.

MY THOUGHTS FOR THE DAY

....

....

....

....

....

....

....

A woman who is loved always has success.
—Vicki Baum

Being loved, and knowing that we are loved, assure us of our connection to the world outside of ourselves, affirming us as participants in the bigger picture. And all of us need to know that we count—that what we say and do matter to others—that we are contributing in an important way.

Often we feel unloved, however. And we search for love. We may have begged for love and still didn't feel it. We have probably become very self-centered in our search. Fortunately, the program helps us to give love to others; the paradox is that love is returned, tenfold.

The wonders of love are many. Love is a healing balm for wounds. And it nurtures, both the one loving and the one loved. Love is an energizer. It spurs us on to successes in work and in play. Love multiplies. If we aren't feeling loved, we can love someone else—and love will visit us, too.

We can help the women in our lives find the successes they deserve. The confidence to tackle new situations is packaged in the gift of love. We need to help one another count.

My love of another is a contributing factor in her success.
Her loving gratitude will enhance my own endeavors.
I will take a moment, today, with a friend who needs my love.

MY THOUGHTS FOR THE DAY

....

....

....

....

....

....

MARCH 18

Noble deeds and hot baths are the best cures for depression.
—DODIE SMITH

Depression feeds on itself. With attention it worsens, but there are places for our attention. We can move our focus to a woman who is close by, a woman who is struggling to determine her direction in life. We can offer our ears. Or we can observe attentively, today, all the women, children, and men we see on the streets. When we notice their expressions, we realize they, too, may be suffering.

Doing something for someone else will lessen our own problems, no matter what the cause. In fact, just doing something will lift our spirits. Depression becomes habitual, and habits, even those that are detrimental, are easy to hang on to. When we take an action, even a small one, we can note the change: Action that benefits another is guaranteed to benefit us as well.

Depression does get worse with self-pitying attention; however, attention to ourselves that is nurturing has its place. We can pamper ourselves, but not pity ourselves. Pampering reflects approval, caring, self-respect; three attitudes inconsistent with depression. Even more than inconsistent, pampering and depression are incongruent.

*Depression must be coddled to maintain it. It's my choice to
move beyond it at any moment. I can put something
besides my problem at my center today and enjoy the results.*

MY THOUGHTS ❀ FOR THE DAY

....

....

....

....

....

....

*I realized a long time ago that a belief which does not spring from a conviction
in the emotions is no belief at all.*
—EVELYN SCOTT

From pillar to post we bounced, most of us not knowing what we actually believed about nearly any situation before getting to this program. Perhaps we believed what was most convenient at the time because of the people we were with. And maybe we jumped the fence quickly when in a new setting. Values were sometimes talked about but not defined, and certainly not adhered to.

It's difficult to develop a strong sense of self, to have a very secure self-image when the parameters offered by a value system are lacking. Our values define who we are. They offer us direction when making choices. They quietly demand that we behave responsibly. Living in concert with our values brings peace to our souls.

Gone are the days when we rode first one fence and then another, never knowing what side of any issue we honestly believed in. The program has offered us a plan for living, a plan that erases the many uncertainties, the inner turmoil of past years.

*Today will have a clarity about it that I can appreciate. I know who I am.
I know what I believe. All I need do is act accordingly.*

MY THOUGHTS ❀ FOR THE DAY

MARCH 20

*There's a period of life where we swallow a knowledge of ourselves and it
becomes either good or sour inside.*
—PEARL BAILEY

For too many of us, feelings of shame, even self-hatred, are paramount. No one of us has a fully untarnished past. Every man, every woman, even every child experiences regret over some action. We are not perfect. Perfection is not expected in the Divine plan. But we are expected to take our experiences and grow from them, to move beyond the shame of them, to celebrate what they have taught us.

Each day offers us a fresh start at assimilating all that we have been. What has gone before enriches who we are now, and through the many experiences we've survived, we have been prepared to help others, to smooth the way for another woman, perhaps, who is searching for a new direction.

We can let go of our shame and know instead that it sweetens the nuggets of the wisdom we can offer to others. We are alike. We are not without faults. Our trials help another to smoother sailing.

*I will relish the joy at hand. I can share my wisdom.
All painful pasts brighten someone's future, when openly shared.*

M Y   T H O U G H T S   ❧   F O R   T H E   D A Y

....

....

....

....

....

....

....

MARCH 21

Children are surely one of God's greatest gifts and truest challenges. To share your life with a child is to humble yourself so that you may learn from them and discover with them the beautiful secrets that are only uncovered in searching.
—KATHLEEN TIERNEY CRILLY

Humility accompanies every experience wherein we let ourselves fully listen to others, to learn from them, to be changed by their words, their presence. Each opportunity we take to be fully present to other people, totally with them in mind and spirit, will bless us while it blesses them. Offering and receiving the gift of genuine attention is basic to the emotional growth of every human being.

Before recovering, many of us so suffered from obsessive self-centered pity that we seldom noted the real needs or pain of the people close to us. We closed ourselves off, wallowing in our own selfish worries, and our growth was stunted.

Some days we still wallow. But a new day has dawned. The Steps offer us new understanding. They are helping us look beyond ourselves to all the children of God in our daily lives. From each of them we have many secrets to learn.

I will be joyous today. Many secrets about life are mine to learn if I will stay close to all the people who cross my path. I will be mindful they are there because they have something to give me. I will be ready to receive it.

MY THOUGHTS FOR THE DAY

....

....

....

....

....

....

....

Reared as we were in a youth and beauty oriented society,
we measured ourselves by our ornamental value.
—JANET HARRIS

Rare is the woman who doesn't long for a svelte body, firm breasts, pretty teeth, a smooth complexion. Rare is the woman who feels content, truly satisfied with her total person. We are often torn between wanting to be noticed and yet not wanting eyes to gaze upon us.

We are all that we need to be today, at this moment. And we have an inner beauty, each of us, that is our real blessing in the lives of others. Our inner beauty will shine forth if we invite it to do so. Whatever our outer appearance, it doesn't gently touch or bring relief where suffering is—like our words which come from the heart, the home of our inner beauty.

Perhaps a better mirror for reflecting our true beauty is the presence or absence of friends in our lives. We each have known stunning women who seemed to cast only cold glances our way and handsome men who arrogantly belittled others. It's our inner beauty that is valued by others. The surprise in store for each of us is discovering that the glow of our inner beauty transforms our outer appearance too.

My beauty today will be enhanced by my gentle attention
to the other people sharing my experiences.

M Y   T H O U G H T S   ❧   F O R   T H E   D A Y

....

....

....

....

....

....

....

On occasion I realize it's easier to say the serenity prayer and take that leap of faith than it is to continue doing what I'm doing.
—S.H.

The pain of change is a reality. But so is the pain of no change—when change is called for. In spite of our desires, changing others will never be an option, whereas changing ourselves takes only a decision and is a choice always available.

We can take an inventory for a moment. What are we presently doing that makes us ashamed or angry or fearful? We can let go of that behavior and responsibly choose a new tack. If strength is needed, or confidence to try a new behavior, we can simply ask that it be ours. The Third Step promises that our lives are in God's care and our needs are always being attended to—not always our wants, but in every instance our needs.

Most of our struggles, today as in the past, are attached to persons and situations we are trying to forcibly control. How righteous our attitudes generally are! And so imposing is our behavior that we are met with resistance, painful resistance. Our recourse is now and always to accept those things we cannot change, and willingly change that which we can. Our personal struggles will end when we are fully committed to the Serenity Prayer.

The wisdom "to know the difference" is mine today.

M Y   T H O U G H T S   ❦   F O R   T H E   D A Y

MARCH 24

Love has a hundred gentle ends.
—LEONORA SPEYER

Letting go is a process that is seldom easy. For many, its meaning is elusive. How do we "let go"? Letting go means removing our attention from a particular experience or person and putting our focus on the here and now. We hang on to the past, to past hurts, but also to past joys. We have to let the past pass. The struggle to hang on to it, any part of it, clouds the present. You can't see the possibilities today is offering if your mind is still drawn to what was.

Letting go can be a gentle process. Our trust in our higher power and our faith that good will prevail, in spite of appearances, ease the process. And we must let each experience end, as its moment passes, whether it is good or bad, love or sorrow. It helps to remember that all experiences contribute to our growth and wholeness. No experience will be ignored by the inner self who is charting our course. All are parts of the journey. And every moment has a gentle end, but no moment is forgotten.

My journey today is akin to yesterday's journey and tomorrow's too.
I will savor each moment and be ready for the next.

MY   THOUGHTS ❧ FOR   THE   DAY

....

....

....

....

....

....

....

....

MARCH 25

When I slow down long enough to smell the roses,
I usually see the beauty and all else that is ours to share.
—MORGAN JENNINGS

We overlook so many joys, so many hidden treasures, when we hurry from place to place, person to person, experience to experience, with little attention anywhere. All that matters passes before us now, at this moment. And assuredly, we will not pass this way again.

It has been said the greatest gift we can give one another is rapt attention; additionally, living life fully attentive to the breezes, the colors, the sorrows and the thrills as well, is the most prayerful response any of us can make in this life. Nothing more is asked of us. Nothing less is expected.

We have just this one life to live, and each day is a blessing. Even the trials we shall understand as blessings in the months, the years ahead, as we can see now how the painful moments of the past played their part. Our attitude toward the lessons life has offered makes all the difference in the world.

I will look closely at everything in my path today.
The women and children, the trees and squirrels, the silent neighbors.
I will never see them again as I see them today. I will be at attention.

MY THOUGHTS FOR THE DAY

MARCH 26

To believe in something not yet proved and to underwrite it with our lives;
it is the only way we can leave the future open.
—LILLIAN SMITH

Today stands before us, ready for our involvement. And it will offer us opportunities for personal growth and occasions to help another make progress on her path to the future. Challenges are to be expected. They further our purpose. They foster our maturity.

How different it is, for many of us, to look forward today with secure anticipation, to trust in what the future holds! We can still remember, all too vividly perhaps, the darker periods in our lives, periods that seemed to hold no promise; a time when we dreaded the future, fearing it would only compound those awful times.

The fear and the dread are not gone completely. They hover about us, on occasion. They no longer need to darken all of a day, however. We can recognize their presence as parts of our whole, not all of it. How free we are, today! Our choices are many.

I can step toward today with assurance, reaching out to others along the way,
trusting that my accumulated steps add stability to my future.

MY THOUGHTS FOR THE DAY

....

....

....

....

....

....

....

....

MARCH 27

It takes time, love, and support to find peace with the restless one.
—DEIDRA SARAULT

Restlessness is born of frustration. Perhaps we want to move ahead with our lives more quickly. Does a job have us trapped? Do past troubles haunt us still? Maybe perfectionism tarnishes every attempt to achieve. We can learn from our restlessness, if we let it guide us to our inner reservoir of peace and spiritual support.

The search for serenity often takes us farther from it. We mistakenly think a different job or home or relationship will answer all our needs. But we find that our restlessness has accompanied us to our new surroundings. Peace has its home within. And prayer opens the door to it. In the stillness of our patience, we are privy to its blessing.

Restlessness indicates our distance from our higher power. It may be time for a change in our lives. Change is good; however, our relationship with God will vouchsafe any needed changes. Restlessness is self-centered and will only hamper the steps we may need to take.

Restlessness is a barometer that reveals my spiritual health.
Perhaps prayer is called for today.

MY THOUGHTS ❦ FOR THE DAY

....

....

....

....

....

....

....

....

MARCH 28

Is there ever any particular spot where one can put one finger and say,
"It all began that day, at such a time and such a place, with such an incident"?
—AGATHA CHRISTIE

No experience of our lives is pure, unadulterated, set apart from all other experiences. There is an eternal flow in our lives. It carries us from one moment, one experience, into the next. Where we are today, the growth we have attained as recovering women and the plans we have for further changes are prompted by the same driving desires that contributed to our many actions in years gone by.

We can reflect on a particular experience and tag it a turning point. However, neither a lone prescription nor a single martini opened the door we passed through when we chose recovery. But they each may have played a part, and it's the many parts of our lives, past and present, that guarantee us the turning points that nudge us further up the mountain. We will see the summit. And we will understand how, each time we stumbled, new strength was gained.

Every day is a training ground. And every experience trains
me to recognize the value of succeeding experiences.
With richness, I am developing, one moment at a time.

MY THOUGHTS ❧ FOR THE DAY

Love is an expression and assertion of self-esteem,
a response to one's own values in the person of another.
—AYN RAND

The struggle to love one another may be a daily one for us, and it is made more difficult because we are still stumbling in our attempts at self-love. Many of us have lived our whole adult lives feeling inadequate, dull, unattractive, fearing the worst regarding our relationships with others.

But this phase, this struggle, is passing. We see a woman we like in the mirror each morning. We did a task or a favor yesterday that we felt good about. And when we feel good about our accomplishments, we look with a loving eye on the persons around us. Self-love does encourage other love.

Self-love takes practice. It's new behavior. We can begin to measure what we are doing, rather than what we haven't yet managed to do, and praise ourselves. Nurturing our inner selves invites further expression of the values that are developing, values that will carry us to new situations and new opportunities for accomplishments, and finally to loving the woman who looks back at us every morning.

Self-love makes me vulnerable and compassionate towards others. It's the balm
for all wounds; it multiplies as it's expressed. It can begin with my smile.

M Y   T H O U G H T S   F O R   T H E   D A Y

The pure relationship, how beautiful it is! How easily it is damaged,
or weighted down with irrelevancies—not even irrelevancies,
just life itself, the accumulations of life and of time.
—ANNE MORROW LINDBERGH

Many of us are presently rebuilding old relationships and searching for new ones, ones that we hope we can protect. We can't survive without relationships, some intimate, some close, some casual. And we discover ourselves through our relationships with others.

The purity of a relationship is directly proportional to the undivided attention we both give to those shared moments, hours, experiences, to being there with one another. This communion with another is the celebration of life and God that quickens hearts and ushers in serenity.

Each day I can look for those chances to give myself wholly.
And gifts will abound.

M Y   T H O U G H T S   F O R   T H E   D A Y

....

....

....

....

....

....

....

....

....

Anger repressed can poison a relationship as surely as the cruelest words.
—Joyce Brothers

Anger is familiar to us all. We feel it toward others and from others. The expression and acceptance of anger are where we often falter. Most of us were told when we were small girls that we shouldn't be angry, but we were. And we are, even yet. However, we often still feel like a little girl when it comes to angry feelings.

We need to accept our anger and learn to express it, honestly, openly and assertively, not aggressively. We can't afford to hang on to anger. It grows and then festers and then boils. Soon it is interfering in all our relationships, and it provides a ready excuse for an old, self-destructive pattern we don't want to entertain for even a moment.

Nothing we set out to do today will have the right outcome if we carry anger within us. How we interpret life, how we treat our friends, what we do with our opportunities and our challenges—all these are determined by our attitudes. Repressed anger always blocks the way to a positive attitude.

Every experience can uplift me if anger doesn't weigh me down.

M Y   T H O U G H T S   FOR   T H E   D A Y

April

APRIL 1

To be wildly enthusiastic, or deadly serious—both are wrong.
Both pass. One must keep ever present a sense of humor.
—KATHERINE MANSFIELD

How familiar wild enthusiasm and deadly seriousness are to most of us. We experience life within the extremes. The thrill of wild enthusiasm we try to trap, to control. We are exhilarated and feel good. Our serious side traps us, controls us, lowers a pall on all our activities. Both expressions keep us stuck. Neither expression allows the freedom of spontaneity so necessary to a full, healthy life.

Through our addiction—the liquor, the upper, the person, the food—we were searching for a feeling we didn't feel. We were searching for an unnatural state of happiness, even perhaps wild enthusiasm, because we had so little of any enthusiasm for life. Our search failed. Again and again we'd "catch it," only to have it elude us.

We may not have given up the search. But we will come to accept both states of mind as temporary and search instead for the middle ground. A sense of humor will make all of life's loads easier to bear. A sense of humor will offer us the balance that has been missing for so many years.

Today will offer me a chance to be wildly enthusiastic and a chance to be deadly serious. I'll try to focus on the middle ground and cultivate my sense of humor.

MY THOUGHTS FOR THE DAY

....

....

....

....

....

....

....

APRIL 2

Courage is the price that life exacts for granting peace.
—AMELIA EARHART

We have learned from experience that a wave of peacefulness washes over us after we have successfully finished a task that was difficult to face. Courage has its reward. However, from time to time, and from task to task, we find we need the reminder that peace will come once the loose ends have been tied by us.

Our search for peace was desperate and unending in past years. Our fears overwhelmed us more often than not. Courage was seldom displayed. Tasks were often left half done or not done at all. Challenges went unmet. And peace eluded us.

We are so lucky that the program found us, and that we found the program! We are looking forward, at last, with the courage that trusting a higher power has given us. Peace is ours, now and always, as we go forth with the strength of the program to bolster us. New jobs, new friends, new situations may still elicit our old fears. But their hold on us is gone. We have learned that we face nothing alone. What relief that simple truth brings.

Courage is one of the program's gifts. I will have courage to go forward:
to meet the new day, to handle whatever confronts me.
Peace is coupled with courage, now and forever.

MY THOUGHTS FOR THE DAY

....

....

....

....

....

....

....

APRIL 3

Those who do not know how to weep with their whole heart
don't know how to laugh either.
—GOLDA MEIR

We all know people who live on the fringes of life. They seem uninvolved with the activity in their midst, as though a pane of glass separated them from us. And there are times when we join the persons standing alone away from the vibrancy of life. Fears keep people apart, particularly the fear of letting go of the vulnerable self and joining in the feelings of the moment.

To fully reap the benefits of life, we have to risk full exposure to one another and to the experience of the moment. Full involvement in the ebb and flow of life will bring the weeping that accompanies both the pain and the joy of life. It will also bring the fruits of laughter.

Both laughter and weeping cleanse us. They bring closure to an experience. They make possible our letting go. And we must let go of pain, as well as joy, to ready ourselves for the next blessing life offers us.

When we keep ourselves apart, when we hold off the tears or the laughter, we cheat ourselves of the richness of life. We have to go through an experience fully in order to learn all it can teach us and then be free of it.

Past experiences never let me go until I fully grieve those that
need to be grieved or laugh over those that deserve the light touch.
The present is distorted when the past shadows it.

MY THOUGHTS ❧ FOR THE DAY

....

....

....

....

....

....

All we are asked to bear we can bear. That is a law of the spiritual life.
The only hindrance to the working of this law, as of all benign laws, is fear.
—ELIZABETH GOUDGE

There is no problem too difficult to handle with all the help available to us. Let's not be overwhelmed. The program tells us to "Let go and let God," to turn it over. And that's where the solution lies.

Our challenges, the stumbling blocks in our way, beckon us toward the spiritual working-out of the problem, which moves us closer toward being the women we are meant to be. Our fear comes from not trusting in the power greater than ourselves to provide the direction we need, to make known the solution.

Every day we will have challenges. We have lessons to learn, which means growing pains. If we could but remember that our challenges are gifts to grow on and that within every problem lies the solution.

I will not be given more than I and my higher power can handle today, or any day.

M Y   T H O U G H T S   ❧   F O R   T H E   D A Y

....

....

....

....

....

....

....

....

....

A P R I L   5

I came to the conclusion then that "continual mindfulness". . . must mean,
not a sergeant-major-like drilling of thoughts, but a continual
readiness to look and readiness to accept whatever came.
—JOANNA FIELD

Resistance to the events, the situations, the many people who come into our lives blocks the growth we are offered every day. Every moment of every day is offering us a gift: the gift of awareness of other persons, awareness of our natural surroundings, awareness of our own personal impact on creation. And in awareness comes our growth as women.

Living in the now, being present in the moment, guarantees us the protection of God. And in the stretches of time when we anxiously anticipate the events of the future, we cheat ourselves of the security God offers us right now.

We are always being taken care of, right here, right now. Being mindful, this minute, of what's happening, and only this, eases all anxieties, erases all fears. We only struggle when we have moved our sights from the present moment. Within the now lies all peace.

The most important lesson I have to learn, the lesson that will
eliminate all of my pain and struggle, is to receive fully
that which is offered in each moment of my life.

M Y   T H O U G H T S   FOR   T H E   D A Y

....

....

....

....

....

....

....

Treat your friends as you do your pictures, and place them in their best light.
—JENNIE JEROME CHURCHILL

Taking our friends and loved ones for granted, expecting perfection from them in every instance, greatly lessens the value we have in one another's lives. Being hard on those closest to us may relieve some of the tension we feel about our own imperfections, but it creates another tension, one that may result in our friends leaving us behind.

We need the reminder, perhaps, that our friends are special to our growth. Our paths have crossed with reason. We complete a portion of the plan for one another's lives. And for such gifts we need to offer gratitude.

Each of us is endowed with many qualities, some more enhancing than others; it is our hope, surely, that our lesser qualities will be ignored. We must do likewise for our friends. We can focus on the good, and it will flourish—in them, in ourselves, in all situations. A positive attitude nurtures everyone. Let us look for the good, and in time, it is all that will catch our attention.

I can make this day one to remember with fondness. I will appreciate a friend. I will let her know she matters in my life. Her life will be enhanced by my attention.

M Y   T H O U G H T S   FOR   T H E   D A Y

A P R I L   7

It is only when people begin to shake loose from their preconceptions,
from the ideas that have dominated them,
that we begin to receive a sense of opening, a sense of vision.
—BARBARA WARD

A sense of vision, seeing who we can dare to be and what we can dare to accomplish, is possible if we focus intently on the present and always the present. We are all we need to be, right now. We can trust that. And we will be shown the way to become who we need to become, step by step, from one present moment to the next present moment. We can trust that, too.

The past that we hang onto stands in our way. Many of us needlessly spend much of our lives fighting a poor self-image. But we can overcome that. We can choose to believe we are capable and competent. We can be spontaneous, and our vision of all that life can offer will change—will excite us, will cultivate our confidence.

We can respond to life wholly. We can trust our instincts. And we will become all that we dare to become.

Each day is a new beginning. Each moment is a new opportunity to
let go of all that has trapped me in the past. I am free. In the present, I am free.

M Y   T H O U G H T S 🌿 F O R   T H E   D A Y

....

....

....

....

....

....

....

APRIL 8

Life is patchwork—here and there, scraps of pleasure and despair.
Joined together, hit or miss.
—ANNE BRONAUGH

As you look ahead, to this day, you can count on unexpected experiences. You can count on moments of laughter. And you can count on twinges of fear. Life is seldom what we expect, but we can trust that we will survive the rough times. They will, in fact, soften our edges. Pleasure and pain share equally in the context of our lives.

We so easily forget that our growth comes through the challenges we label "problems." We do have the tools at hand to reap the benefits inherent in the problems that may face us today. Let us move gently forward, take the program with us, and watch the barriers disappear.

There is no situation that a Step won't help us with. Maybe we'll need to "turn over" a dilemma today. Accepting powerlessness over our children, or spouse, or co-worker may free us of a burden today. Or perhaps amends will open the communication we seek with someone in our lives. The program will weave the events of our day together. It will give them meaning.

Today, well lived, will prepare me for both the pleasure and the pain of tomorrow.

MY THOUGHTS FOR THE DAY

....

....

....

....

....

....

....

APRIL 9

For is it not true that human progress is but a mighty growing pattern woven
together by the tenuous single threads united in a common effort?
—SOONG MEI-LING (MADAME CHIANG KAI-SHEK)

We each are spinning our individual threads, lending texture, color, pattern, to the "big design" that is serving us all. Person by person our actions, our thoughts, our values complement those of our sisters, those of the entire human race. We are heading toward the same destination, all of us, and our paths run parallel on occasion, intersect periodically, and veer off in singleness of purpose when inspiration calls us.

It's comforting to be reminded that our lives are purposeful. What we are doing presently, our interactions with other people, our goals, have an impact that is felt by many others. We are interdependent. Our behavior is triggering important thoughts and responses in someone else, consistently and methodically. No one of us is without a contribution to make. Each one of us is giving what we are called upon to give when we are in a right relationship with God, who is the master artist in this design we are creating.

Prayer and meditation will direct my efforts today.
My purpose can then be fulfilled.

M Y   T H O U G H T S   ✿   F O R   T H E   D A Y

....

....

....

....

....

....

....

....

Even though I can't solve your problems,
I will be there as your sounding board whenever you need me.
—SANDRA K. LAMBERSON

The prize we each have been given is our ability to offer full and interested attention to people seeking our counsel. And seldom does a day pass that we aren't given the opportunity to listen, to nurture, to offer hope where it's been dashed.

We are not separate, one from another. Interdependence is our blessing; however, we fail to recognize it at our crucial crossroads. Alone we ponder. Around us, others, too, are often suffering in silence. These Steps that guide our lives push us to break the silence. The secrets we keep, keep us from the health we deserve.

Our emotional well-being is enhanced each time we share ourselves—our stories or our attentive ears. We need to be a part of someone else's pain and growth in order to make use of the pain that we have grown beyond. Pain has its purpose in our lives. And in the lives of our friends, too. It's our connection to one another, the bridge that closes the gap.

We dread our pain. We hate the suffering our friends must withstand. But each of us gains when we accept these challenges as our invitations for growth and closeness to others.

Secrets keep us sick. I will listen and share and be well.

M Y   T H O U G H T S   ❧   F O R   T H E   D A Y

....

....

....

....

....

....

....

APRIL 11

*An element of recovery is learning that we deserve success, the good things
that come to us, and also that pain is a reality. We have the strength to deal
with that pain without medicating, and it will pass.*
—DUDLEY MARTINEAU

Many of us didn't understand the changing variables in being human. Our coping skills
were at a minimum until we discovered what alcohol or pills, even food, could do for us.
And then, a drink or two—or six, maybe—got us through many a lonely evening.

The desire for an easy solution might still haunt us, but time, new experiences, and program friends have taught us that our past habits weren't really easy solutions. In reality,
they increased our problems and led us nowhere.

The Steps and the principles of the program, if applied, guarantee success, living success.
We come to believe that strength enough to handle any situation is ours for the asking. And
experience with these principles shows us that when we live the way our conscience dictates, the rewards are many.

Every day, especially this one facing us, our choices and decisions will be many. But there
is only one solution to any problem, and that's the one our higher power guides us to. The
answer, the choice, always lies within, and the good life will accompany our thoughtful,
reverent choices.

*The power of the program is mine for the taking.
All of today's problems can be eased, if I choose to do so.*

MY THOUGHTS FOR THE DAY

....

....

....

....

....

....

APRIL 12

*Make yourself a blessing to someone. Your kind smile or
pat on the back just might pull someone back from the edge.*
—CARMELIA ELLIOTT

Someone will be helped today by our kindness. Compassionate attention assures others that they do matter, and every one of us needs that reassurance occasionally. The program has given us the vehicle for giving and seeking the help we need—it's sponsorship.

Not all of the people we encounter share our program, however. Sponsorship as we know it isn't a reality in their lives. Offering words of encouragement to them, or a willing ear, can be unexpected gifts. They will be deeply appreciated.

The real gift, though, is to ourselves. Helping someone in need benefits the helper even more. Our own closeness to God and thus assurance about our own being is strengthened each time we do God's work—each time we do what our hearts direct.

We are healed in our healing of others. God speaks to us through our words to others. Our own well-being is enhanced each time we put someone else's well-being first.

*We're all on a trip, following different road maps, but to the
same destination. I will be ready to lend a helping hand to a
troubled traveler today. It will breathe new life into my own trip.*

MY THOUGHTS ❧ FOR THE DAY

....

....

....

....

....

....

....

A P R I L   1 3

The world is a wheel always turning. Those who are high go down low,
and those who've been low go up higher.
—ANZIA YEZIERSKA

Everything changes. Nothing stays the same. And letting go of the way things are, anticipating instead what they might become, frees us to live each moment more fully.

Time marches on, and our destiny marches with it. There is purpose in how our lives unfold; the ups and downs serve our growth. We must neither resent the doldrums nor savor too long the elation. Giving too much attention to either state interferes with our awareness of the present. And the present has come to teach us.

We must move with time. We must focus our attention on the moment and accept whatever feelings each experience elicits. Emotional maturity is accepting our feelings and letting them go and facing the next moment with fresh receptivity. Our lessons are many, and they accompany the lows as well as the highs. We can be grateful for both.

The program has taught us freedom from lingering lows. It has given us the tools to move confidently forward, trusting that all is well. Nothing lasts forever, and within each struggle is the opportunity for real growth.

The highs will pass away, just as will the lows. They visit us purposefully.
I will give them their freedom and find mine as well.

M Y   T H O U G H T S   ❀   F O R   T H E   D A Y

....

....

....

....

....

....

....

APRIL 14

Only those who dare, truly live.
—RUTH P. FREEDMAN

We receive from life, from every experience, from each interaction, according to what we have given. When we commit ourselves fully to an experience, it will bless us. When we give ourselves wholly to any moment, our awareness of reality will be heightened. When we risk knowing others, truly knowing them, we will find ourselves.

How common, and how unfortunate, that so many of us "escape" life! We escape through hiding, hiding from ourselves and others. We fear self-disclosure, our own and someone else's. Before choosing abstinence, our escape was easier. Now, the Steps make escape hard, fortunately.

Having a sponsor—and being one—helps. Taking the Fifth Step and working the Twelfth help. Going to meetings and sharing help. Our experiences today won't come around again—in just the same way. The people in our lives won't say again just what they'll say today. We must not miss out on what life offers. We can risk feeling it all, hearing it all, seeing it all.

The riches of a full life are so easily mine, and so deservedly mine.

MY THOUGHTS ❧ FOR THE DAY

APRIL 15

It seems to me that I have always been waiting for something better—sometimes to see the best I had snatched from me.
—DOROTHY REED MENDENHALL

Gratitude for what is prepares us for the blessings just around the corner. What is so necessary to understand is that our wait for what's around the corner closes our eyes to the joys of the present moment.

We have only the 24 hours ahead of us. In fact, all we can be certain of having is the moment we are presently experiencing. And it is a gift to be enjoyed. There is no better gift just right for us than this moment, at this time.

We can, each of us, look back on former days, realizing that we learned too late the value of a friend or an experience. Both are now gone. With practice and a commitment to ourselves, we can learn to reap the benefits of today, hour by hour. When we detach from the present and wait for tomorrow, or next week, or look to next year, we are stunting our spiritual growth. Life can only bless us now, one breath at a time.

I can live in the present if I choose to. Gentle reminders are often necessary, however. I will step into my life, today. It can become a habit, one I will never want to break.

MY THOUGHTS FOR THE DAY

APRIL 16

In the face of an obstacle which is impossible to overcome, stubbornness is stupid.
—SIMONE DE BEAUVOIR

Sudden obstacles, barriers in the way of our progress, doors that unexpectedly close, may confuse, frustrate, even depress us. The knowledge that we seldom understand just what is best for us comes slowly. And we generally fight it, even after we've begun to understand. Fortunately, the better path will keep drawing us to it.

We may wonder why a door seems to have closed. Our paths are confounded only when our steps have gone astray. Doors do not close unless a new direction is called for. We must learn to trust that no obstacle is without its purpose, however baffling it may seem.

The program can help us understand the unexpected. We perhaps need to focus on the first three Steps when an obstacle has surfaced. We may need to accept our powerlessness, believe there is a higher power in control, and look to it for guidance. We may also need to remind ourselves that fighting an obstacle, pushing against a closed door, will only heighten our frustration. Acceptance of what is will open our minds and our hearts to the better road to travel at this time.

The obstacles confronting me invite me to grow, to move beyond
my present self. They offer me chances to be the woman
I always dreamed of being. I will be courageous. I am not alone.

M Y   T H O U G H T S   🌸   F O R   T H E   D A Y

APRIL 17

I can stand what I know. It's what I don't know that frightens me.
—FRANCES NEWTON

Fear of the unknown, often referred to as free-floating anxiety, catches up to us on occasion. But it needn't. The program offers us strength whenever we need it, and faith diminishes all fear. It is said that fear cannot exist where there is faith.

We have many days when we feel strong, in touch with our higher power, able to meet all situations. On those days, we are seldom conscious of how our faith is guiding us. But the hours of fear that we experience on other days make us aware of faith's absence. There is a simple solution: We can reach out to a friend. We can be attentive to her needs, and the connection to God will be made.

Shifting our focus from self-centered fears to another person's needs offers us a perspective on our own life. It also offers us a chance to let God work through us. Our own faith is strengthened each time we offer our services to God and to a friend in need. What may frighten us seems less important the closer we are to the people in our lives.

When I touch someone else, God touches me in return.

MY THOUGHTS FOR THE DAY

....

....

....

....

....

....

....

....

APRIL 18

To oppose something is to maintain it.
—URSULA K. LEGUIN

Most of our struggles are with other persons or perhaps situations we want to change. We discover that our continual opposition adds fuel to the fires (at least our own internal ones). But can we turn our backs when we feel justified in our opposition? There's perhaps no more difficult action to take than to walk away from those situations we feel so strongly about, but the wisdom of this program says, "Let go and let God." And when we do let go, as if by magic, relief comes. The fires die out. That which we opposed is less troubling, maybe even gone. We no longer feel the need to struggle today. The need may rise again, but again we can turn to our higher power. Trusting that relief awaits us, ensures its arrival.

As women we discover many opportunities for opposition, too many persons and situations that make our changing roles difficult—too many persons who don't easily accept our changing characters. We must share with one another the strength to let go and let God.

I maintain my struggles with righteous behavior.
They lose their sting when they lose my opposition. I will step aside and let God.

M Y   T H O U G H T S   F O R   T H E   D A Y

....

....

....

....

....

....

....

....

APRIL 19

In the process of defining myself, I have a tendency to set up rules and
boundaries and then forget that rules are made to be broken,
as are boundaries to be expanded and crossed.
—KATHLEEN CASEY THEISEN

Recovery has given us the freedom to address life honestly, with forethought and a certainty about the rightness of our actions. We need be mindful that what is right today may not be right tomorrow or thereafter. As we move through our experiences, we are changed, and then we look with a new perspective on old conditions. Our new perspective hones our value systems, and yesterday's rules and boundaries no longer fit today's situations.

Our growth as women is an unending process. What we confront today with assurance, we prepared for yesterday. And tomorrow will be eased by our definition of today. The program has gifted us with clarity—clarity about ourselves, clarity regarding others, and clarity on how to continue our growth.

My value system awaits finer definition, and every experience today
presents me with an opportunity for that definition.

M Y   T H O U G H T S   ❀   F O R   T H E   D A Y

....

....

....

....

....

....

....

....

One has to grow up with good talk in order to form the habit of it.
—HELEN HAYES

Our habits, whatever they may be, were greatly influenced, if not wholly formed, during childhood. We learned our behavior through imitation—imitation of our parents, our siblings, our peer group. But we need not be stuck in habits that are unhealthy. The choice to create new patterns of behavior is ours to make—every moment, every hour, every day. However, parting with the old pattern in order to make way for the new takes prayer, commitment, determination.

All of us who share these Steps have broken away from old patterns. We have chosen to leave liquor and pills alone. We may have chosen to leave unhealthy relationships. And we are daily choosing to move beyond our shortcomings. But not every day is a successful one. Our shortcomings have become ingrained. Years of pouting, or lying, or feeling fearful, or overeating, or procrastinating beckon to us; the habit invites itself.

We can find strength from the program and one another to let go of the behavior that stands in the way of today's happiness. And we can find in one another a better, healthier behavior to imitate.

The program is helping me to know there is a better way, every day, to move ahead. I am growing up again amidst the good habits of others, and myself.

M Y   T H O U G H T S   F O R   T H E   D A Y

....

....

....

....

....

....

....

APRIL 21

To look backward for a while is to refresh the eye, to restore it,
and to render it the more fit for its prime function of looking forward.
—MARGARET FAIRLESS BARBER

When we contemplate last month, last year, the period of time just before we came into this Twelve Step program, we can see many changes, good changes, have come our way. But we take the changes for granted sometimes. Or maybe we fail to reflect on them at all. We get caught up in the turmoil of the present, believing it will last forever, forgetting that yesterday's turmoil taught us much that we needed to know.

The past, for most of us, was rife with pain. But now we have hope. We have gained on life. We may be back in the good graces of our family. Perhaps we have patched up some failed relationships. A career has beckoned to us. Good experiences have come to pass. But we aren't free of difficulties. They need not get us down again. Hindsight assures us that this, too, will pass. It also guarantees that we will move forward, just as we have again and again, if only we have faith.

I will take this moment to look back at last year or the last binge.
I can rest assured that I am moving forward. I will continue to do so.

MY THOUGHTS FOR THE DAY

....

....

....

....

....

....

....

....

Our own rough edges become smooth as we help a friend smooth her edges.
—SUE ATCHLEY EBAUGH

Focusing on a good point in every person we encounter today will benefit us in untold ways. It will smooth our relations with that person, inviting her to respond kindly also. It will increase our awareness of the goodness all around us. It will help us realize that if everyone around us has positive traits, then we must also have them. But perhaps the greatest benefit of focusing on good points is that it enhances us as women; a healthy, positive attitude must be cultivated. Many of us had little experience with feeling positive before the turning point, recovery.

Recovery is offering us a new lease on life every moment. We are learning new behaviors, and we are learning that with the help of a higher power and one another, all things that are right for us are possible. It is energizing to focus on the good points of others, to know that their good points don't detract from our own.

In the past, we may have secretly hated other women's strengths because we felt inferior. We are free from that hate now, if we choose to be. A strength we can each nurture is gratitude for being helped by, and privy to, the strengths of our friends and acquaintances.

Bad points get worse with attention. My good points will gain strength.

M Y T H O U G H T S F O R T H E D A Y

A P R I L   2 3

When you cease to make a contribution, you begin to die.
—ELEANOR ROOSEVELT

We need to take note, today, of all the opportunities we have to offer a helping hand to another person. We can notice too the many times a friend, or even a stranger, reaches out to us in a helpful way. The opportunities to contribute to life's flow are unending.

Our own vibrancy comes from involvement with others, from contributing our talents, our hearts, to one another's daily travels. The program helps us to know that God lives in us, among us. When we close ourselves off from our friends, our fellow travelers, we block God's path to us and through us.

To live means sharing one another's space, dreams, sorrows; contributing our ears to hear, our eyes to see, our arms to hold, our hearts to love. When we close ourselves off from each other, we have destroyed the vital contribution we each need to make and to receive in order to nurture life.

We each need only what the other can give. Each person we meet today needs our special contribution.

What a wonderful collection of invitations awaits me today!

M Y   T H O U G H T S   ❧   F O R   T H E   D A Y

....

....

....

....

....

....

....

....

APRIL 24

She knows omnipotence has heard her prayer and cries
"it shall be done—sometime, somewhere."
—OPHELIA GUYON BROWNING

Patience is a quality that frequently eludes us. We want what we want when we want it. Fortunately, we don't get it until the time is right, but the waiting convinces us our prayers aren't heard. We must believe that the answer always comes in its own special time and place. The frustration is that our timetable is seldom like God's.

When we look back over the past few weeks, months, or even years, we can recall past prayers. Had they all been answered at the time of request, how different our lives would be. We are each on a path unique to us, offering special lessons to be learned. Just as a child must crawl before walking, so must we move slowly, taking the steps in our growth in sequence.

Our prayers will be answered, sometime, somewhere. Of that we can be sure. They will be answered for our greater good. And they will be answered at the right time, the right place, in the right way.

I am participating in a much bigger picture than the one in my
individual prayers. And the big picture is being carefully orchestrated.
I will trust the part I have been chosen to play. And I can be patient.

M Y   T H O U G H T S   F O R   T H E   D A Y

....

....

....

....

....

....

....

APRIL 25

Everything has its wonders, even darkness and silence, and I learn,
whatever state I may be in, therein to be content.
—HELEN KELLER

There is wonder in the moment, if we but look for it, let it touch us, believe in it. And with the recognition and celebration of the wonder comes the joy we desire and await.

Being wholly in tune with the present moment is how we'll come to know the spiritual essence that connects all of life. We search for peace, happiness, and contentment outside of ourselves. We need instead to discover it within us, now and always, in whatever we are experiencing.

We can let our experiences wash over us. Longing for a different time, a distant place, a new situation breeds discontent. It prevents us from the thrill, the gifts offered in this present moment. But they are there.

We can practice feeling joyful in the present, be thrilled with the realization that right now, all is well. All is always well. Life is full of mystery and wonder and each moment of our awareness adds to the wonder.

I am moving forward; we all are. I am on target. I am participating in a glorious,
wonderful drama. Let me jump for joy. I have been specially blessed.

M Y   T H O U G H T S   ❀   F O R   T H E   D A Y

....

....

....

....

....

....

....

APRIL 26

. . . pain is the root of knowledge.
—SIMONE WEIL

We don't want pain in our lives. We dread the situations we anticipate will be painful. We probably even pray to be spared all painful experiences. But they come anyway, at times in profusion. And we not only survive the pain, we profit from it.

It seems that pain stretches us to our limits, generally forcing us to look for guidance from others, and it pushes us to consider new choices in our present situation. Pain is our common denominator as women, as members of the human family. It softens us to one another. It fosters empathy. It helps us to reach out and realize our need for one another.

New knowledge, new awarenesses, are additional benefits of accepting, rather than denying, the pain that accompanies life. This journey that we're on is moving us further and further along the path of enlightenment. We can consider that each problem, each crisis, is our necessary preparation for moving another step down the road.

I learn out of necessity. And when the student is ready, the teacher will appear.

MY THOUGHTS FOR THE DAY

APRIL 27

So much to say. And so much not to say! Some things are better left unsaid.
But so many unsaid things can become a burden.
—VIRGINIA MAE AXLINE

The occasions are many when we'd like to share a feeling, an observation, perhaps even a criticism with someone. The risk is great, however. She might be hurt, or he might walk away, leaving us alone.

Many times, we need not share our words directly. Weighing and measuring the probable outcome and asking for some inner guidance will help us decide when to speak up and when to leave things unsaid. But if our thoughts are seriously interfering with our relationships, we can't ignore them for long.

Clearing the air is necessary sometimes, and it freshens all relationships. Deciding when to take the risk creates consternation. But within our quiet spaces, we always know when we must speak up. And the direction will come. The right moment will present itself. And within those quiet spaces the right words can be found.

If I am uncomfortable with certain people, and the feelings don't leave,
I will consider what might need to be said. I will open myself to the way
and ask to be shown the steps to take. Then, I will be patient.

MY THOUGHTS 🌿 FOR THE DAY

APRIL 28

. . . suffering . . . no matter how multiplied . . . is always individual.
—ANNE MORROW LINDBERGH

Knowing that others have survived experiences equally devastating gives us hope, but it doesn't diminish our own personal suffering. Nor should it; out of suffering comes new understanding. Suffering also encourages our appreciation of the lighter, easier times. Pain experienced fully enhances the times of pleasure.

Our sufferings are singular, individual, and lonely. But our experiences with it can be shared, thereby lessening the power they have over us. Sharing our pain with another woman also helps her remember that her pain, too, is survivable.

Suffering softens us, helps us to feel more compassion and love toward another. Our sense of belonging to the human race, our recognition of the interdependence and kinship of us all, are the most cherished results of the gift of pain.

Each of our sufferings, sharing them as we do,
strengthens me and heals my wounds of alienation.

MY THOUGHTS ❧ FOR THE DAY

....

....

....

....

....

....

....

....

....

APRIL 29

Love between two people is such a precious thing. It is not a possession. I no longer need to possess to complete myself. True love becomes my freedom.
—ANGELA L. WOZNIAK

Self-doubt fosters possessiveness. When we lack confidence in our own capabilities, when we fear we don't measure up as women, mothers, lovers, employees, we cling to old behavior, maybe to unhealthy habits, perhaps to another person. We can't find our completion in another person because that person changes and moves away from our center. Then we feel lost once again.

Completion of the self accompanies our spiritual progress. As our awareness of the reality of our higher power's caring role is heightened, we find peace. We trust that we are becoming all that we need to be. We need only have faith in our connection to that higher power. We can let that faith possess us, and we'll never need to possess someone else.

God's love is ours, every moment. Recognition is all that's asked of us. Acceptance of this ever-present love will make us whole, and self-doubt will diminish. Clinging to other people traps us as much as them, and all growth is hampered, ours and theirs.

Freedom to live, to grow, to experience my full capabilities is as close as my faith. I will cling only to that and discover the love that's truly in my heart and the hearts of my loved ones.

MY THOUGHTS FOR THE DAY

A P R I L   3 0

Accustomed as we are to change, or unaccustomed,
we think of a change of heart, of clothes, of life, with some uncertainty.
—JOSEPHINE MILES

Being used to a situation, even a painful one, carries with it a level of comfort. Moving away from the pain, changing the situation, be it job, home, or marriage, takes courage and support from other persons. But even more it takes faith that the change will benefit us. For most of us, the pain will need to worsen.

In retrospect, we wonder why it took us so long. We forget, from one instance to the next, that a new door cannot open until we've closed one behind us. The more important fact is that a new one will always open without fail. The pain of the old experience is trying to push us to new challenges, new opportunities, new growth. We can handle the change; we can handle the growth. We are never given more than we can handle, and we are always given just what we need.

Experience can't prepare us for the ramifications of a new change. But our trust in friends, and our faith in the spiritual process of life, can and will see us through whatever comes.

If a change of any kind is facing me today, I will know that I am not alone.
Whatever I am facing is right for me and necessary to my well-being.
Life is growth. The next stage of my life awaits me.

M Y   T H O U G H T S   ❧   F O R   T H E   D A Y

....

....

....

....

....

....

....

May

MAY 1

Insight is cheap.
—MARTHA ROTH

For years we kept ourselves in a split condition: With one part of our minds we looked at ourselves and said, "I do some self-destructive things because I don't believe I deserve love." When we became involved with unsuitable people or abused our bodies, we said, "I am punishing myself—I am expecting too much—I neglect my own needs."

We may see clearly how and why we get in our own way. But unless we have faith in a power greater than ourselves, we won't step aside. We won't let go. We'll do the same thing and "understand" ourselves in the same ways. We may even use our "insight" to keep ourselves stuck—to protect ourselves from the risk of change.

Now, having had a spiritual awakening, having come to believe that a higher power can restore us, we possess a gift more powerful than the keenest insight—faith in our ability to grow and change. We are children of God. All the creative power of the universe streams through us, if we don't block it.

Today, I will have faith, and all will be well.

MY THOUGHTS FOR THE DAY

....

....

....

....

....

....

....

....

MAY 2

One must be leery of words because they turn into cages.
—VIOLA SPOLIN

We defeat ourselves with labels. We hem ourselves in; we shorten our vision; we cut off opportunities in the making. We influence how others think of us, too. Someone wise said that we teach others how to treat us. Are we teaching people to expect nothing great from us—because we are always afraid? Do we shatter their vision of our potential—by never thinking we can handle what may come?

We become the persons we have programmed ourselves to be. We can revamp the program, anytime. And right now is a good time to begin. We are surrounded by persons who have done just that.

It's time for praise. We are all that we need to be, and more. We will be helped to do all we are asked to do. We have an inner beauty that only needs encouragement to shine forth. If we smile from within today, we will free ourselves from our negative cages. A new life awaits us.

To catch myself each time I insult myself will be a challenge,
but one worth taking on. And it's one I can win!

MY THOUGHTS FOR THE DAY

....

....

....

....

....

....

....

....

MAY 3

. . . love is a great beautifier.
—LOUISA MAY ALCOTT

Meeting life head-on, with a smile, attracts people and situations to us. Our attitudes shape our world—which is not to deny that problems do occur. However, problems can be viewed as special opportunities for personal growth—as gifts, more or less, that we are ready to receive. When the student is ready, the teacher appears. The stumbling blocks we encounter push us beyond our present awareness. They teach us that we are stronger and more creative than we'd thought. Problem solving is esteem-building.

Negatively confronting the day is sure to complicate any experiences. A simple misunderstanding can be exaggerated into a grave situation, requiring the energy of many people to handle it. On the other hand, a patient, trusting, loving attitude can turn a grave situation into a positive learning experience for all affected.

We can beautify the day by smiling throughout all the experiences it offers us. The expression of love to everyone we meet guarantees to make us more lovable in return.

How great is my influence today! I can go forth feeling love,
if I choose to—guaranteeing an enjoyable day for me and everyone I meet.

MY THOUGHTS ❦ FOR THE DAY

....

....

....

....

....

....

....

M A Y 4

The rare and beautiful experiences of divine revelation are moments of
special gifts. Each of us, however, lives each day with special gifts which
are a part of our very being, and life is a process of discovering and
developing these God-given gifts within each one of us.
—JEANE DIXON

Have we discovered what our gifts are? We assuredly have them, and now that we are abstinent we have opportunities, daily, to share them with others. Sharing them knowingly will bring joy to us, but more than that, we will grow in appreciation of ourselves. And we do need to realize how very important we are to others.

Many of us came into this program nearly feet first. Most of us were filled with rage, shame, or both. Life had dumped on us. We had survived only minimally. The knowledge that we had something to offer the human race was not ours, then. It may still be knowledge that escapes us, from time to time. But we can learn to acknowledge it.

We have many talents that are ours alone to offer the world. Perhaps we express ourselves adroitly; maybe we write particularly well. Listening when it's most needed by a friend may be our finest talent today. We might have gifts as a musician or a manager. Our inner self knows our strengths. We can listen for that voice.

God is trying to get my attention today,
to direct my energies to make the most of my special talents. I will be aware.

M Y   T H O U G H T S   FOR   T H E   D A Y

....

....

....

....

....

....

MAY 5

. . it is a peaceful thing to be one succeeding.
—GERTRUDE STEIN

Success is at hand. While we read these words, we are experiencing it. At this very instant, our commitment to recovery is a sign of success, and we feel peace each time we let go of our struggle, turning to another for help, for direction. Because we strive only for perfection, we recognize nothing less; we block our awareness of the ordinary successes that are ours again and again. Thus, the serenity the program promises us eludes us. But we are succeeding. Every day that we are abstinent, we succeed.

We can think of the times—perhaps only yesterday—when we listened to a friend in need, or finished a task that was nagging at us. Maybe we made an appointment to begin a project we've been putting off. Success is taking positive action, nothing more.

Many of us, in our youth, were taught that success only came in certain shapes and sizes. And we felt like failures. We need new definitions; it's time to discard the old. Luckily for us, the program offers us new ones.

Every person, every situation, can add to my success today.
My attitude can help someone else succeed, too.

MY THOUGHTS FOR THE DAY

....

....

....

....

....

....

....

....

M A Y 6

I stand before you as a tower of strength, the weight of the world
on my shoulders. As you pass through my life, look, but not too close,
for I fear I will expose the vulnerable me.
—DEIDRA SARAULT

Vulnerability is as much a part of being human as is strength. Our vulnerability prevents our strength from becoming hard, brittle, self-serving. Our soft edges invite others' openness and their expressions of love.

We learned long ago to be "strong." We were encouraged to need no help, to need nobody. Now, we struggle to ask for help. As we grow in understanding of our human needs, and as we become more aware of the spiritual help available, the difficulty of reaching out to others is eased.

No longer need we look to pills, booze, food, or lovers for strength. All the strength we'll ever need is as close as our thoughts. At this moment, we are a tower of strength, not one weighted with burdens. Rather, our strength is a gift of our connection to a spiritual power that can free us from all the troubles we shoulder. Our vulnerable selves will open our souls to the flood of strength just waiting for our prayers.

I will be as strong as I need to be when I tap the spiritual source
that awaits my call. I will risk my vulnerable self today.

M Y T H O U G H T S ❧ F O R T H E D A Y

....

....

....

....

....

....

....

MAY 7

*We tend to think of the rational as a higher order, but it is the
emotional that marks our lives. One often learns more from
ten days of agony than from ten years of contentment.*
—MERLE SHAIN

Pain stretches us. It pushes us toward others. It encourages us to pray. It invites us to rely on many resources, particularly those within.

We develop our character while handling painful times. Pain offers wisdom. It prepares us to help other women whose experiences repeat our own. Our own pain offers us the stories that help another who is lost and needs our guidance.

When we reflect on our past for a moment, we can recall the pain we felt last month or last year; the pain of a lost love, or the pain of no job and many bills; perhaps the pain of children leaving home, or the death of a near and dear friend. It might have seemed to us that we couldn't cope. But we did, somehow, and it felt good. Coping strengthened us.

What we forget, even now, is that we need never experience a painful time alone. The agony that accompanies a wrenching situation is dissipated as quickly and as silently as the entrance of our higher power, when called upon.

*I long for contentment. And I deserve those times. But without life's pain
I would fail to recognize the value of contentment.*

MY THOUGHTS FOR THE DAY

....

....

....

....

....

....

....

MAY 8

The battle to keep up appearances unnecessarily, the mask—whatever
name you give creeping perfectionism—robs us of our energies.
—ROBIN WORTHINGTON

How familiar we are with trying to be women other than ourselves; ones more exciting, we think, or sexier, or smarter. We have probably devoted a great deal of energy to this over the years. It's likely that we are growing more content with ourselves now. However, aren't there still situations in which we squirm, both because we want to project a different image, and because we resent our desire to do so?

We each have been blessed with unique qualities. There is no other woman just like ourselves. We each have special features that are projected in only one way, the way we alone project them.

Knowing that we are perfect as we are is knowledge that accompanies recovery. How much easier life is, how much more can be gained from each moment, when we meet each experience in the comfort of our real selves. The added gift of simply being ourselves is that we'll really hear, see, and understand others for the first time in our lives.

I can fully focus on only one thing, one person at a time. I will free my focus
from myself today and be filled up by my experiences with others.

MY THOUGHTS FOR THE DAY

....

....

....

....

....

....

....

MAY 9

*To expect too much is to have a sentimental view of life, and this is a softness
that ends in bitterness.*
—FLANNERY O'CONNOR

Having too-high expectations is a setup for disappointment. Expectations that are high lend themselves to a fantasy life, and reality can never match our fantasies. When we get hooked on the fantasies, somehow thinking they are reality, or should be reality, we are vulnerable to the hurt that accompanies the emergence of "the real." Then we feel cheated—bitter: "Why did this have to happen to me?"

Having too-high expectations was a familiar feeling before recovery. And it remains familiar to us, even now. Dreams and aspirations aren't wrong. In fact, they beckon us on to better and greater things. But dreams of what we can become through responsible choices are quite different from idle expectations of what will or should be.

*Every moment of every day opens the way to my aspirations that enhance reality.
I will be open and receptive to reality and its gifts.*

MY   THOUGHTS 🌻 FOR   THE   DAY

....

....

....

....

....

....

....

....

....

MAY 10

To wait for someone else, or to expect someone else to make my life richer, or fuller, or more satisfying, puts me in a constant state of suspension; and I miss all those moments that pass. They never come back to be experienced again.
—KATHLEEN TIERNEY CRILLY

The steps we are taking today will never again be taken in exactly the same way. The thoughts we are thinking are fresh, never to be repeated. All that these moments offer will never pass our way again.

We each have to grab our own happiness, create our own richness through experiences. We may share what we capture with loved ones, but like us, they too must search their own avenues for the satisfaction that lasts. We can neither give happiness to another, like a gift, nor expect it in return.

The fullness of life we all long for is the natural by-product of living every moment as fully as possible. Our higher power will never direct us into waters too deep. When we have willingly turned our lives and our wills over, we'll find an abundance of the rich, the full, the satisfying. Faith in God answers all questions, solves all problems.

I will cherish every moment today.
Each one is special and will not visit me again.

MY THOUGHTS ❧ FOR THE DAY

....

....

....

....

....

....

....

MAY 11

Bad moments, like good ones, tend to be grouped together.
—EDNA O'BRIEN

Rough times may be pouring in on us at the moment, and they may seem unending. Difficulties appear to attract more difficulties, problems with loved ones, problems at work, problems with our appearance. A negative attitude, something that we all struggle with at times (some of us more than others), is the culprit.

When the good times come, as they always do, they are accompanied by a positive attitude. We do find what we look for.

Our attitude is crucial. It determines our experiences. A trying situation can be tolerated with relative ease when we have a positive, trusting attitude. We forget, generally, that we have an inner source of strength to meet every situation. We forget the simple truth—all is well, at this moment, and at every moment. When the moments feel good, our presence is light, cheery. When the moments are heavy, so are we.

I can turn my day around. I can change the flavor of today's experiences.
I can lift my spirits and know all is well.

MY THOUGHTS 🍂 FOR THE DAY

....

....

....

....

....

....

....

MAY 12

Every human being has, like Socrates, an attendant spirit;
and wise are they who obey its signals. If it does not always tell us what to do,
it always cautions us what not to do.
—LYDIA M. CHILD

Our Spirit is our inner guide. And our Spirit never, never, gives us wrong directions. Because we're human, it's all too easy to deny the voice from within. Some call it conscience. And our behavior, maybe frequently, maybe occasionally, belies what our conscience knows is right. We suffer for it.

We are trying to be healthy—emotionally, spiritually, physically. Each day we can make progress. With each action we take, we have a choice. Our Spirit, our conscience, should be consulted. Right choices make for right actions that will emotionally and spiritually benefit us and the other persons close to us.

It's comforting to rely on the inner voice. It assures us we're never alone. No decision has to be made alone. No wrong action need ever be taken. A sense of security accompanies the partnership between each of us and our Spirit.

I will let the partnership work for me today.

MY THOUGHTS ❀ FOR THE DAY

MAY 13

Your sense of what will bring happiness is so crude and blundering.
Try something else as a compass. Maybe the moralists are right
and happiness doesn't come from seeking pleasure and ease.
—JOANNA FIELD

We think we know what will make us happy. Seldom do we readily accept that painful moments are often the price tags for peaceful, happy times. Nor do we appreciate that happiness lives within each of us; never is it intrinsic to the events we experience. Because we look for happiness "out there" and expect it gift-wrapped in a particular way, we miss the joy of being fully alive each passing moment. How distorted our sense of happiness was before finding our way to this program! How futile our search!

The way still isn't easy every Step we take, but we will find happiness in those fleeting moments when we can get outside of ourselves long enough to be fully attentive to the people in our lives. We'll find it because it's been there all the time. It flows between us when we open our hearts to give and to receive compassion. Being truly there for another person is the key which unlocks the gate holding happiness back.

I will let someone in today and feel the rush of happiness.

MY THOUGHTS ❀ FOR THE DAY

M A Y 1 4

Miracles are instantaneous, they cannot be summoned, but come of themselves,
usually at unlikely moments and to those who least expect them.
—KATHERINE ANNE PORTER

Each of us has miraculously been summoned to the road to recovery. We no doubt felt hopeless many times. We no doubt pleaded, aimlessly and to no one in particular, for help. And then it came. Many of us probably do not know just how. But we can look around at one another and appreciate the miracle in our lives.

We still have days when the going is rough. Days when we feel twelve years old, unable to handle the responsibility of our lives, in need of a mother to nurture us and assure us that the pain will pass. We can look to a sponsor on those days. We can look for someone else to help. We can also reflect on how far we've come. In the midst of distress, gratitude for all the gifts of recovery eases the pain, the fear, the stress of the moment.

The miracles continue in my life. Every day offers me a miracle.
Thankfulness today will help me see the miracles at work in my life
and in the lives of other women on the road to recovery.

M Y T H O U G H T S 🌸 F O R T H E D A Y

MAY 15

Difficulties, opposition, criticism—these things are meant to be overcome, and there is a special joy in facing them and in coming out on top. It is only when there is nothing but praise that life loses its charm, and I begin to wonder what I should do about it.
—Vijaya Lakshmi Pandit

To be alive means to experience difficulties, conflicts, challenges from many directions. What we do with adverse conditions both determines and is determined by who we are. Resistance, most of us have learned, heightens the adversity. Acceptance of the condition, trusting all the while the lesson it offers us is for our benefit, ensures that we'll "come out on top."

Difficulties are opportunities for advancement, for increased self-awareness, for self-fulfillment. So often we hear and remind one another that we grow through pain. We can face any situation knowing we have the strength of the program to shore us up. Strangely, we need challenges in order to grow; without growth we wither. Happiness is the bounty for facing the momentarily unhappy conditions.

Any difficulty I meet today offers me a chance for even greater happiness; it guarantees my growth.

MY THOUGHTS FOR THE DAY

MAY 16

*It is only the women whose eyes have been washed clear with tears who get the
broad vision that makes them little sisters to all the world.*
—Dorothy Dix

The storms of our lives benefit us like the storms that hit our towns and homes and wash clean the air we breathe. Our storms bring to the surface the issues that plague us. Perhaps we still fear a job with responsibilities. Perhaps we still struggle with the significant other persons in our lives. Possessiveness is a particular storm that often haunts our progress. Storms force us to acknowledge these liabilities that continue to stand in our way, and acknowledgment is the step necessary to letting go.

Recovery is a whole series of storms, storms that help to sprout new growth, storms that flush clean our own clogged drains. The peace that comes after a storm is worth singing about.

Each storm can be likened to a rung on the ladder to wholeness, the ladder to full membership in the healthy human race. The storms make climbing tough, but we get strength with each step. The next storm will be more easily weathered.

If today is a stormy day, let me remember it will freshen the air I breathe.

MY THOUGHTS FOR THE DAY

....

....

....

....

....

....

....

....

MAY 17

Loving allows us to live and through living we grow in loving.
—Evelyn Mandel

Many days it seems too easy to be centered on ourselves, wondering if others love us rather than loving others. On those days, we may have to act "as if" we love the persons who live on our pathways. The unexpected gift is that we do begin to feel both love and loved. Living becomes easier, and so does loving. Acting "as if" is a good way of learning those behaviors that don't feel natural. And in time, acting "as if" is necessary no more.

I can behave in any way I decide to. I can choose to think about others,
and love them. I can choose to forget myself today.

MY THOUGHTS FOR THE DAY

MAY 18

. . . in order to feel anything you need strength . . .
—ANNA MARIA ORTESE

Strength for any task, to withstand any pressure, to find the solution to any problem, is always as close as our very breath. We expend all our energy, wearing ourselves down, even getting sick from worry when we fail to turn to the source of strength that is ours for the taking.

We are offered, moment by moment, opportunities to experience the rapture of life. We have the chance, with recovery, to trust our senses, to turn ourselves over to the moment, knowing we can survive every experience, knowing we are guaranteed new knowledge, a greater awareness of the meaning of our own lives when we're fully attuned to the experiences that are uniquely our own, right here, right now.

Our strength increases as we flex it, not unlike muscles. The more we turn to that greater power, the more available that source of strength becomes. With practice, it becomes habitual to let God help us withstand all pressures, solve every problem. In time, the pressures and problems seem to exist no more. We learn to let our higher power circumvent the difficulties in our lives. Free at last, we become free at last to feel the real joys of living.

All the strength I need to face anything that's worrying me is at hand.
I will let go and let God help me today.

MY THOUGHTS 🌸 FOR THE DAY

....

....

....

....

....

....

....

. . . if we are suffering illness, poverty, or misfortune, we think we shall be
satisfied on the day it ceases. But there too, we know it is false,
so soon as one has got used to not suffering, one wants something else.
—SIMONE WEIL

Perhaps it's the human condition never to be satisfied and yet always to think, "If only . . ." However, the more we look within for wholeness, the greater will be our acceptance of all things, at all times.

So frequently we hear that happiness is within. But what does that mean when we may have just lost the job that supported us and our children? Or when the car won't start and funds are low? Or when we are feeling really scared and don't know whom to talk to or where to go? "Happiness is within" is such a grand platitude at those times.

Nevertheless, our security in any situation is within, if we but know how to tap it. It is within because that is where the strength we are blessed with resides, the strength given us from the power greater than ourselves. "Going within" first takes a decision. Next, it takes stillness, and then, patience. But peace will come.

We will quit wanting when we have learned how to turn to our inner strength. We will find serenity rather than suffering.

I will go within whenever I feel the rumblings of dissatisfaction today. I will look
there for my joy and sense of well-being and know that divine order is in charge.

M Y   T H O U G H T S   F O R   T H E   D A Y

M A Y   2 0

It only takes one person to change your life—you.
—Ruth Casey

Change is not easy, but it's absolutely unavoidable. Doors will close. Barriers will surface. Frustrations will mount. Nothing stays the same forever, and it's such folly to wish otherwise. Growth accompanies positive change; determining to risk the outcome resulting from a changed behavior or attitude will enhance our self-perceptions. We will have moved forward; in every instance our lives will be influenced by making a change that only each of us can make.

We have all dreaded the changes we knew we had to make. Perhaps even now we fear some impending changes. Where might they take us? It's difficult accepting that the outcome is not ours to control. Only the effort is ours. The solace is that positive changes, which we know are right for us and other people in our lives, are never going to take us astray. In fact, they are necessary for the smooth path just beyond this stumbling block.

When we are troubled by circumstances in our lives, a change is called for, a change that we must initiate. When we reflect on our recent as well as distant past, we will remember that the changes we most dreaded again and again have positively influenced our lives in untold ways.

Change ushers in glad, not bad, tidings.

M Y   T H O U G H T S   F O R   T H E   D A Y

Our friends were not unearthly beautiful, Nor spoke with tongues of gold;
our lovers blundered now and again when we most sought perfection . . .
—ADRIENNE RICH

So often our expectations exceed reality. We want more than we have; our homes, our loved ones, perhaps our jobs seem not to measure up. "If only"—we say to ourselves. The time has come to quit saying "if only" and be glad, instead, for what is.

We are recovering. We do have friends and family who care about us. We do have exactly what we need at this moment.

We each can make a contribution today for the good of someone else and thus for ourselves. And in the act of looking to this day—to giving something to another human being—we will sense the inner perfection we mistakenly long for in our outer selves.

I can look around me today and be thankful. I will tell someone close
that I'm glad we share one another's world.

M Y   T H O U G H T S   F O R   T H E   D A Y

....

....

....

....

....

....

....

....

MAY 22

The change of one simple behavior can affect other behaviors
and thus change many things.
—JEAN BAER

Our behavior tells others and ourselves who we are. Frequently, we find ourselves behaving in ways that keep us stuck or embarrass us. Or we may feel deep shame for our behavior in a certain instance. Our behavior will never totally please us. But deciding we want to change some behavior and using the program to help us is a first step.

Remember, imperfections are human and very acceptable. However, changing a particular behavior, maybe deciding to take a walk every morning rather than sleeping 30 extra minutes, will change how we feel about ourselves. And a minor change such as this can have a remarkable effect on our outlook, our attitudes.

The dilemma for many of us for so long was the fear we couldn't change. But we can. And we can help each other change, too.

One small change today—a smile at the first person I meet—meditation before
dinner—a few minutes of exercise—will help me chart a new course. I will
encourage another woman to join me in this effort too, and I will be on my way.

MY THOUGHTS ❀ FOR THE DAY

MAY 23

*Give as much of yourself as you can to as much of
your higher power as you can understand.*
—S.H.

The more we are in concert with God, the greater will be our pleasures in life. Recognizing our partnership with our higher power makes every decision easier, facilitates the completion of every task, and removes all uncertainty about our value to this world, particularly to those persons around us.

Knowledge that we are never alone, that in every circumstance our best interests are being cared for, softens whatever blow we encounter. The blows teach us; they are the lessons the inner self has requested, and let us never forget we have a ready tutor to see us through every assignment.

The more we rely on God to see us through the mundane activities as well as the troubling experiences, the greater will be our certainty that all is well, our lives are on course, and a plan is unfolding little by little that has our best interests at its center.

*My understanding of God and the power of that presence is
proportionate to my reliance on that power. Not unlike the power
of electricity, I can plug into the source of the "light" of understanding
and for the strength to see my way through any experience today.*

MY   THOUGHTS   FOR   THE   DAY

....

....

....

....

....

....

....

MAY 24

It's ironic, but until you can free those final monsters within the
jungle of yourself, your life, your soul is up for grabs.
—RONA BARRETT

We all have monsters. Maybe it's depression over the past or present circumstances, or resentment about another's behavior, or fear of new situations. Maybe it's jealousy of other women. The more attention we give the monsters, the more powerful they get. The harder we try to resist the jealousy or depression or fear, the greater it becomes.

The program offers us the way to let go. And we find the way through one another. When we share ourselves fully with one another, share our monsters with one another, they no longer dominate us. They seek the dark recesses of our minds, and when we shine the light on them, they recoil. The program offers us an eternal light.

I will let the program shine its light in my life today.
My monsters will flee for the day.

MY THOUGHTS ❧ FOR THE DAY

....

....

....

....

....

....

....

....

MAY 25

One is happy as a result of one's own efforts, once one knows the necessary
ingredients of happiness—simple tastes, a certain degree of courage,
self-denial to a point, love of work, and above all, a clear conscience.
Happiness is no vague dream, of that I now feel certain.
—GEORGE SAND

We are as happy as we make up our minds to be, so goes the saying. But happiness is the result of right actions. We prepare for it daily. We chart our course. Many of us have to first determine where we want to go before we can decide on the chart. We have perhaps passively floated along for years. But now the time is right to navigate, to move toward a goal.

We may have fears about moving ahead. We can be courageous, however. Strength is at hand, always, if we but ask for it. We can make a small beginning today. And every day, we can do at least one thing we need to do to bring us closer to our goal. Accomplishment, however small, nurtures good feelings. Happiness is the by-product.

Today is wide open. I will decide on a course of action and move ahead.
All around me help is available for the asking.

MY THOUGHTS FOR THE DAY

Out of every crisis comes the chance to be reborn, to reconceive ourselves as individuals, to choose the kind of change that will help us to grow and to fulfill ourselves more completely.
—NENA O'NEILL

Before choosing to recover, most of us lived through crisis after crisis. Many days we sought the oblivion of alcohol and drugs rather than face fears that ate away at us. It probably wasn't possible for most of us to realize that a crisis was a tool for growth.

Even today, even in our recovery program, even though the clouds are clearing and we are feeling better about ourselves, a crisis may overwhelm us for a time. We do find help for it, though. We can breathe deeply, look to our higher power, listen for the messages that are coming through from our friends. And we can choose among the many options for the right action to take at this time.

Life is a series of lessons. Crises can be seen as the homework. They aren't there to defeat us but to help us grow—to graduate us into the next stage of life.

Today, I will look for my lessons and feel exhilarated by the growth that is guaranteed.

M Y   T H O U G H T S   F O R   T H E   D A Y

MAY 27

*As the wheel of the decades turns, so do a person's needs, desires,
and tasks. Each of us does, in effect, strike a series of "deals" or compromises
between the wants and longings of the inner self, and an outer environment
that offers certain possibilities and sets certain limitations.*
—MAGGIE SCARF

What life has measured out may not be what we had dreamed of. Life's lessons may not be those we'd have chosen to learn. Wisdom dictates that the joy of life is proportional to the ease with which we accept those possibilities for growth that have grown out of our inner desires.

Our desires are like an outline for a written assignment, a research project. They help us to see where we want to go at any one time, but as we move, the direction may need to change. The natural flow of "the assignment" will help to refine it.

We may not have tried to "realize" many of our desires in the past. But the time has come. One of the joys of recovery is that we understand our desires are closely related to our spiritual program and our recovery. And we know we are not alone. We need to attend to the inner desires that beckon to us. They are calling us to move forward.

Today, I can take the first few steps.

MY THOUGHTS 🌺 FOR THE DAY

....

....

....

....

....

....

....

MAY 28

Spiritual power can be seen in a person's reverence for life—hers and all others, including animals and nature, with a recognition of a universal life force referred to by many as God.
—VIRGINIA SATIR

Taking the time, daily, to recognize the spiritual force in everyone and everything that is all about us encourages us to feel humble, to feel awe. Reflecting on our interconnections, our need for one and all to complete the universe, lessens whatever adversity we might feel as we struggle with our humanity.

Our spiritual power is enhanced with each blessing we give. And as our spiritual power is enhanced, life's trials are fewer. Our struggle to accept situations, conditions, and other people, or our struggle to control them, lessens every day that we recognize and revere one another's personhood, one another's existence.

I can teach myself reverence, and I can begin today. I will look for "the Spirit" everywhere, and I will begin to see it.

MY THOUGHTS ✿ FOR THE DAY

....

....

....

....

....

....

....

....

MAY 29

Women sometimes gossip when they want to get close to people.
—JOAN GILBERTSON

Feeling alone and lonely heightens our fears of inadequacy. In our alienation from others, paranoia grips us. We yearn to feel a connection with someone, and gossip about another someone can draw two lonely people close. We are bonded.

We need a sense of belonging, every one of us: belonging to the neighborhood; belonging to the staff where we work; belonging to the group we call friends. Knowing that we do belong fosters the inner warmth that accompanies security, well-being. And our fears are melted.

The program's Fifth, Ninth, and Tenth Steps guarantee that we'll feel the closeness we long for when we work them. Self-revelation strengthens our ties to the people we long to connect with. Gossip loses its appeal when we know we share a closeness already. Mingling our vulnerabilities secures our closeness.

We need to be attentive to our judgments of others, be they verbalized in gossip or only savored in silence. These judgments act as barometers of our own self-image. Our security in knowing we belong, that we are one, relieves us of the need to judge others unfairly.

Loneliness pushes me to behavior that even compounds the loneliness.
Real closeness will come when I talk about myself rather than someone else.

M Y   T H O U G H T S   ❀   F O R   T H E   D A Y

MAY 30

In anxiety-provoking situations, many women feel unable to act. They find themselves at a loss to come up with an effective response, or any response at all.
—STANLEE PHELPS AND NANCY AUSTIN

Feeling unable to act is a humiliation, perhaps an embarrassment, and it is habit-forming. Perhaps our inertia is due to our need to act "correctly" and the accompanying fear that we'll err. Unfortunately, our fear of action reinforces itself. The only way to end the vicious cycle is to act—right or wrong. The surprise in store for us is that no action we take will be truly wrong. We will learn not only from the action itself, but from its ripples.

The response to life we make through action will gratify us; it will nourish us and will make us dread less the next situation that calls for a response.

Opportunities for action are the stepping stones to emotional maturity. The more we "act," the more able we are to act. And a new habit is formed.

Taking action, even when I fear it's wrong, is growth-producing.
Without growth there is no life. Today, I will live!

MY THOUGHTS FOR THE DAY

....

....

....

....

....

....

....

....

....

MAY 31

That reality of life and living—movement from one place to another either in a project or in a state of mind, does not conform with what we imagine or expect or think we deserve so we often leave things hanging unfinished or unstarted.
—SANDRA EDWARDS

Being dissatisfied—discontented with the experiences life gives us—forever hampers our growth. Reality is not our bane but our gift. The particular reality perceived by any one of us is of special significance because in that reality are our lessons—the very lessons that will awaken us to the awareness that what life offers is just what we deserve, and more.

It's our interpretation of life's realities that is at fault. But as we grow spiritually the clouds will disappear. We'll come to understand the interplay between our realities. And we'll willingly move ahead, fulfilling our part in life's bigger picture.

Sometimes all I can do is trust that all is well, even though it's not as I had hoped. On bad days I need only to reflect on the past to know that I am moving in the right direction.

MY THOUGHTS FOR THE DAY

....

....

....

....

....

....

....

....

....

June

....

....

....

....

....

....

....

J U N E   1

One cannot collect all the beautiful shells on the beach; one can collect
only a few, and they are more beautiful if they are few.
—ANNE MORROW LINDBERGH

Being selective in choosing activities, in choosing friends, in choosing material posses-
sions fosters unexpected appreciation. Too much of any one thing negates whatever specialness might have been realized. If we surround ourselves with acquaintances, we never fully
share in knowing a few people well. If we surround ourselves with "toys," we never learn
how we really want to spend our time.

When we don't take life slowly, piece by piece (one shell at a time), we avoid the greatest
discovery of all, the person within. When our attention to persons, places, things is deliberate and steady, the beauty within the object of our focus shines forth, and we, too, are made
more beautiful in the process.

Today, I will take time to smell the flowers.

M Y   T H O U G H T S   🌿   F O R   T H E   D A Y

....

....

....

....

....

....

....

....

....

JUNE 2

*I have come to realize that all my trouble with living has
come from fear and smallness within me.*
—ANGELA L. WOZNIAK

We create problems for ourselves because we think we need to be more than we are. We fear that we are inadequate to the task before us, fear that another woman is more attractive, fear that the friends around us are bored by our presence.

Fear hinders us; it prevents full involvement with the experiences we are given to grow on. When we withdraw from a situation in order to save ourselves from failure, we have chosen instead another kind of failure: failure to take all we can from life, failure to be all that we can be. Every experience can move us forward in the understanding of ourselves. When we withdraw, we stay stuck in a world we need to leave behind.

*I will not fear whatever looks like trouble today. Nothing I can't handle—in fact,
nothing I can't grow from—will come my way today.
My inner strength can see me through.*

MY THOUGHTS FOR THE DAY

....

....

....

....

....

....

....

....

....

J U N E   3

Follow your dream . . . take one step at a time and don't settle for less,
just continue to climb.
—AMANDA BRADLEY

Dreams are common to us all. Dreams are special as well. We probably keep to ourselves many of our dreams for fear of derision or misunderstanding. Oftentimes we may have selectively shared some dreams, those we figured would get approval. The ones closest and dearest to us, the ones we feel most vulnerable about, we may choose to treasure to our hearts only, sometimes thinking, "If only you knew," sometimes wondering if we are being silly.

We are coming to believe that our dreams are *spirit-filled*. They are gifts to encourage us. Like a ship at sea needing a "heading" to move forward, our dreams lend direction to our lives. Our frustration may be that we can't realize a dream without many steps and much time. But life is a process of steps. Success in anything comes inch by inch, stroke by stroke, step after step.

My dreams today are meant to guide me.
I will take a first step toward making the dream a reality.

M Y   T H O U G H T S   &   F O R   T H E   D A Y

....

....

....

....

....

....

....

....

JUNE 4

We all live with the objective of being happy;
our lives are all different and yet the same.
—ANNE FRANK

Happiness feels so close and yet so far away. Perhaps we look to a person for it, or to a job, or to a new winter coat. We deserve happiness, we know. Yet, we learn so slowly that happiness can only be found within. The person leaves; the job goes sour; the new coat is quickly out of style. Elusive, all of them.

But the happiness that comes from knowing who we are and how our lives fit in the grand design of the Creator never eludes us. We are one of a kind. And there is no other who can offer to the world of friends just what each of us can. We are needed, and knowing that, really knowing it, brings happiness.

Before we found this program, we no doubt failed to realize our worth. We can celebrate it now. We can glory in our worth, our specialness, and we can cherish the design. We can cherish our parts and cherish the part each person plays.

Combined, we are as one big orchestra. The conductor reads the music and
directs the movements. Being in tune with the conductor feels good.
I can call it happiness. All I need do is play my part.

MY THOUGHTS ❧ FOR THE DAY

JUNE 5

*The level of anxiety I feel when an attractive woman enters the room is the cue
informing me of my closeness to God at that moment.*
—ANONYMOUS

Our security lies now and always in our relationship with God. When we are spiritually connected, we don't lack confidence, self-assurance. We don't doubt our value to those around us. Having an active friendship with our God keeps us ever aware that whatever is right for each of us at this time will be given us, that each other person in our life is also on a divinely ordained path going somewhere special to her growth.

It's unfortunate, but true, that many of us had painful experiences with other women earlier in our lives. Maybe we lost a lover or a husband to someone we knew. And it's difficult to believe that what is right for us will come to us, that we need never fear another woman.

The program offers us daily opportunities to take stock of our assets in order to know that we count. And more importantly, it promises security and serenity if each day we invite our higher power to be our companion. We need never fear someone else's presence. Nor need we fear any new situation. With God at our side, all is well. And we'll know it!

I will make God my friend today and enjoy the ease of living.

MY THOUGHTS 🌹 FOR THE DAY

....

....

....

....

....

....

....

....

JUNE 6

*From early infancy onward we all incorporate into our lives the
message we receive concerning our self-worth, or lack of self-worth, and
this sense of value is to be found beneath our actions and feelings as a
tangled network of self-perception.*
—CHRISTINA BALDWIN

Lifting our self-esteem is not a particularly easy task for most of us. It's probable that again and again our confidence wavered before we sought help from the program. It's also probable that our confidence still wanes on occasion. The old fears don't disappear without effort.

But each day we can do some one thing that will help us to feel better about ourselves. All it takes is one small act or decision, each day. The program can give us the strength we need each day to move forward one step.

*Today, I will do one thing I've been putting off. A whole collection of "one days"
will lay the groundwork for the person I'm building within.*

MY THOUGHTS ❧ FOR THE DAY

....

....

....

....

....

....

....

....

....

JUNE 7

Without discipline, there's no life at all.
—KATHARINE HEPBURN

Procrastination is habitual. It's perhaps a habit we've struggled with over the years, and not one that can be willed away. It eats at us, no doubt. How many times have we gone to bed at night depressed, discouraged, angry with ourselves for not finishing a job we promised ourselves, or someone else, we'd do! Sometimes it feels hopeless. The tasks awaiting our attention pile up, seem impossible to complete. But there is hope. The program has offered us an easy solution.

We have only this day to concern ourselves with. We can break the spell of procrastination, lethargy, immobility, if we choose. We can pick a task that needs attention, any task, preferably a small one for today. Maybe it's writing a letter, or fixing a hem, or making an appointment to see a doctor. Deciding to do something, and then doing it, breaks through the barriers that have caged us. Immediately we will sense the surge of freedom. In this moment we can always act. And any act will free us.

When procrastination blocks us, our senses are dead to the friends close to us. It's as though we have stepped outside of the circle of life. The real gifts of sobriety are beyond our reach when we choose inaction.

I will get free. I will tackle a small task today. It will bless me in special ways.

MY THOUGHTS 🌿 FOR THE DAY

....

....

....

....

....

....

....

The process of living, for each of us, is pretty similar. For every gain
there is a setback. For every success, a failure. For every moment of joy,
a time of sadness. For every hope realized, one is dashed.
—SUE ATCHLEY EBAUGH

The balance of events in our lives is much like the balance of nature. The pendulum swings; every extreme condition is offset by its opposite, and we learn to appreciate the gifts . . . of the bad times as well as the periods of rest.

On occasion we'll discover that our course in life has changed direction. We need not be alarmed. Step Three has promised that we are in caring hands. Our every concern, every detail of our lives, will be taken care of, in the right way, at the right time.

We can develop gratitude for all conditions, good or bad. Each has its necessary place in our development as healthy, happy women. We need the sorrows along with the joys if we are to gain new insights. Our failures keep us humble; they remind us of our need for the care and guidance of others. And for every hope dashed, we can remember, one will be realized.

Life is a process. I will accept the variations with gratitude.
Each, in its own way, blesses me.

M Y   T H O U G H T S   F O R   T H E   D A Y

....

....

....

....

....

....

....

....

J U N E   9

Many of us achieve only the semblance of communication with others;
what we say is often not contingent on what the other has just said,
and neither of us is aware that we are not communicating.
—DESY SAFÁN-GERARD

When we don't listen fully to each other, when we don't revere the Spirit within others that's trying to talk to us, we destroy the connection that wants to be made between our Spirits. Our inner selves have messages to give and messages to receive for the good of all. Our ego selves often keep us from hearing the very words that would unravel a problem in our lives.

How hard it is, how often, to be still and to fully listen to the words, rather than the person. How much more familiar it is to filter the message with our own ongoing inner dialogue—our own ongoing continual assessment of another's personhood at the very time our higher power is trying to reach us through them.

There really are no wasted words. Messages are everywhere. We can learn to listen.

I will hear just what I need to hear today. I will open myself fully to the words.

M Y   T H O U G H T S   ❀   F O R   T H E   D A Y

....

....

....

....

....

....

....

....

JUNE 10

*When we start at the center of ourselves, we discover something worthwhile
extending toward the periphery of the circle. We find again some of the
joy in the now, some of the peace in the here, some of the love in me and
thee which go to make up the kingdom of heaven on earth.*
—G. F. SEAR

Perhaps we have feared discovering our center; perhaps we have feared finding nothing there. The struggle to believe in ourselves, to know we have an important part to play in the circle of life, the circle encompassing all life, is a hard-fought struggle for many of us. But we are learning. We are finding treasures within ourselves. Others are helping us to find those treasures. Sharing special moments in time with loved ones and ones we are learning to love reveals many treasures.

All we have is here—now—us. We are all we ever need to be—here and now. We are, at every moment, what we need to be if only we'd trust revealing our true selves, our centers, to one another. Our centers each need that of another.

This program needs each of us for what we add to it. The worthiness of the program, of the whole circle, is enhanced by the inclusion of our centers.

I will share my center today with you.

MY THOUGHTS ❀ FOR THE DAY

....

....

....

....

....

....

....

JUNE 11

My lifetime listens to yours.
—MURIEL RUKEYSER

Our experiences educate us to help show each other the way. Others' experiences, likewise, will help still others. We need to share our histories. And the program offers us the way. There is no greater honor we can give one another than rapt attention. We each want to be heard, to be special, to be acknowledged. And recognition may well be the balm that will heal someone's hurt today.

A new day faces us, a day filled with opportunities to really listen to someone who needs to be heard. And the surprise is that we will hear a message just right for us, where we are now. A message that may well point us in a new, better direction. Guidance is always at hand, if only we listen for it. But when we are trapped in our own narrow world of problems and confusion, we scramble whatever messages are trying to reach us. And we miss the many opportunities to make another person feel special and necessary to our lives.

My growth is enhanced every time I give my attention fully to another person.
And this process is multiplied over and over and over.
I will be there for someone today.

MY THOUGHTS ❧ FOR THE DAY

JUNE 12

*If people only knew the healing power of laughter and joy,
many of our fine doctors would be out of business. Joy is one of nature's
greatest medicines. Joy is always healthy. A pleasant state of mind
tends to bring abnormal conditions back to normal.*
—CATHERINE PONDER

Feeling joy may not come naturally to us most of the time. We may, in fact, have to act "as if" with great effort. We may not even recognize genuine joy in the beginning. A technique for finding it is living fully in the present and with gratitude for all we can see, touch, and feel.

The open and honest expression of gratitude for the presence of the ones closest to us now creates a rush within our breasts, a rush that will be shared by our friends, too. Joy is contagious. Joy is freeing. Joy brings into focus our distorted perceptions. Greeting life with joy alters every experience for us and for those we share it with.

I will bring joy wherever I go today. I will give the gift of joy to everyone I meet.

MY THOUGHTS FOR THE DAY

JUNE 13

Everyday . . . life confronts us with new problems to be solved which
force us to adjust our old programs accordingly.
—Dr. Ann Faraday

Facing the day straight on is occasionally difficult to do. There are those days we feel like crawling under the covers and staying there, certain that we can't handle whatever might be asked of us. Maybe today is one of those days. Perhaps we feel 12 years old, instead of 42. To consciously behave like a responsible 42-year-old is out of the question. Acting "as if" is the next best thing, the program tells us, and it is.

Acting "as if" also comes in handy when only a minor kink interferes with the day's progression. Most problems don't fit an easy solution or a familiar one. However, most problems are dispensed with by seeing them as opportunities for creative response, calmly seeking guidance and then moving ahead slowly, being aware of the effects of our actions.

Today, and every day, I will have an opportunity to think creatively and to rely
on my inner guide. Instead of dreading the unfamiliar, I will be glad for it.
It's moving me ever closer to understanding life's mysteries.

MY THOUGHTS ❧ FOR THE DAY

JUNE 14

All of us have unique talents and gifts. No obstacle, be it physical, mental or emotional, has the power to destroy our innate creative energies.
—LIANE CORDES

Believing this fully is difficult at times; for some of us, most of the time. But it is true. What each of us can contribute to the world is unlike every other contribution. Each talent is slightly different from every other talent. And they are all needed. We are all needed.

Creativity—any kind—writing, photography, cooking, child care, weaving, managing, woodworking—nourishes the self that feels isolated and worthless. And as the self is nourished, it grows; it recovers.

Recovery means changing our lifestyle. It means reaching out to others and being there for one another. It means rejoining the human race by giving of ourselves. Our talents are the gifts the human race awaits—needs, in fact. Do we know our talents?

I will search out my secret dreams today. In them lie my talents.
I will develop them. Help awaits me.

MY THOUGHTS FOR THE DAY

JUNE 15

For many years I was so flexible I didn't know who I was, and now that I'm discovering who I am, I think "OK, I know where I stand on that issue. Now on to the next one." But I have to remind myself that all issues are interrelated—no one is separate.
—Kathleen Casey Theisen

Today flows from yesterday, the day before, the day before that. Tomorrow repeats the pattern. What we are given on any one day will have its beginning in the past and its finale in the future. No incident is isolated entirely; no issue is self-contained.

Maturity is being able to let go of outgrown attitudes, stifling opinions, no matter how good and right they were at one time. Our egos often get too attached to some of our opinions, and new ideas can't filter in. Some will try to get our attention today. We are ready for new growth. The choice not to hamper it is ours to make.

The opinions we held certain yesterday may not be adequate to the problems of today. They need not be. They served us well. They are not for naught.

Today's issues need today's fresh responses. I will be unafraid. Today flows from yesterday, the day before, and the day before that. Tomorrow follows suit.

MY THOUGHTS ❧ FOR THE DAY

....

....

....

....

....

....

....

JUNE 16

The pain of love is the pain of being alive. It's a perpetual wound.
—MAUREEN DUFFY

We live in one another's company. We grow to yearn for one another's company at a deeper level. The yearning reciprocated opens the way to a love relationship, a relationship both blessed and torn by intimacies.

It's human to long for love, to want to shower it and receive it. But the pain of waiting for it doesn't match the pain that accompanies its arrival. Love heightens our sensitivities. Any separations, any discrepancies, physical or emotional, wound the partners in love. The pain that accompanies never having something is less than the pain of projected loss after its arrival.

Love should bring only happiness, we mistakenly think. But love, giving it and receiving it, beckons us to bare our souls, to expose our hidden selves. The fear of rejection, the anxiety that we'll be rejected "when they know the real me," is large and looms over our shoulders.

How lucky we are to have this program, these Steps, which if practiced in all our affairs will prepare us for love and loving. They will help us to live with the pain of love, knowing that it increases our humanity—that it deepens our awarenesses and thus heightens our appreciation of all of life.

The pain of love increases my rapture.

MY THOUGHTS 🌿 FOR THE DAY

....

....

....

....

....

....

J U N E   1 7

Wisdom never kicks at the iron walls it can't bring down.
—OLIVE SCHREINER

God grant us the serenity to accept the things we cannot change. Many times—yesterday, last week, today, and even tomorrow—we'll come face-to-face with a seemingly intolerable situation. The compulsion to change the situation, to demand that another person change the situation, is great. What a hard lesson it is to learn we can change only ourselves! The hidden gift in this lesson is that as our activities change, often the intolerable situations do, too.

Acceptance, after a time, smooths all the ripples that discourage us. And it softens us. It nurtures wisdom. It attracts joy and love from others. Ironically, we often try to force changes that we think will "loosen" love and lessen struggle. Acceptance can do what our willpower could never accomplish.

As we grow in wisdom, as we grow in understanding, as we realize the promises of this program, we'll stand ready, as women, to weather all our personal storms. Like the willow in the wind, we'll bend rather than break. And we'll be able to help our sisters become wise through our example.

My lessons are not easy. But they will ease my way. Better days begin today.

M Y   T H O U G H T S   ❧   F O R   T H E   D A Y

JUNE 18

. . . we could never learn to be brave and patient if there
were only joy in the world.
—HELEN KELLER

We chase after joy, like a child after a firefly, being certain that in joy all problems are solved, all questions are answered. Joy has its rewards, and we deserve them. But life has more to teach us.

We need to learn patience; through patience we come to respect time and its passage, and we are mellowed. We need to learn tolerance; through tolerance our appreciation of another's individuality is nurtured. We need to learn self-respect; self-respect prepares us to contribute more freely to our experiences, and we find wholeness.

Life's travails are our opportunities for lasting, enriching joy. The rough spots deepen our understandings. And these help us to bring joy to the lives of friends near and dear.

I need not turn my back on joy. But I will be glad for all life's experiences.
The panorama will sustain me more fully.

MY THOUGHTS ❀ FOR THE DAY

....

....

....

....

....

....

....

....

....

One receives only that which is given. The game of life is a game of
boomerangs. Our thoughts, deeds and words, return to us sooner or later,
with astounding accuracy.
—FLORENCE SCOVEL SHIN

Each of us can attest to the truth of this passage. During the difficult times, however, it is not uppermost in our minds that "what goes around, comes around." It feels all too easy to be justifiably resentful or to gossip or to ignore another's presence. And the repercussions are seldom immediate. They will come, though.

Goodness is likewise repaid. Giving love, attention, and respect to the individuals who share our lives and to the people who cross our paths by chance will smooth our own passage day by day. The effects of our goodness will often be felt quickly. A smile elicits a smile. Kind thoughts bless us as well as the receiver. Life events do come full circle.

With a bit of effort, I can smile at someone today,
even though I'm frowning inside. Both will be better for it.

M Y   T H O U G H T S   F O R   T H E   D A Y

JUNE 20

There were deep secrets, hidden in my heart, never said for fear others
would scoff or sneer. At last I can reveal my sufferings, for the strength
I once felt in silence has lost all its power.
—Deidra Sarault

There is magic in sharing ourselves with someone else. We learn from Steps Four and Five that what we thought were heinous acts are not unusual. Our shameful acts are not unique, and this discovery is our gift when we risk exposure.

Realizing how much we are like others gives us strength, and the program paves the way for us to capture that strength whenever and wherever we sense our need. Secrets block us from others and thus from God too. The messages we need to hear, the guidance offered by God, can't be received when we close ourselves off from the caring persons in our lives. They are the carriers of God's message.

How freeing to know we share the same fears, the same worries. Offering our story to someone else may be the very encouragement she needs at this time. Each of us profits from the sharing of a story. We need to recognize and celebrate our "sameness." When we share ourselves, we are bonded. Bonding combines our strength.

Silence divides us. It diminishes our strength.
Yet all the strength we need awaits us. I will let someone else know me today.

M Y   T H O U G H T S   FOR   T H E   D A Y

....

....

....

....

....

....

....

JUNE 21

There is no such thing as conversation. It is an illusion.
There are interesting monologues, that is all.
—REBECCA WEST

How often we want to be heard, to be truly listened to by our spouse, our children, friends and co-workers. And we deserve to be fully attended to. So do the other persons in our lives who come to us to be heard. We let our minds wander in the midst of important messages. And we may miss the very phrase that we need to hear—the answer to a problem, perhaps. Our minds wander, randomly, looking for a place to light, unconsciously searching for peace, the serenity promised by the Twelve Steps.

Living fully in the present, soaking up all the responses of the life we are immersed in for the moment, is the closest we can get to our higher power, our God. Being there—fully—is conversation with God. How can we know all that God intends for us to know if we don't take advantage of God's many messages? Every moment of every day offers us information, divine information. Each time we turn our minds to self-centered thoughts, we're refusing the chance to grow.

As I come together with friends and family today, I will remember to listen for
God's message. I will hear what I need to hear if I will but listen.

M Y   T H O U G H T S ✿ F O R   T H E   D A Y

JUNE 22

I want to do it because I want to do it. Women must try to do things as men have tried. When they fail, their failure must be but a challenge to others.
—AMELIA EARHART

Fear of failure plagues many women, not just those who get into trouble with drugs, alcohol, food. Those of us in this recovery program may still fear failure. Halting our addiction doesn't solve all our problems, but it does allow us to realistically take stock of our assets. Knowing our assets and accepting them provides the confidence we need to attempt a project, to strive for a goal.

Another plus of this recovery program is the help available from our groups and our higher power. All things become possible when we understand we are not alone. Seeing other women strive and succeed or strive, fail, and strive again, undefeated, creates an energy flow that can spur us on, if we choose. Feeling good about others' accomplishments can motivate each of us.

Today, I will pay particular attention to the accomplishments of other women, those close to me and those I read or hear about. I will believe their example and feel the forward push.

MY THOUGHTS FOR THE DAY

JUNE 23

*. . . How much bondage and suffering a woman escapes when she takes the
liberty of being her own physician of both body and soul.*
—ELIZABETH CADY STANTON

If we listen to ourselves, to the innermost voice of our Spirits, we know that we have the power to heal ourselves. Self-healing begins with making our own decisions—about what we wear, what we do, who we are—and deciding that we will be true to ourselves. With the help of our spiritual guide, we can resist the temptations to betray ourselves, for these temptations are born of fear; the fear that we are not good enough to be our "own physicians."

To give away our powers binds us and causes us to suffer. But we can go to others for help without losing our own strength.

*Today and every day, I will pray for the wisdom to choose wise counselors
and the strength to love and heal myself.*

MY THOUGHTS ❀ FOR THE DAY

....

....

....

....

....

....

....

....

....

....

If you attach yourself to one person, you ultimately end up
having an unhealthy relationship.
—SHIRLEY MACLAINE

Needing people in our lives is healthy, human, and natural. Needing a single person to love at a very deep level is also soothing to the soul's well-being. Love and attachment are not synonymous, however. They are close to being opposites. If we "attach" ourselves to others, our movements as separate individuals are hampered. Attachment means dependency; it means letting our movements be controlled by the one we are "hooked" to.

Dependency on mood-altering chemicals, on food, on people, means unmanageability in our individual lives. Many of us in this recovery program, though abstinent, still struggle with our dependency on a certain person or a certain friend.

The tools we are learning apply in all cases of dependency. It is healthy independence we are striving for—taking responsibility for our own lives—making choices appropriate for our personal selves. Loving others means letting them make their own choices unhampered by our "attachment."

Are my relationships attachments or are they based on love?
I will take an inventory of them today.

M Y   T H O U G H T S   F O R   T H E   D A Y

....

....

....

....

....

....

....

JUNE 25

I have a simple philosophy. Fill what's empty. Empty what's full.
And scratch where it itches.
—ALICE ROOSEVELT LONGWORTH

All too often, we complicate our lives. We can wonder and worry our way into confusion; obsession or preoccupation it's often called. "What if?" "Will he?" "Should I?" "What do you think?" We seldom stop trying to figure out what to do, where to do it, how to meet a challenge, until someone reminds us to "keep it simple."

What we each discover, again and again, is that the solution to any problem becomes apparent when we stop searching for it. The guidance we need for handling any difficulty, great or small, can only come into focus when we remove the barriers to it, and the greatest barrier is our frantic effort to personally solve the problem. We clutter our minds; we pray for an answer and yet don't become quiet enough, for long enough, to become aware of the direction to go, or the steps to take. And they are always there.

Inherent in every problem or challenge is its solution. Our greatest lesson in life may be to keep it simple, to know that no problem stands in our way because no solution eludes a quiet, expectant mind.

I have opportunities every day to still my mind.
And the messages I need will come quietly. My answers are within me, now.

MY THOUGHTS ❀ FOR THE DAY

....

....

....

....

....

....

....

JUNE 26

Mental health, like dandruff, crops up when you least expect it.
—ROBIN WORTHINGTON

We're responsible for the effort but not the outcome. Frequently, a single problem or many problems overwhelm us. We may feel crazy, unable to cope and certain that we have made no progress throughout this period of recovery. But we have. Each day that we choose sobriety, that we choose abstinence from pills or food, we are moving more securely toward mental health as a stable condition.

We perhaps felt strong, secure, on top of things last week, or yesterday. We will again tomorrow, or maybe today. When we least expect it, our efforts pay off—quietly, perhaps subtly, sometimes loudly—a good belly-laugh may signal a glimmer of our mental health.

No one achieves an absolute state of total mental health. To be human is to have doubts and fears. But as faith grows, as it will when we live the Twelve Steps, doubts and fears lessen. The good days will increase in number.

Meeting a friend, asking for a raise, resolving a conflict with my spouse,
or friend, will be handled more easily, when I least expect it.
Looking forward with hope, not backward, is my best effort—today.

M Y   T H O U G H T S   ❧   F O R   T H E   D A Y

....

....

....

....

....

....

....

....

JUNE 27

Often God shuts a door in our face, and then subsequently
opens the door through which we need to go.
—CATHERINE MARSHALL

We try and try to control the events of our lives. And not seldom the events in others' lives, too. The occasions are frequent when our will conflicts with God's. Then for a time we feel at a loss. Our direction is uncertain. But always, always, another door opens. A better way beckons. How stubborn we are! And how simple life would be were we to daily, fully, turn our will and our lives over to the care of God. God's help and direction in all things are always available. Turning a deaf ear is like trying to find a seat in a darkened movie theater unaided by the usher.

Every experience is softened when we face it accompanied by our higher power. Any past struggle, any present fear, is a testament to our attempts to do it alone. Too frequently we forge ahead, alone, only to have our way blocked. The detours need never be there. No door closes unless there is a better way. Divine order will prevail.

There is no need to struggle today. I will breathe deeply and take my higher
power with me wherever I go. And the doors will be open for as far as I can see.

MY THOUGHTS 🌿 FOR THE DAY

....

....

....

....

....

....

....

....

JUNE 28

Joy fixes us to eternity and pain fixes us to time. But desire and fear
hold us in bondage to time, and detachment breaks the bond.
—SIMONE WEIL

We live both in the material realm and the spiritual. In our material dimension we seek material pleasures, inherent in which is pain. Our human emotions are tied to our material attachments, and joy, at its fullest, is never found here. Real joy lies outside of the material dimension and lives fully within us in the secret, small place inside where we always know that all is well.

We are on a trip in this life. And our journey is bringing us closer to full understanding of joy with every sorrowful circumstance. When we are one with God, have aligned our will with the will of God, we know joy. We know this, fully, that all is well. No harm can befall us.

Each circumstance in the material realm is an opportunity for us to rely on the spiritual realm for direction, security, understanding. As we turn within to our spiritual nature we will know joy.

Every day in every situation I have an opportunity to discover real joy.
It's so close and so ready for my invitation.

MY THOUGHTS ❀ FOR THE DAY

....

....

....

....

....

....

....

JUNE 29

*I am convinced, the longer I live, that life and its blessings are
not so entirely unjustly distributed [as] when we are suffering
greatly we are so inclined to suppose.*
—MARY TODD LINCOLN

Self-pity is a parasite that feeds on itself. Many of us are inclined toward self-pity, not allowing for the balance of life's natural tragedies. We will face good and bad times—and they will pass. With certainty they will pass.

The attitude "Why me?" hints at the little compassion we generally feel for others' suffering. Our empathy with others, even our awareness of their suffering, is generally minimal. We are much too involved in our own. Were we less self-centered, we'd see that blessings and tragedies visit us all, in equal amounts. Some people respond to their blessings with equanimity, and they quietly remove the sting from their tragedies. We can learn to do both.

Recovery is learning new responses, feeling and behaving in healthier ways. We need not get caught by self-pity. We can always feel it coming on. And we can let it go.

Self-pity may beckon today. Fortunately, I have learned I have other choices.

M Y   T H O U G H T S   F O R   T H E   D A Y

....

....

....

....

....

....

....

....

J U N E   3 0

. . . in silence might be the privilege of the strong, but it was certainly a danger
to the weak. For the things I was prompted to keep silent about were nearly
always the things I was ashamed of, which would have been far better aired . . .
—JOANNA FIELD

It has been said, "We are only as sick as the secrets we keep." Our emotional health as recovering women is hindered, perhaps even jeopardized, each time we hold something within that we need to talk over with others.

Sharing our fears, our hurts, our anger, keeps open our channel to God. Secrets clutter our mind, preventing the stillness within where our prayers find answers. Secrets keep us stuck. Our health, emotional and spiritual, depends on our commitment to shared experiences.

Every secret we have and tell someone frees that person also to be herself and to grow. Sharing experiences relieves us of our shame and invites the forgiveness we must allow ourselves.

Steps Four and Five facilitate the process of sharing those secrets that block our path to God and to one another. Never can we be fully at peace with secrets left untold. Self-revelation cleanses the soul and offers us life.

I will be alert to the opportunities to share myself and cherish the freedom offered.

M Y   T H O U G H T S   FOR   THE   DAY

....

....

....

....

....

....

....

July

....

....

....

....

....

....

....

J U L Y   1

It's quite uncomfortable to be an adolescent at age thirty-two.
—PEGGY CAHN

Our lives are in process every moment, which means change is ever-present. As new information is sorted and acquired, old habits are discarded. We don't let go of some old behaviors easily, however. They are like comfortable shoes. They may be worn thin, and they probably embarrass us in certain company, but we slip them on unconsciously—and then it's too late.

Maturity is an "as if" behavior, initially. Emotional development was stunted, for most of us, with the onset of our addictive behavior, thus, we often respond to situations like adolescents. Application of the "as if" principle will result both in new personal attitudes and unfamiliar, yet welcome, responses from others. Acting as if we are capable, strong, confident, or serene will pave the way for making those behaviors real, after a time. If we believe in ourselves and our ability to become the women we strive to be, we can then move forward confidently.

When my behavior embarrasses or shames me, I will accept the responsibility for changing it. Changing it offers immediate rewards. The people around me will react in refreshing ways, and I'll feel more fully alive.

M Y   T H O U G H T S   **❀**   F O R   T H E   D A Y

....

....

....

....

....

....

....

JULY 2

Humor is such a strong weapon, such a strong answer.
Women have to make jokes about themselves, laugh about themselves,
because they have nothing to lose.
—AGNES VARDA

Laughter can cure a physical condition; it can and will positively affect an emotional illness as well. Laughter ushers in a new perspective which gives vent to a changed attitude. And our attitude toward any situation, any individual, is all-powerful.

A negative, critical attitude toward our financial situation, toward our disease, toward our boss, or spouse, or children determines how we feel moment by moment. In like manner, when we raise our sights, look at the world with lightness in our hearts, expecting to enjoy the day, the people, the activity, we'll succeed.

Finding humor in a situation, any situation, prevents us from succumbing to feelings of powerlessness. Feeling powerless, behaving as victims, came easily for many of us before we chose this program and the Twelve Steps to live by. Choosing a humorous response, opting to laugh at our situation, at any point in time, keeps our personal power where it belongs—with ourselves.

My emotional health depends on my active involvement in
deciding who I am, right now. Deciding to chuckle rather
than snarl will give me an unexpected emotional boost.

MY   THOUGHTS   FOR   THE   DAY

JULY 3

No one can build (her) security upon the nobleness of another person.
—WILLA CATHER

Where do we look for our security? Do we look to our husbands or our lovers? Do we look to a parent or our children? Perhaps we seek our security in our jobs. But none of these avenues brings lasting contentment, as we've each probably discovered, just as pills, alcohol, or maybe food failed to give us lasting security.

Security of the spirit is with us from our birth. It's just that we haven't tapped into the source. Perhaps we don't even know the source, but it's been with us always, awaiting our realization of it.

No step do we ever take alone. Each breath we take is in partnership with the eternal source of strength and security within us. We have the choice to accept this partnership any time. And this guarantee of security in all things at all times is the gift of freedom.

Our desire for security is God-given. The security we desire is also given by God to us. We are secure today and every day.

Each step I take is in concert with my higher power. I need experience nothing alone. I can breathe in and tap the plentiful source of strength awaiting me, now.

MY THOUGHTS FOR THE DAY

JULY 4

One doesn't recognize in one's life the really important
moments—not until it's too late.
—AGATHA CHRISTIE

Every moment is special and offers us an opportunity—to let an experience change us in an important way, to invite another person into our life, to nurture the growing, changing woman within. Life's events move so rapidly we seldom relish the moments individually, but each day teems with tiny gifts divinely designed for our well-being. The woman smiled at in the grocery store yesterday or the man acknowledged on the bus last week felt special. And we were softened, too, by our expression.

We change, and we change our world when we acknowledge one another's presence in it. The wonderful reality is that we are in another's world because of the special qualities we each have and are able to share with one another.

For many of us, in times past, no moment felt important. The days were simply long and painful. But now, we can relish even the past pain for what it taught us. We know now that we can look to this day before us with expectation. We can be conscious of every moment, thankful for every experience and every person we encounter.

In this inner game of life, I share the court, and I will have my turn to serve.
To really live, I must participate fully.

MY THOUGHTS ❧ FOR THE DAY

....

....

....

....

....

....

....

J U L Y 5

*There are really only two ways to approach life—as victim or as gallant
fighter—and you must decide if you want to act or react, deal your
own cards or play with a stacked deck. And if you don't decide
which way to play with life, it always plays with you.*
—MERLE SHAIN

Being the victim is, or was, uncomfortably familiar to many of us. Perhaps some of us are only now realizing we have choices, that we need not let life happen to us. Becoming responsible to ourselves, choosing behavior, beliefs, friends, activities, that please us, though unfamiliar at first, soon exhilarates us. The more choices we make, the more alive we feel. The more alive we feel, the healthier our choices.

Our aim is recovery. Recovering means participating fully in our lives. It means self-assessment and self-direction. It means trusting to move forward, step-by-step, choice-by-choice, knowing all the while that no thoughtful action can trouble us.

*Many opportunities to make choices will present themselves today. The choices
I make will satisfy me; they will move me toward my goal of recovery.*

M Y   T H O U G H T S   F O R   T H E   D A Y

....

....

....

....

....

....

....

....

J U L Y   6

Peace, she supposed, was contingent upon a certain disposition of the soul, a disposition to receive the gift that only detachment from self made possible.
—ELIZABETH GOUDGE

Self-centeredness, egocentrism, and selfishness are familiar to most of us. We have judged our world and all the situations and people in it in terms of how their existence affects our own. We have become tied to him or to her or to a situation just as surely as an anchor to a boat. Most of us learned in very early childhood to read others' behaviors. And we determined our own worth accordingly.

As adult women we still struggle, trying to read another's actions, hoping to find acceptance. Which means we are always vulnerable, exposing our "self" to the whims of other, equally vulnerable "selves." What we search for is peace and security. We think if others love and accept us, we'll be at peace. We'll know serenity. A most important lesson for us to learn in this life is that peace is assured when we anchor ourselves to our God. Peace, well-being, serene joy will accompany our every step when we expose our vulnerable selves to God's care and only God's care. We'll no longer need to worry about the self we try to protect. It will be handled with care.

Peace awaits me today. I will look to God, and only God, to know that all is well, that I am all that I need to be.

M Y   T H O U G H T S   F O R   T H E   D A Y

JULY 7

. . . that is what learning is. You suddenly understand something
you've understood all your life, but in a new way.
—DORIS LESSING

As we are changed by our experiences, that which we know also changes. Our experiences foster growth and enlightenment, and all awarenesses give way to new understandings. We are forever students of life blessed with particular lessons designed only for us. There is joy in knowing that learning has no end and that each day offers us a chance to move closer to becoming the persons we are meant to be.

To understand something more deeply requires that we be open to the ideas of others, willing to part with our present opinions. The program offers us many opportunities to trade in the understandings we've outgrown. Throughout our recovery we have discovered new interpretations of old ideas. And we will continue to expand our understanding.

Every situation, every person, every feeling, every idea has a slightly different hue each time we encounter it. The wonder of this is that life is forever enriched, forever fresh.

Each moment offers me a chance to know better who I am and to understand
more fully the real contribution that is mine to make in this life.
I will let the anticipation of my changing ideas excite me.

MY THOUGHTS ❧ FOR THE DAY

....

....

....

....

....

....

....

JULY 8

Women like to sit down with trouble as if it were knitting.
—ELLEN GLASGOW

How often we turn minor challenges into monumental barriers by giving them undue attention, forgetting that within any problem lies its solution! However, the center of our focus must be off the problem's tangle if we are to find the solution's thread. The best remedy for this dilemma is the Serenity Prayer.

We cannot change our children, our husbands or partners, not even the best friends who we know love us. But with God's help we can change the attitude that has us blocked at this time. A changed attitude, easing up on ourselves, lessening our expectations of others, will open the door to the kind of relationships we seek, the smooth flowing days we long for.

We need not take life so seriously. In fact, we shouldn't take it so seriously. We can measure our emotional health by how heartily we laugh with others and at ourselves. The 24 hours stretching before us at this time promises many choices in attitude. We can worry, be mad, depressed, or frustrated, or we can trust our higher power to see us through whatever the situation. So, we can relax. It is our decision, the one decision over which we are not powerless.

I will be in control of my attitude today. I can have the kind of day I long for.

MY THOUGHTS ❧ FOR THE DAY

....

....

....

....

....

....

....

Of course, fortune has its part in human affairs,
but conduct is really much more important.
—JEANNE DETOURBEY

It's not infrequent that we are faced with a dilemma; what is the best action to take in a certain situation? We can be guided, rightly, in every situation if we but turn inward and let our conscience direct our behavior. We have often heard it said at meetings that when we long for a message from God we will hear it, either through our conscience or in the words of our friends. Thus we can never really be in doubt; our conduct can always be above reproach if we but listen.

Right behavior leads to fortunate opportunities for those who look for them. Behavior that we're proud of seems to attract blessings in our lives. One's good fortune is really God-given and in proportion to one's willingness to act well toward others in all situations.

Simply, what goes around, comes around. Our behavior comes back to us, manyfold. In our encounters with others today, we'll have numerous occasions to decide about the best behavior for the particular circumstance. We must not forget that our behavior elicits the responses we receive.

I will invite blessings today. I will also shower blessings on my friends.

M Y   T H O U G H T S   F O R   T H E   D A Y

....

....

....

....

....

....

....

JULY 10

No one can make you feel inferior without your consent.
—ELEANOR ROOSEVELT

We are competent women. We made a wise choice for ourselves when we decided to recover. Each day that we continue working this program our Spirits are strengthened. And our gifts will multiply.

Feeling inferior can become a habit. Being passive and feeling inferior go hand-in-hand, and they prepare us for becoming dependent on alcohol, pills, food, and people. We didn't understand, instinctively, that we are just who we're meant to be. We grew up believing we were not smart enough, not pretty enough, not capable enough. We grew up too distant from the source of our real strength.

How wonderful for us that we found the program! How lucky we are to have, for the taking, all the strength we'll ever need to face any situation, to handle any problem, to resolve any personal relationship conflict. Feeling inferior can be only a bad memory. The choice is ours. The program promises a better life. The Steps promise the strength to move forward. Our friends promise us outstretched hands.

*I will look forward to the challenges of today with hope and strength
and know that I am able to meet them.*

MY THOUGHTS ❧ FOR THE DAY

....

....

....

....

....

....

....

JULY 11

I have listened to the realm of the Spirit. I have heard my own soul's voice, and
I have remembered that love is the complete and unifying thread of existence.
—MARY CASEY

The act of loving someone else brings us together, closes whatever the gap between us. It draws us into the world of another, making richer the world we call our own. Love is the great equalizer.

We no longer wish to conquer or dominate those whom we love. And our love for one increases our capacity for loving others. Love heals another, and love heals ourselves, both giving it and receiving it.

Love from another acknowledges our existence, assuring us that we do count, that our presence is valued by someone else. It is human to need these reminders, these assurances. But our need for them is lessened each time we acknowledge another person in our midst.

Where love is absent, people, even in a crowd, feel alone, forgotten, unimportant. No doubt we can each recall times of quiet desperation—moments of alienation. We must reach out to someone and send thoughts of love to someone who may need to be remembered. Our loving thoughts for persons close and far away always reach their destination. They do unify us.

Love is powerful. It can change the complexion of the universe.
It will change the direction of my life.

M Y   T H O U G H T S   F O R   T H E   D A Y

....

....

....

....

....

....

JULY 12

*. . . those interested in perpetuating present conditions are always in tears
about the marvelous past that is about to disappear,
without having so much as a smile for the young future.*
—SIMONE DE BEAUVOIR

Hanging on to any moment, once it's gone, deadens us to the joys and lessons of the present. We must learn to let go, to let go of persons, painful situations, even meaningful experiences. Life goes on, and the most fruitful lesson before us is to move with the vibrations, to be in tune with them.

Being open to the present is our only chance for growth. These experiences today in our lives beckon us forward along the path meant for us. We are not guaranteed only joy today. But we are promised security. We may not be free of twinges of fear or confusion, but we can learn to trust even in the midst of adversity. We can remember that power greater than ourselves whenever and wherever our steps are uncertain.

Dwelling, as we are wont to do, on our rebuffs, our rejections, invites further criticism. But neither should we dwell on past joys. Attention to now and to the persons *here, now*, is the only rightful response to life. Not being here, now, invites others to turn away, just as we have turned away.

*I will celebrate the thrill of the present, squeeze the moments of today,
and trust the outcome to God.*

MY THOUGHTS ❧ FOR THE DAY

JULY 13

The trouble is not that we are never happy—it is that happiness is so episodical.
—RUTH BENEDICT

Happiness is our birthright. The decision to be happy is ours to make, every day, when confronted with any experience. Too many of us grew up believing that life needed to be a certain way for us to be happy. We looked for the right lover, the right job, the right dress. We looked outside of ourselves for the key to happiness. In time, we even looked to alcohol, drugs, food perhaps—to no avail.

Happiness lies within. We must encourage it to spring forth. But first we need to believe that happiness is fully within our power. We must trust that the most difficult circumstances won't keep it from us when we have learned to tap the source within.

Life is a gift we are granted moment by moment. Let us be in awe of the wonder of it, then revel in it. We can marvel at creation for a moment and realize how special we are to be participants. Happiness will overcome us if we let it. We can best show our gratitude for the wonder of this gift by smiling within and without.

That I am here is a wonderful mystery to which joy is the natural response.
It is no accident that I am here.

M Y   T H O U G H T S   F O R   T H E   D A Y

....

....

....

....

....

....

....

JULY 14

Through spontaneity we are reformed into ourselves. Freed from handed-down frames of reference, spontaneity becomes the moment of personal freedom when we are faced with a reality, explore it, and act accordingly.
—VIOLA SPOLIN

Living in the here and the now opens up untold possibilities for new growth. Our inner self is enticed in new directions when our attention is fully in the present. When our minds are still on last night's argument or tomorrow's board meeting, we wear blinders to the activity at hand. And God, as our teacher and protector, resides in *this* experience, in the hearts of *these* people present.

Every single moment has something for us. Maybe a new piece of information. A piece that solves a problem that's been puzzling us. Perhaps a chance to make a new friend, one who will be there in a time of need.

Letting go of yesterday frees us. We need not be burdened. It is gone. Our lives could be eased, so much, if we kept our focus on the experience at hand, where the problems we ponder have their solutions. Always.

I will greet today, skipping, smiling, ready for the answers, the truths, the directions meant only for me. The wonders of today will bless me.

MY THOUGHTS FOR THE DAY

JULY 15

If I can stop one heart from breaking, I shall not live in vain;
If I can ease one life the aching, Or cool one pain,
Or help one fainting robin Into his nest again, I shall not live in vain.
—EMILY DICKINSON

The gift of attention to each other is "passing on" the love of God. In order to feel love, we have to give it away. We will know love when we give love.

Our attachment to the world, the sense of belonging most of us longed for the many years prior to recovery, awaits us, is showered upon us even as we reach out to someone else. We are no longer alone, scared, alienated when we let others know they are not alone. We can heal one another. The program opens the way for our healing.

Each day, each one of us can ease the pain of a friend, a co-worker, a child. The beauty of the program, the beauty of God's plan for us all, is that our own pain is relieved in the process of easing the pain of another. Love is the balm. Loving others makes our lives purposeful.

No day is lived in vain, if I but cherish someone else's presence.

M Y   T H O U G H T S   F O R   T H E   D A Y

....

....

....

....

....

....

....

....

JULY 16

*I have come to believe in the "Sacrament of the Moment," which
presupposes trust in the ultimate goodness of my creator.*
—RUTH CASEY

The moment, realized, is like a bud blossoming. The day unfolds and with each minute we are moved along to the experiences right for us at this place and this time. Our resistance to certain experiences and particular people creates the barrier that blocks the good in store for us.

We can rest assured, our higher power is caring for us. Each breath we take is Spirit-filled, and the plan for our lives is an accumulation of necessary experiences that are helping us to grow and develop our special talents. What we often forget is that the difficult periods of our lives stretch us, enlighten us, ready us to be the women we desire within to be.

This moment is sacred. All moments are sacred. They will not come again. What is offered this moment for us to grow on will not be offered in exactly this way again. Our higher power knows our needs and is caring for them. We can trust the goodness of today.

*Whatever situation I encounter today, I will believe in its goodness.
It is right for me. It may stretch my patience rather than
elicit laughter, but it is right for me at this time.*

MY THOUGHTS ❧ FOR THE DAY

....

....

....

....

....

....

....

JULY 17

*The problem is not merely one of woman and career, woman and the home,
woman and independence. It is more basically: how to remain whole in the
midst of the distractions of life; how to remain balanced, no matter what
centrifugal forces tend to pull one off center; how to remain strong, no matter
what shocks come in at the periphery and tend to crack the hub of the wheel.*
—ANNE MORROW LINDBERGH

Before getting into this recovery program, many of us didn't cope with life's distractions except with the help of our addiction. We had no sense of wholeness and were constantly bouncing from one crisis to another. We may still feel pulled. The crises may still trip us up. But we have a center now that we are beginning to understand and rely upon. That center is our spiritual selves.

Slowing down, going within to our center, listening to the message therein, unravels our problem, smooths the waves of the storm. The strength to go forward awaits us.

We can absorb the shocks that "crack the hub of the wheel" and be enriched by them. Each moment we are weaving our tapestry of life. Each experience colors our design. Our pain and sorrow and joy give the depth that one day will move us to say, "I see, I understand."

I will be grateful for the experiences today that give my tapestry its beauty.

M Y   T H O U G H T S   F O R   T H E   D A Y

....

....

....

....

....

....

....

J U L Y 1 8

Have the courage to act instead of react.
—DARLENE LARSON JENKS

Taking the time to be thoughtful about our responses to the situations we encounter offers us the freedom to make choices that are right for us. Impulsive behavior can be a thing of our past, if we so choose. It seldom was the best response for our well-being.

Decision-making is morale boosting. It offers us a chance to exercise our personal powers, an exercise that is mandatory for the healthy development of our egos. We need to make careful, thoughtful choices because they will further define our characters. Each action we take clearly indicates the persons we are becoming. When we have consciously and deliberately chosen that action because of its rightness for us, we are fully in command of becoming the persons we choose to be.

Our actions reveal who we are, to ourselves and others. We need never convey an inaccurate picture of ourselves. We need only take the time and risk the courage necessary to behave exactly as we choose. We will know a new freedom when we are in control.

I will exercise my power to act and feel the fullness of my being.

M Y T H O U G H T S F O R T H E D A Y

....

....

....

....

....

....

....

....

J U L Y   1 9

At fifteen life had taught me undeniably that surrender, in its place,
was as honorable as resistance, especially if one had no choice.
—Maya Angelou

We had to surrender to a power greater than ourselves to get to where we are today. And each day, we have to turn to that power for strength and guidance. For us, resistance means struggle—struggle with others as well as an internal struggle.

Serenity isn't compatible with struggle. We cannot control forces outside of ourselves. We cannot control the actions of our family or our co-workers. We can control our responses to them. And when we choose to surrender our attempts to control, we will find peace and serenity.

That which we abhor, that which we fear, that which we wish to conquer seems suddenly to be gone when we decide to resist no more—to tackle it no more.

The realities of life come to us in mysterious ways. We fight so hard, only to learn that what we need will never be ours until the struggle is forsaken. Surrender brings enlightenment.

Life's lessons are simple once I give up the struggle.

M Y   T H O U G H T S   &   F O R   T H E   D A Y

JULY 20

It is ironic that the one thing that all religions recognize as separating us from our Creator—our very self-consciousness—is also the one thing that divides us from our fellow creatures.
—ANNIE DILLARD

Getting outside of ourselves, moving beyond our own egos, opens the door to real communication with the people we'll meet today. We have to learn to look with loving appreciation into the soul of that person or child who stands before us. We have to practice being concerned with their needs before our own, and in time our concern will be genuine. The separation between us will exist no more.

This division from others, the barrier that keeps us apart, comes from our individual insecurities. We have grown accustomed to the quick comparisons of ourselves with those we meet. We determine them to be either inferior or superior to ourselves. Whatever gifts we have to offer each other are left unwrapped, at least for now.

Let's come together, truly together, with someone we've been holding off until now. We can trust that the people who have come into our lives are there by design. We are equal to them, and they to us. We need what they have to offer us, and their growth needs our gifts, too.

I will appreciate the design of my life today. I will draw myself close to the day.

MY THOUGHTS ❦ FOR THE DAY

....

....

....

....

....

....

....

J U L Y   2 1

I wake each morning with the thrill of expectation and the joy of being truly alive. And I'm thankful for this day.
—ANGELA L. WOZNIAK

Being open to the day's offering, all of it, and looking for the positive experiences therein, become habits only after a firm commitment and dedicated practice. Today is special for each of us.

These next twenty-four hours will be unlike all others. And we are not the persons we were, even as recently as yesterday. Looking forward to all of the day's events, with the knowledge that we are in the care of our higher power, in every detail, frees us to make the most of everything that happens.

We have been given the gift of life. We are survivors. The odds against survival in our past make clear we have yet a job to do and are being given the help to do it. Confidence wavers in all of us, but the strength we need will be given to each of us.

In this day that stands before me, I can be certain that I'll have many chances for growth, for kindness to others, for developing confidence in myself. I will be thoughtful in my actions today. They are special and will be repeated no more.

M Y   T H O U G H T S   ❀   F O R   T H E   D A Y

....

....

....

....

....

....

....

....

JULY 22

How I relate to my inner self influences my relationships with all others.
My satisfaction with myself and my satisfaction with other
people are directly proportional.
—SUE ATCHLEY EBAUGH

Hateful attitudes toward others, resistance to someone's suggestions, jealousy over another woman's attractiveness or particular abilities are equally strong indications of the health of our spiritual programs. Our security rests with God. When that relationship is nurtured, the rewards will be many and satisfactions great.

Our inner selves may need pampering and praise. They have suffered the abuse of neglect for many years, no doubt. In many instances we have chided ourselves, perhaps shamed ourselves. Learning to love our inner selves, recognizing the value inherent in our very existence, takes effort, commitment, patience—assets we may only just now be developing in this recovery program.

Our inner selves are the home of our Spirit wherein our attachment to all strength, all courage, all self-esteem, all serenity resides. Our Spirit is one with our higher power. We must acknowledge the presence and utilize the comforts offered.

My relationships with others are as healthy and
fulfilling as my communication with God.

MY   THOUGHTS   FOR   THE   DAY

JULY 23

For this is wisdom; to live,
To take what fate, or the Gods, may give.
—LAURENCE HOPE

We can't control the events of our lives, but we do have mastery over our attitudes. The chances will be many, today, to react negatively or positively to circumstances we find ourselves in. We can consider that each circumstance has something special in it for us.

Positive expectations regarding the planned as well as spontaneous activities of the day will influence the activity's flow, our involvement with it, and our interactions with the other people involved. A positive attitude seems to breed positive experiences. In other words, we attract into our lives that which we expect. How often do we get up angry, feeling behind when the day has only begun, short-tempered with our children, "ready" for a tough one at work? And we generally find it.

The Serenity Prayer offers us all the knowledge, all the wisdom we'll ever need. We can accept what has to be, change what we can, and not get confused between the two. We can inventory our attitude. Are we taking charge of it? Our attitude is something we can change.

I won't get trapped today by a negative attitude.
I will accept the challenge of turning my day around.

M Y   T H O U G H T S   ❦   F O R   T H E   D A Y

JULY 24

*. . . The idea has gained currency that women have often been handicapped
not only by a fear of failure—not unknown to men either—but by a
fear of success as well.*
—SONYA RUDIKOFF

It was our practice, before coming to this program, to eat, drink, and smoke our fears away. What we came to realize, profoundly, was that the fears couldn't be escaped even while high. This program is helping us to understand that fears are human, normal and survivable when we let God and our friends in the program lend a helping hand.

Drugs and alcohol distorted our perceptions. Our fears, whether large or small, were distorted. And we still distort those fears, on occasion, because we move away from the spiritual reality of our lives. Remember, we are confronted with no situation too big to handle, no experience for which we are unprepared, if we but turn to that greater power that the program offers us.

We cannot fail in whatever we try today. The outcome of any task attempted is just as it should be. And however we succeed today, we will be shown the steps, at the right time, to make use of that success.

*I shall not fear failure or success. I am not alone in experiencing either;
both are stepping stones on my life's journey.*

MY THOUGHTS 🌺 FOR THE DAY

....

....

....

....

....

....

....

JULY 25

I have a clear choice between life and death, between reality and fantasy, between health and sickness. I have to become responsible—responsible for mistakes as well as accomplishments.
—EILEEN MAYHEW

Choosing to participate actively in our own lives ushers in joy and sometimes fear. We are energized by our conscious involvement; making thoughtful choices regarding our development heightens our sense of well-being. But occasionally we may fear potential failure. About as frequently, we may fear probable success.

Not every day do we want the responsibility for our lives; but we have it. On occasion we only want the loving arms of a caretaker. The beauty of our lives at this time is that we do have a caretaker at our beck and call, a caretaker who has demonstrated repeatedly a concern for our safety, a caretaker who will help us shoulder every responsibility we face.

Clearly, our coming to this program shows that we have chosen to act responsibly. And just as clearly, every day that we ask for the guidance to live to the best of our abilities, we will be helped to accomplish the tasks right for us in this stage of our lives.

All I have to do is make the right choices.
I will always know which they are, when I ask for guidance.

MY THOUGHTS FOR THE DAY

JULY 26

We want the facts to fit the preconceptions. When they don't,
it is easier to ignore the facts than to change the preconceptions.
—JESSAMYN WEST

To live fully and creatively, to contribute what is only ours to give, requires that we be receptive, wholly, to the reverberations of each present moment. Even anticipation of what may transpire next can prejudice our minds, our level of awareness. Preconceptions cloud our senses. They prevent the actual situation from being fully realized. And it is only in the *now*, as sensed moment by moment, that we find our cues to proceed along the path chosen for us.

As we grow more comfortable with Step Three, daily turning our lives and wills over to the care of God, we'll see how much more rewarding our experiences are. We'll see, too, how much greater are our own contributions. Preconceptions of any situation, persons, anticipated experience dulls the magic, the depth of the moment. And only when we attune ourselves to the invitation of the moment do we give of ourselves, wholly. Our partnership with God lives now, as we go forth in this moment.

I will look to each moment with child-like eyes. I'll find joy and contentment.

M Y   T H O U G H T S   ❧   F O R   T H E   D A Y

....

....

....

....

....

....

....

....

JULY 27

To keep a lamp burning we have to keep putting oil in it.
—MOTHER TERESA

Our spiritual nature must be nurtured. Prayer and meditation lovingly kindle the flame that guides us from within. Because we're human, we often let the flame flicker and perhaps go out. And then we sense the dreaded aloneness. Fortunately, some time away, perhaps even a few moments in quiet communion with God, rekindles the flame.

For most of us, the flame burned low, or not at all, for many years. The flickering we may feel today, or tomorrow, or felt yesterday, will not last, so we may put away our fears. We can listen to the voice of our higher power in others. We can listen, too, as we carry the message. Prayer surrounds us every moment. We can fuel our inner flame with the messages received from others. We can let our spirit spring forth, let it warm our hearts and the hearts of others.

We each have a friend whose flame may be flickering today. I will help her and thus myself. A steady flame can rekindle one that's flickering.

MY THOUGHTS ❀ FOR THE DAY

....

....

....

....

....

....

....

....

JULY 28

The beauty of loving someone is the feeling of "wholeness" that I experience.
The need for that individual in my life, the "I'm part of you and you're part of
me" feeling that connects two people and makes them necessary to each other.
—Kathleen Andrus

All that is asked of us by our Creator is that we love one another. Where love doesn't flow easily, perhaps we can just decide to not hurt someone. If we each avoided hurting all people, for just one day, lives would be transformed. We'd each see the world with a fresh perspective.

The more we love others, any others, the deeper our love will grow for all others. Loving lifts our hearts and lightens our burdens. Every day's tribulations can become triumphs when we carry love in our hearts. Love fills us up, and the more we share it, the fuller we become.

We are connected—each of us to one another, all of us together. Our contributions to the whole are necessary. Its completion is made perfect by our presence.

As I pass a friend today, I will be grateful for
her contribution to my wholeness, too.

M Y   T H O U G H T S   FOR   T H E   D A Y

J U L Y   2 9

Harmony exists in difference no less than in likeness,
if only the same key-note governs both parts.
—MARGARET FULLER

Harmony exists everywhere, as an entity of itself. Our personal attitudes bring the disharmony to a situation. An attitude of love can bless all situations and all people.

The converse is likewise true. We all desire harmony in our relationships. And we will find it, every time we bring an attitude of honest gratitude into a situation.

How we feel, today, about this person or that situation, reflects the strength of our relationship with God. When we experience life in the company of our higher power, we will let life flow. We will observe harmony, then, even in the midst of difference.

All of life's elements are moving toward a state of total and perfect harmony. We need not fear. We can trust the company of our higher power and know that every situation, no matter how adverse its appearance, is contributing to a harmonious outcome if we'd but lend a trusting attitude.

Harmony is everywhere. I will celebrate it.
I will trust the present. I will trust the future.

M Y   T H O U G H T S   ❦   F O R   T H E   D A Y

JULY 30

It is the creative potential itself in human beings that is the image of God.
—MARY DALY

God's presence is within us, now and always, even though we feel alone, alienated, scared, and forgotten much of the time. We often overlook God's presence because we don't recognize it. Our talents, our desires, and our pursuits are the evidence—all the evidence we'll ever need once we understand it—that God is present within and about us all the time.

The creative potential goes unrealized among so many of us, perhaps because we have a rigid definition of what creativity is. We are creative. We are all, each of us, creative. We must be because God's presence is here now. When we choose to let it guide us, we'll be able to offer our own unique gifts to the world of friends around us. Encouraging creativity, our own and someone else's, may mean breaking old habits. It surely does mean stepping out of our own way. It also means giving ourselves fully to the experience of the moment and trusting that God's presence will prompt the deliverance of our special gift.

In the moment lives God within us. In the moment I am creative,
blessed with gifts like no other. I will stay in the moment
and offer them, guided by the God within.

MY THOUGHTS 🌸 FOR THE DAY

....

....

....

....

....

....

....

....

JULY 31

Love doesn't just sit there like a stone, it has to be made, like brick;
re-made all the time, made new.
—URSULA K. LEGUIN

We love to be loved; we love to be held; we love to be caressed. A show of appreciation we love too. And we love to know we've been heard. The friends, the spouses, the children in our lives want the same from us. Like a garden that needs water, sun, weeding to nurture the growth, so does love need attending to. To become whole and healthy women, we need tender nurturing. And we also need to give away what we get. Those we nurture will bless our growth.

Love is dynamic, not static. It is always changing, and it always changes those it enfolds. Since coming into this program where the sharing of oneself, the open expression of love, is profoundly evident, we each have changed. And our presence has changed others. We have learned to accept love and give it. But better yet, we have learned that we deserve love.

I will look around me today at others, and I will remember, my growth and theirs
depends on loving and being loved. I will reach out. I can make love new.

M Y   T H O U G H T S   F O R   T H E   D A Y

August

....

....

....

....

....

....

....

A U G U S T   1

The secret of seeing is to sail on solar wind. Hone and spread your spirit, till
you yourself are a sail, whetted, translucent, broadside to the merest puff.
—ANNIE DILLARD

Our progress today, and certainly our serenity, is enhanced by our willingness to accept all that we are blessed with today. Not only to accept, but to celebrate, trusting that these events are moving us toward our special destiny.

Flowing with the twists and turns in our lives, rather than resisting them, guarantees smooth sailing, helps us to maximize our opportunities, increases our serenity. Accepting our powerlessness over all but our own attitude is the first step we need to take toward finding serenity.

Resistance, whether it is against a person or a situation in our lives, will compound the problem as we perceive it. We can believe in the advantages for growth that all experiences offer. We can sail with our experiences. We can be open to them so they can carry us to our destination. We can trust, simply trust, that all is well and in our favor, every moment.

My serenity is in my control today. I will look to this day
with trust and thanksgiving. And my Spirit will soar.

M Y   T H O U G H T S   FOR   T H E   D A Y

....

....

....

....

....

....

....

....

AUGUST 2

Though we be sick and tired and faint and worn—Lo, all things can be borne!
—Elizabeth Chase Akers

What bothered us most a year ago? A month ago? Even a week ago? It's probable that whatever it was, we were obsessed with it, certain that our futures were ruined, that there was no reasonable solution. It's also probable that we feared we simply couldn't survive the complexity of the situation. But we did. And we always will be able to survive any and all difficulties. We are never, absolutely never, given more than we can handle. In fact, we are given exactly what we need, at any given time.

We have many lessons to learn. Fortunately, we have the structure of the Twelve Steps to guide us through the lessons. We need mainly to remember what we are powerless over, that there is a power greater than ourselves, and that life will become simple; we'll need no extra homework when we've turned it over to the care of God.

Whatever my problem today, I will let God have it. A solution is in the making.
I'll see it just as quickly as I can let go of the problem.

MY THOUGHTS FOR THE DAY

....

....

....

....

....

....

....

....

....

A U G U S T   3

All that is necessary to make this world a better place to live is to love—to love as Christ loved, as Buddha loved.
—ISADORA DUNCAN

To be unconditionally loved is our birthright, and we are so loved by God. We desire just such a love from one another, and we deserve it; yet, it's a human quality to look for love before giving it. Thus many of us search intently for signs of love.

Too many of us are searching, rather than loving. Truly loving another means letting go of all expectations. It means full acceptance, even celebration of another's personhood. Not easy, but so rewarding, to ourselves as well as to the one who is the focus of our love.

Love is a balm that heals. Loving lightens our burdens, whatever they are. It invites our inner joy to emerge. But most of all, it connects us, one with another. Loneliness leaves. We are no longer alienated from our environment. Love is the mortar that holds the human structure together. Without the expression of love, it crumbles. This recovery program has offered us a plan for loving others, as well as ourselves. Love will come to us, just as surely as we give it away.

Each and every expression of love I offer today will make smooth another step I take in this life.

M Y   T H O U G H T S   FOR   T H E   D A Y

....

....

....

....

....

....

....

AUGUST 4

Let me tell thee, time is a very precious gift of God;
so precious that it's only given to us moment by moment.
—AMELIA BARR

Where are our minds right now? Are we focused fully on this meditation? Or are our minds wandering off to events scheduled for later today or tomorrow perhaps? The simple truth is that this moment is all God has allowed right now. It's God's design that we will live fully each moment, as it comes. Therein lies the richness of our lives. Each moment contributes to the full pattern that's uniquely our own.

We must not miss the potential pleasure of any experience because our thoughts are elsewhere. We never know when a particular moment, a certain situation, may be a door to our future. What we do know is that God often has to work hard getting our attention, perhaps allowing many stumbling blocks in order to get us back on target.

Being in tune with now, this moment, guarantees a direct line of communication to God. It also guarantees a full, yet simple life. Our purpose becomes clear as we trust our steps to God's guidance. How terribly complicated we make life by living in the past, the present, and many future times, all at once!

One step, one moment, and then the next step and its moment
How the simple life brings me freedom!

M Y   T H O U G H T S   ❧   F O R   T H E   D A Y

....

....

....

....

....

....

....

The bottom line is that I am responsible for my own well-being,
my own happiness. The choices and decisions I make regarding
my life directly influence the quality of my days.
—KATHLEEN ANDRUS

There is no provision for blaming others in our lives. Who we are is a composite of the actions, attitudes, choices, decisions we've made up to now. For many of us, predicaments may have resulted from our decisions to not act when the opportunity arose. But these were decisions, no less, and we must take responsibility for making them.

We need not feel utterly powerless and helpless about the events of our lives. True, we cannot control others, and we cannot curb the momentum of a situation, but we can choose our own responses to both; these choices will heighten our sense of self and well-being and may well positively influence the quality of the day.

I will accept responsibility for my actions, but not for the
outcome of a situation; that is all that's requested of me.
It is one of the assignments of life, and homework is forthcoming.

M Y T H O U G H T S F O R T H E D A Y

....

....

....

....

....

....

....

....

A U G U S T   6

They sicken of the calm, who knew the storm.
—DOROTHY PARKER

Variety in experiences is necessary for our continued growth. We mistakenly think that the "untroubled" life would be forever welcome. It's the deep waves of life that teach us to be better swimmers.

We don't know how to appreciate the calm without the occasional storm that pushes us to new limits of ourselves. The calm following the storm offers us the time we need to become comfortable with our new growth. We are ever changing, refining our values, stepping gingerly into uncharted territories. We are forever in partnership in these new territories, let us not forget.

We long for challenge even in the midst of the calm that blesses us. Our inner selves understand the journey; a journey destined to carry us to new horizons; a journey that promises many stormy seasons. For to reach our destination, we must be willing to weather the storms. They are challenges, handpicked for us, designed to help us become all that we need to be in this earthly life.

The mixture of the calm with the storm is not haphazard. Quite the contrary.
My growth is at the center of each. I will trust its message.

M Y   T H O U G H T S   F O R   T H E   D A Y

....

....

....

....

....

....

....

A U G U S T   7

*To have one's individuality completely ignored is like being pushed
quite out of life. Like being blown out as one blows out a light.*
—EVELYN SCOTT

We need to know that we matter in this life. We need evidence that others are aware of our presence. And thus, we can be certain that others need the same attention from us. When we give it, we get it. So the giving of attention to another searching soul meets our own need for attention as well.

Respectful recognition of another's presence blesses her, ourselves, and God. And we help one another grow, in important ways, each time we pay the compliment of acknowledgment.

We're not sure, on occasion, just what we have to offer our friends, families, co-workers. Why we are in certain circumstances may have us baffled, but it's quite probably that the people we associate with regularly need something we can give them; the reverse is just as likely. So we can begin with close attention to people in our path. It takes careful listening and close observation to sense the message another soul may be sending to our own.

*I will be conscious of the people around me. I shall acknowledge them
and be thankful for all they are offering me.*

M Y   T H O U G H T S   ❧   F O R   T H E   D A Y

....

....

....

....

....

....

....

AUGUST 8

I'm a most lucky and thankful woman. Lucky and thankful for each morning I wake up. For three wonderful daughters and one son. For an understanding and very loving husband with whom I've shared 52 blessed years, all in good health.
—THELMA ELLIOTT

Gratitude for what's been offered us in our lives softens the harsh attitudes we occasionally harbor. Life presents us with an assortment of blessings; some bring us immediate joy; some invite tears; others foster fear. What we need help in understanding is that all experiences are meant for our good, all bless us in some manner. If we are able to see the big picture, we'd greet all situations, large and small, with a thankful heart.

It's so very easy to wish away our lives, never finding satisfaction with our families, our jobs, our friends. The more we find fault with life, the more fault we are guaranteed to find. Negative attitudes attract negative experiences, while positive attitudes lighten whatever burden we may be learning from.

The years pass so quickly. Our chances to enjoy life pass quickly too. We can grab what comes our way and be grateful. We are never certain that this experience offered now might not be our last.

Each morning I awake is blessing number one.

MY THOUGHTS FOR THE DAY

For me, stopping smoking wasn't a matter of will power, but being will-less.
—JOAN GILBERTSON

Most of us have struggled, willfully, with untold numbers of addictions; liquor, uppers, downers, sugar, chocolate, cigarettes, men. The more we became determined to control our use or to abstain, the greater the compulsion felt for one drink, one bite, one puff. Giving in completely was the turning point.

This recovery program helps each of us find relief from our primary addiction once we humble ourselves, accept our powerlessness, and ask for help. It can help us equally effectively, every day, with any problem we are willfully trying to control. Is a family member causing us grief? Is a co-worker creating anxiety? Has a close friend pulled away? We expend so much energy trying to manage outcomes! In most cases, our attempt to control will invite even more resistance.

The program offers the way out of any frustrating situation. We can be mindful of our powerlessness and cherish the opportunities offered by our higher power. We can turn over whatever our problem to God and quietly, trustingly, anticipate the resolution. It's guaranteed.

How much easier I will find life's experiences if I will let go of my willful ways.
The right outcome in all cases will more quickly surface.

M Y   T H O U G H T S   ❧   F O R   T H E   D A Y

....

....

....

....

....

....

....

AUGUST 10

*. . . the growth of understanding follows an ascending spiral
rather than a straight line.*
—JOANNA FIELD

We each are traveling our own, very special path in this life. At times our paths run parallel to each other. On occasion they may intersect. But we do all have a common destination: knowledge of life's meaning. And we'll arrive at knowledge when we've arrived at the mountain's summit, separately and yet together.

We do not go straight up the side of the mountain on this trip. We circle it, slowly, carefully, sometimes losing our footing, sometimes backtracking because we've reached an impasse. Many times we have stumbled, but as we grow in understanding, as we rely more and more on our inner strength, available for the taking, we become more sure-footed.

We have never needed to take any step alone on this trip. Our troubles in the past were complicated because we did not know this; but now we do. Our lifeline is to our higher power. If we hang on to it, every step of the way will feel secure. The ground will be stable under us.

*I am on a path to full understanding. I am learning to trust the
lifeline offered by the program and God and my friends. As I learn,
my footing is less tentative, and it supports me more securely.*

MY THOUGHTS ❀ FOR THE DAY

....

....

....

....

....

....

....

AUGUST 11

Imagination has always had powers of resurrection that no science can match.
—INGRID BENGIS

In the imagination are transmitted messages, from God to us. Inspiration is born there. So are dreams. Both give rise to the goals that urge us forward, that invite us to honor this life we've been given with a contribution, one like no other contribution.

Our imagination offers us ideas to ponder, ideas specific to our development. It encourages us to take steps unique to our time, our place, our intended gifts to the world. We can be alert to this special "inner voice" and let it guide our decisions; we can trust its urgings. It's charged with serving us, but only we can decide to "listen."

The imagination gives us another tool: belief in ourselves. And the magic of believing offers us strength and capabilities even beyond our fondest hopes. It prepares us for the effort we need to make and for handling whatever outcome God has intended.

My imagination will serve me today.
It will offer me the ideas and the courage I need to go forth.

MY THOUGHTS ❀ FOR THE DAY

....

....

....

....

....

....

....

....

A U G U S T   1 2

*When a woman has love, she is no longer at the mercy of forces greater than
herself, for she, herself, becomes the powerful force.*
—VERONICA CASEY

The need for love is universal. Each of us longs for the affirmation that assures us we are
needed, appreciated, desired. We are strengthened by the strokes others give us, and when
no strokes are forthcoming, we sometimes falter.

With emotional and spiritual maturity comes the understanding that we are loved, unconditionally, by God. And the awareness of that love, the realization of its abiding presence,
will buoy us up when no other love signals to us. Most of us still lose our connection to the
omnipresent God, however. Thus, our buoyancy is tentative.

Until that time when we are certain about our value, about the presence of God's love,
we'll need to practice self-affirmation. But learning how to nurture ourselves, how to be
gentle and caressing to the woman within, may be painstaking. Patience will ease the
process. Unconditionally loving ourselves will become natural in time. In fact, we'll sense
our inner person growing, changing. Our wholeness will become apparent to others as well
as to ourselves.

*Love breeds love. I will shower it upon myself and others and
relish the growing sense of self that emerges.*

M Y   T H O U G H T S   🌸   F O R   T H E   D A Y

....

....

....

....

....

....

....

A U G U S T   1 3

Anything forced into manifestation through personal will is always
"ill got" and has "ever bad success."
—FLORENCE SCOVEL SHINN

The main thrust of our recovery is to attune ourselves to God's will, struggling no longer to impose our own. The pain we've endured in past years was often of our own making. We controlled situations until we managed to force the outcome we desired, only to realize it didn't offer happiness. It was, instead, a bitter ending to the struggle.

When we want something or someone to play by our rules, we can expect barriers. And when the barriers don't give way with a gentle push, we should consider it a clue that we are off course. When we want what God wants for us, the bafflers, if any, will fall away.

What God wants for us at every moment is growth and happiness. When we step away from our ego and develop a selfless posture toward life, we'll find serenity in the midst of any turmoil. Serenity is God's promise. When we get in line with God's will, we'll find peace.

I will know God's will if I will listen to my inner voice.
I will do what feels right, and peace will be my reward.

M Y   T H O U G H T S   FOR   T H E   D A Y

....

....

....

....

....

....

....

....

AUGUST 14

Often when we're being tough and strong, we're scared. It takes a lot of
courage to allow ourselves to be vulnerable, to be soft.
—DUDLEY MARTINEAU

We've developed defenses for protection because we have felt the need for protection from the abuses of others, parents on occasion, bosses, spouses, even strangers. And in certain situations, our defenses served us well for a time. However, they have taken their toll. Hiding behind them for long makes them habitual, and we move farther and farther away from our center, from the woman each of us needs and wants to be.

Exposing who we really are invites judgment, sometimes rejection, oftentimes discounting. It's a terribly hard risk to take, and the rewards are seldom immediate. But with time, others respect us for our vulnerability and begin to imitate our example. We are served well by our integrity, in due time.

Letting others see who we really are alleviates confusion, theirs and ours. We no longer need to decide who we should be; we simply are who we are. Our choices are simplified. There is only one appropriate choice to every situation—the one that is honest and wholly reflective of who we are at that moment.

Rewards will be forthcoming when I am honest.

MY THOUGHTS FOR THE DAY

Life does not need to mutilate itself in order to be pure.
—SIMONE WEIL

How terribly complicated we choose to make life's many questions. Should we call a friend and apologize or wait for her call? Are the children getting the kind of care they must, right now? That we "Came to believe in a power greater than ourselves" is often far from our thoughts when we most need it.

Our need to make all things perfect, to know all the answers, to control everything within our range, creates problems where none really exist. And the more we focus on the problem we've created, the bigger it becomes.

Inattention relieves the tension; last week's problems can seldom be recalled. The one we are keeping a problem with our undivided attention can be turned loose, at this moment. And just as quickly, the turmoil we've been feeling will be beyond recall too.

The program offers us another way to approach life. We need not mutilate it or ourselves. We can learn to accept the things we cannot change, and change the things we can . . . with practice.

I will pray for wisdom today. I shall expect wisdom, not problems,
and the day will smoothly slip by.

M Y   T H O U G H T S   FOR   T H E   D A Y

....

....

....

....

....

....

....

AUGUST 16

Love is a force. It is not a result; it is a cause. It is not a product; it produces.
It is a power, like money, or steam or electricity.
It is valueless unless you can give something else by means of it.
—ANNE MORROW LINDBERGH

Love and feeling loved—how often both elude us! We have taken the first step, though. Let's be grateful for our recovery; this is an act of love. We have chosen to love ourselves, and the program opens the way to our loving others. Love and loving are balms for the soul sickness we experience. We are being healed. We are healing one another.

Loving others means going beyond our own selfish concerns, for the moment, and putting others' concerns first. The result is that others feel our love. They feel a caring that is healing. And our spiritual natures are likewise soothed.

We find God and ourselves through touching the souls of one another. Our most special gift is being loved and giving love. Every moment we spend with another person is gift-giving time.

Every day is a gift-giving holiday, if I will but make it so.

M Y T H O U G H T S 🌸 F O R T H E D A Y

AUGUST 17

Life is not always what one wants it to be,
but to make the best of it as it is, is the only way of being happy.
—JENNIE JEROME CHURCHILL

We are generally so certain that we know what's best for ourselves. And we are just as often certain that what we think is best will guarantee happiness. Perhaps we should reflect on all the times in the past when our wishes didn't come true—fortunately.

Did any one of us expect to be doing, today, what we each are doing? We may have expected children, a particular kind of home, a certain career, but did we really anticipate all that life has wrought? Addiction, and then recovery from it, was probably not in our pictures. But it does fit into the big picture. The happiness we experience today probably doesn't visit us in the way we anticipated a few years back. But it is measured out according to our needs. The choice to be happy with what is, is ours to make, every moment.

I can take life as it is, and trust that it is just right, just what
it needs to be. The big picture guarantees me lasting happiness.
Today's experiences will move me a step closer.

MY THOUGHTS ❧ FOR THE DAY

....

....

....

....

....

....

....

....

AUGUST 18

Today was like a shadow. It lurked behind me. It's now gone forever.
Why is it that time is such a difficult thing to befriend?
—MARY CASEY

Each passing minute is all that we are certain of having. The choice is ever present to relish the moment, reaping fully whatever its benefits, knowing that we are being given just what we need each day of our lives. We must not pass up what is offered today.

Time accompanies us like a friend, though often a friend denied or ignored. We can't recapture what was offered yesterday. It's gone. All that stands before us is here, now.

We can nurture the moment and know that the pain and pleasures offered us with each moment are our friends, the teachers our inner selves await. And we can be mindful that this time, this combination of events and people, won't come again. They are the gift of the present. We can be grateful.

We miss the opportunities the day offers because we don't recognize the experiences as the lesson designed for the next stage of our development. The moment's offerings are just, necessary, and friendly to our spiritual growth.

I will take today in my arms and love it.
I will love all it offers; it is a friend bearing gifts galore.

MY THOUGHTS ❦ FOR THE DAY

....

....

....

....

....

....

....

AUGUST 19

Exaggerating the negative element in our lives is familiar behavior for all too many of us. But this obsession is our choice. We can stop at any moment. We can decide to let go of a situation that we can't control, turn it over to God, and be free to look ahead at the possibilities for happiness.

Perhaps we can learn to accept a serious situation in our lives as a special opportunity for growth first of all, but even more as an opportunity to let God work in our lives. We learn to trust by giving over our dilemmas to God for solutions. With patience, we will see the right outcomes, and we will more easily turn to God the next time.

Crises will lessen in number and in gravity in direct proportion to the partnership we develop with our higher power. The stronger our dependence on that power, for all answers and all directions, the greater will our comfort be in all situations.

Serenity is the gift promised when we let God handle our lives. No crisis need worry us. The solution is only a prayer away.

I will take action against every crisis confronting me—I will turn to God.
Each crisis is an invitation to serenity.

MY THOUGHTS ✿ FOR THE DAY

....

....

....

....

....

....

....

Everything in life that we really accept undergoes a change.
So suffering must become love. That is the mystery.
—KATHERINE MANSFIELD

Acceptance of those conditions that at times plague us changes not only the conditions but, in the process, ourselves. Perhaps this latter change is the more crucial. As each changes, as we all change into more accepting women, life's struggles ease. When we accept all the circumstances that we can't control, we are more peaceful. Smiles more easily fill us up.

It's almost as though life's eternal lesson is acceptance, and with it comes life's eternal blessings.

Every day offers me many opportunities to grow in acceptance and thus
blessings. I can accept any condition today and understand it as an
opportunity to take another step toward serenity, eternal and whole.

M Y   T H O U G H T S   F O R   T H E   D A Y

....

....

....

....

....

....

....

....

....

A U G U S T   2 1

With each new day I put away the past and discover the
new beginnings I have been given.
—ANGELA L. WOZNIAK

We can't recapture what is no more. And the minutes or hours we spend dwelling on what was or should have been only steal away from all that presently is. Today stands before us with promise. The opportunities for growth are guaranteed, as is all the spiritual help we need to handle any situation the day offers.

If today offers us a challenge, we can be grateful. Our challenges are gifts. They mean we are ready to move ahead to new awarenesses, to a new sense of our womanhood. Challenges force us to think creatively; they force us to turn to others; they demand that we change. Without challenges, we'd stagnate, enjoying life little, offering life nothing.

We each are making a special contribution, one that only we can make, each time we confront a new situation with courage. Each time we dare to open a new door. What we need to do today is to close the door on yesterday. Then we can stand ready and willing to go forward.

This day awaits my full presence. I will be the recipient of its gifts.

M Y   T H O U G H T S   FOR   T H E   D A Y

....

....

....

....

....

....

....

....

AUGUST 22

We're only as sick as the secrets we keep.
—SUE ATCHLEY EBAUGH

Harboring parts of our inner selves, fearing what others would think if they knew, creates the barriers that keep us separate, feeling different, certain of our inadequacies.

Secrets are burdens, and they weigh heavily on us, so heavily. Carrying secrets makes impossible the attainment of serenity—that which we strive for daily. Abstinence alone is not enough. It must come first, but it's not enough by itself. It can't guarantee that we'll find the serenity we seek.

This program of recovery offers self-assurance, happiness, spiritual well-being, but there's work to be done. Many steps to be taken. And one of these is total self-disclosure. It's risky, it's humbling, and it's necessary.

When we tell others who we really are, it opens the door for them to share likewise. And when they do, we become bonded. We accept their imperfections and love them for them. And they love us for ours. Our struggles to be perfect, our self-denigration because we aren't, only exaggerates even more the secrets that keep us sick.

Our tarnished selves are lovable; secrets are great equalizers when shared. We need to feel our oneness, our sameness with other women.

Opportunities to share my secrets will present themselves today.
I will be courageous.

MY THOUGHTS FOR THE DAY

....

....

....

....

....

....

AUGUST 23

Were our knowledge of human relationships a hundredfold more
reliable than it is now, it would still be foolish to seek ready-made
solutions for problems of living in the index of a book.
—MIRRA KOMAROVSKY

The problems each of us experience have within their own parameters the solutions most fitting. And we each must discover those solutions, understand their appropriateness, and absorb them into the body of information that defines who we are and who we are becoming.

We learn experientially because only then is our reality significantly affected. Others' experiences are helpful to our growth and affirm how similar is our pain, but each of us must make our own choices, take responsible action in our own behalf.

How fortunate that we are now in a position to make healthy decisions about our relationships! No longer the victim, we have the personal power to choose how we want to spend our time and with whom. Through active participation in all our relationships, we can discover many of the hidden elements in our own natures and develop more fully all the characteristics unique to our personhood. Our growth as recovering women is enhanced in proportion to our sincere involvement within the relationships we've chosen.

I can inform myself about who I am within my relationships.
Therein lie the solutions to my problems.

MY THOUGHTS ❦ FOR THE DAY

....

....

....

....

....

....

AUGUST 24

*There were many ways of breaking a heart. Stories were full of
hearts broken by love, but what really broke a heart was taking
away its dream—whatever that dream might be.*
—PEARL S. BUCK

No new door is opened without the inner urge for growth. Dreams guide us, encourage us, stretch us to new heights—and leave us momentarily empty when they are dashed.

Recovery has given us resilience and a multitude of reasons for living. We have come to understand that when one dream serves us no longer, it is making way for an even better one. Our dreams are our teachers. When the student is ready, a new one comes into focus.

Dreams in our earlier years often come to nought. They couldn't compete for our attention as effectively as the self-pity. The direction they offered was lost. Each day that we look forward with positive anticipation, we put the wreckage of the past farther from our minds.

Our dreams are like the rest areas on a cross-country trip. They refresh us, help us to gauge the distance we've come, and give us a chance to consider our destination.

*Today's dreams and experiences are points on the road map of my life.
I won't let them pass unnoticed.*

M Y   T H O U G H T S   ❀   F O R   T H E   D A Y

AUGUST 25

*In soloing—as in other activities—it is far easier to
start something than it is to finish it.*
—AMELIA EARHART

Procrastination plagues us all, at one time or another. But any activity that is worthy of our effort should be tackled by bits and pieces, one day at a time. We are too easily overwhelmed when we set our sights only on the accomplished goal. We need to focus, instead, on the individual elements and then on just one element at a time. A book is written, word by word. A house is built, timber by timber. A college degree is attained, course by course.

By the time we got to this program, most of us had accumulated a checkered past, much of which we wanted to deny or forget. And the weight of our past can stand in the way of the many possibilities in the present.

Our past need not determine what we set out to do today. However, we must be realistic: We can't change a behavior pattern overnight. But we can begin the process. We can decide on a reasonable, manageable objective for this 24-hour period. Enough days committed to the completion of enough small objectives will bring us to the attainment of any goal, large or small.

*I can finish any task I set my sights on, when I take it one day at a time.
Today is before me. I can move forward in a small way.*

MY THOUGHTS FOR THE DAY

....

....

....

....

....

....

....

A U G U S T   2 6

A woman who has no way of expressing herself and of realizing herself as a full human has nothing else to turn to but the owning of material things.
—ENRIQUETA LONGEAUX Y VASQUEZ

Each of us struggling with these Twelve Steps is finding self-expression and self-definition. Introspection, coupled with self-revelation through sharing with others, affords us the awareness of how like others we are. How human we are. And what we receive from others who respond to our vulnerability diminishes our need for "things" to fill our lives.

The love that we receive freely from a trusting, caring friend or group fills up the empty places in our souls, the places we used to try filling up with alcohol or cookies or sex. New clothes, maybe even a new home or a different job served their terms as void fillers too. Nothing succeeded for long, and then the program found us.

The program is the filler for all times. Of this we can be certain. Time will alleviate any doubts we may have. All that is asked of us is openness, honesty, and attention to others' needs as well as our own.

I can share our likenesses and relish whatever differences may surface.
The chain of friendship I've created makes me the proud owner
of my wholeness. I am a succeeding woman who is moving
forward with courage and self-awareness on this, my road of life.

M Y   T H O U G H T S   ❧   F O R   T H E   D A Y

....

....

....

....

....

....

....

A U G U S T 2 7

Acceptance is not submission; it is acknowledgment of the facts of a situation.
Then deciding what you're going to do about it.
—KATHLEEN CASEY THEISEN

Recovery offers us courage to make choices about the events of our lives. Passive compliance with whatever is occurring need no longer dominate our pattern of behavior. Powerlessly watching our lives go by was common for many of us, and our feelings of powerlessness escalated the more idle we were.

Today, action is called for, thoughtful action in response to the situations begging for our attention. Recovery's greatest gift is the courage to take action, to make decisions that will benefit us as well as the people who are close to us. Courage is the by-product of our spiritual progress, courage to accept what we cannot change, believing that all will be well, courage to change in ourselves what we do have control over.

An exhilaration about life accompanies the taking of action. The spell that idleness casts over us is broken, and subsequent actions are even easier to take. Clearly, making a choice and acting on it is healthful. The program has given us the tools to do both.

Decisions will be called for today. I will be patient with myself, and thoughtful.
I will listen closely to the guidance that comes from those around me.

M Y T H O U G H T S FOR T H E D A Y

....

....

....

....

....

....

....

AUGUST 28

There are sounds to seasons. There are sounds to places,
and there are sounds to every time in one's life.
—ALISON WYRLEY BIRCH

Life is rich and full. Your life. My life. Even when the day feels flat or hollow, there's a richness to it that escapes our attention. We see only what we choose to see. We hear selectively, too. Our prejudgment precludes our getting the full effects of any experience. Some days we hear only the drum of the humdrum.

But the greater our faith in the program and a loving God, the clearer our perceptions become. We miss less of the day's events; we grow in our understanding of our unfolding, and we perceive with clarity the role others are playing in our lives.

We can see life as a concert in progress when we transcend our own narrow scope and appreciate the variety of people and situations all directed toward the same finale. The more we're in tune with the spiritual activity surrounding us, the more harmoniously we will be able to perform our parts.

I will listen to the music of today. I will get in tune, in rhythm.
I am needed for the concert's beauty.

MY THOUGHTS ❧ FOR THE DAY

....

....

....

....

....

....

....

....

AUGUST 29

Life is either a daring adventure or nothing.
—HELEN KELLER

The next 24 hours are guaranteed to excite us, to lift us to new levels of understanding, to move us into situations with others where we can offer our unique contributions. All that is asked of us is a willingness to trust that we will be given just what we need at each moment.

We can dare to live, fully, just for today. We can appreciate the extraordinariness of every breath we take, every challenge we encounter. Within each experience is the invitation for us to grow, to reach out to others in caring ways, to discover more fully the women we are capable of being. We must not let a single moment go by unnoticed.

When we withdraw from life, we stunt our growth. We need involvement with others, involvement that perturbs us, humors us, even stresses us. We tap our internal resources only when we have been pushed to our limits, and our participation in life gifts us, daily, with that push. How necessary the push!

None of us will pass this way again. What we see and feel and say today are gone forever. We have so much to regret when we let things slip away unnoticed or unappreciated.

A special series of events has been planned for me today. I shall not miss it.

MY THOUGHTS 🌼 FOR THE DAY

AUGUST 30

I like my friend for what is in her heart, not for the way she does things.
—SANDRA K. LAMBERSON

We find good in situations, experiences, and people when we look for it. Generally we find just what we expect to find. The power attaching to our attitudes is awesome. Often it is immobilizing; too seldom is it positive.

We each create the personal environment that our soul calls home, which means that at any moment we have the power to change our perspective on life, our response to any particular experience and most of all, our feelings about ourselves. Just as we will find good in others when we decide to look for it, we'll find good in ourselves.

We are such special women, all of us. And in our hearts we want joy. What the program offers is the awareness that we are the creators of the joy in our hearts. We can relinquish the past and its sorrows, and we can leave the future in the hands of our higher power. The present is singular in its importance to our lives, now.

Behavior generally reveals attitudes which are of the mind and frequently in conflict with the heart. I will strive for congruence. I will let my heart lead the way. It will not only find the good in others, it will imitate it.

MY THOUGHTS ❦ FOR THE DAY

Tears are like rain. They loosen up our soil so we
can grow in different directions.
—Virginia Casey

Full self-expression softens our being, while self-reservation makes us brittle. Our wholeness is enhanced each time we openly acknowledge our feelings and share our many secrets. The tears that often accompany self-disclosure, self-assessment, or the frustration of being "stuck" seem to shift whatever blocks we have put in our paths.

At each stage of our lives, we are preparing for yet another stage. Our growth patterns will vary, first in one direction, and then another. It's not easy to switch directions, but it's necessary. We can become vulnerable, accept the spiritual guidance offered by others and found within, and the transition from stage to stage will be smooth.

Tears shed on the rocky places of our lives can make tiny pebbles out of the boulders that block our paths. But we also need to let those tears wash away the blinders covering our eyes. Tears can help us see anew if we're willing to look straight ahead—clearly, openly, and with expectation of a better view.

Tears nurture the inner me. They soften my rootedness to old behavior.
They lessen my resistance to new growth.

MY THOUGHTS FOR THE DAY

September

SEPTEMBER 1

Success can only be measured in terms of distance traveled.
—Mavis Gallant

We are forever moving from one experience to another, one challenge to another, one relationship to another. Our ability to handle confidently all encounters is a gift of the program, and one that accompanies us throughout every day, providing we humbly express gratitude for it. Success is ours when we are grateful.

We are not standing still. No matter how uneventful our lives may seem, we are traveling toward our destiny, and all the thrills and tears, joys and sorrows, are contributing to the success of our trip. Every day, every step, we are succeeding.

We can reflect on yesterday, better yet, on last week or even last year. What were our problems? It's doubtful we can even remember them. We have put distance between them and us. They were handled in some manner. We have succeeded in getting free of them. We have succeeded in moving beyond them.

How far we have come! And we will keep right on traveling forward. As long as we rely on the program, we are assured of success.

I can do whatever I need to do, today, with success,
when I humbly accept the program's gifts.

MY THOUGHTS ❀ FOR THE DAY

....

....

....

....

....

....

....

SEPTEMBER 2

If I had to describe something as divine it would be what happens between people when they really get it together. There is a kind of spark that makes it all worthwhile. When you feel that spark, you get a good feeling deep in your gut.
—JUNE L. TAPP

How lucky we are, that we can experience that divine spark with one another, and with all recovering women. The program offers us the chance, every moment of our lives from this day forward, to experience divinity. All we are asked to do is be there, for one another, to share fully who we are. Vulnerability gets easier as we learn that we can trust each other, that we can share pain, that it's okay to pull and prod and follow, first you and then me and then her.

What a thrill it is to leave our competition behind! The program bonds us together, and the bond will strengthen each of us, but it can elude us, too. It often does when we forget to be there, in one another's presence, when the opportunity comes.

I need these sparks to nurture my growth, singly and collectively.
I will be part of a divine experience today.

MY THOUGHTS ❧ FOR THE DAY

....

....

....

....

....

....

....

....

. . . satisfaction is a lowly thing, how pure a thing is joy.
—MARIANNE MOORE

Our perfectionism generally dashes all hopes of self-satisfaction. But the program is here to show us that we can make progress. We can learn to believe that we are doing any task as well as we need to do it, at this time. Our job is the effort. The outcome is part of a larger plan, one that involves more than ourselves.

We'll find joy when we find acceptance of ourselves and our efforts and the belief that we are spiritual beings whose lives do have purpose and direction.

The wisdom that accompanies spiritual growth offers us security, that which we have sought along many avenues. And when we feel secure, we can trust that the challenges confronting us are purposeful and to our advantage.

One day at a time, one small prayer at a time, move us ever closer to spiritual security. We can look with glad anticipation at our many responsibilities and activities today. They are our opportunities for spiritual security. We can trust our growing inner resources by simply asking for guidance and waiting patiently. It will find us.

I must exercise my prayers if I want the spiritual security where I can find joy.
I will ask for guidance with every activity today.

M Y   T H O U G H T S   ❀   F O R   T H E   D A Y

For all the sadness of closure, there is a new and joyful
unfolding in the process of becoming.
—MARY CASEY

We must let go of people, places, memories, and move on to new experiences. The doors of the past must be closed before we can enter those that are opening to us today. However, no experience is gone forever. All of our experiences are threaded together, each one contributing to the events that claim our attention now.

Recovery has offered us a chance to be aware of our process of becoming. With each day, each experience, each new understanding, we are advancing along the path of personal growth. Let us remember that each of us has a particular path, like no other. Thus, our experiences are ours alone. We need not envy what comes to someone else.

Life is unfolding for us. The pain of the present may be necessary for the pleasure of tomorrow. We can accept the unfolding. Our inner selves have a goal; experiences of the past must be left in the past; experiences at hand will lead us to our destination today.

I am moving and changing and growing, at the right pace.
The process can be trusted. What is right for me will come to me.
I will let the joy of becoming warm me.

MY THOUGHTS ✿ FOR THE DAY

....

....

....

....

....

....

....

Pity is the deadliest feeling that can be offered to a woman.
—VICKI BAUM

We must move forward with confidence, trusting that the strength we need will be given us, having faith in our visions to guide us. Problems need not daunt us. Rather, they can spur us on to more creative activity. They challenge our capabilities. They insist that we not stand still.

Pity from others fosters inaction, and passivity invites death of the soul. Instead, our will to live is quickened through others' encouragement. All else dampens the will. Pity feeds the self-pity that rings the death knell.

We can give strokes wherever we are today and know that we are helping someone live. And each time we reach out to encourage another, we are breathing new life into ourselves, new life that holds at bay the self-pity that may appear at any moment.

We can serve one another best, never by commiserating with sadnesses, but by celebrating life's challenges. They offer the opportunities necessary to our continued growth.

Someone needs a word of encouragement from me.
I will brighten her vision of the future.

MY THOUGHTS ❦ FOR THE DAY

We can build upon foundations anywhere if they are well and firmly laid.
—Ivy Compton-Burnett

Recovery is a process, one which rebuilds our lives. And the Twelve Steps provide the foundation to support our growth as healthy, productive women. But each Step must be carefully and honestly worked, or the whole foundation will be weakened.

How lucky we are to have found this program and the structure it offers. We looked for structure in our past. We searched, maybe for years, running from one panacea to another, hoping to find ourselves. Booze—pills—food—lovers—causes; none gave us the security we longed for. We couldn't find ourselves because we hadn't defined ourselves. At last we've come home. Self-definition is the program's guarantee. Not only can we discover who we are, now, but we can change, nurture those traits that we favor, diminish those that attract trouble.

My actions today are the key. They tell who I am at this moment.
Who I become is up to me. I will pick a Step and reflect before I move ahead.
The strength of my foundation depends on it.

M Y   T H O U G H T S   FOR   T H E   D A Y

....

....

....

....

....

....

....

....

SEPTEMBER 7

*Remember your good memories, but live for today and
keep the memories behind you.*
—JODI K. ELLIOTT

The stuff of our memories comprise who we have become. Each recollection is akin to an ingredient in a simmering pot of stew. The full flavor of our lives is enhanced by each additional experience whether it be painful or joyful.

Our experiences have a way of dovetailing, of grouping themselves, perhaps even tailoring themselves, to provide us the best advantage. So human is our tendency to linger in thought on past times that we fail to take advantage, to be fully present in the moment which is assuredly making a necessary contribution to the total panorama of our lives.

Who are we to judge the value of any single experience? It's how all experiences have mingled, that we must trust. We can be certain, in retrospect, that those situations that created the most inner turmoil also offered us the most as growing, developing women.

*The experiences offered today, in the 24 hours ahead, are significant because they
are unique. I will cherish them for the addition they are making to my total person.*

MY THOUGHTS FOR THE DAY

....

....

....

....

....

....

....

....

*It's astonishing in this world how things don't turn out
at all the way you expect them to!*
—AGATHA CHRISTIE

Probably every day of our lives, a plan goes awry. Often we have counted heavily on a particular outcome. We generally assume we have all things under control and know exactly what's best for us, and everyone else as well. But such is not the case. There is a bigger picture than the one we see. The outcome of that picture is out of our hands.

Our vision is limited, and again divinely so. However, we are able to see all that we need to see, today. And more important, if we can trust our inner guidance regarding the events of today, we'll begin to see how each day fills in a shade more of the bigger picture of our lives. In retrospect we can see how all events have contributed, in important ways, to the women we are becoming. Where today's events are leading we can't know, for certain, but we can trust the divine plan.

*I will anticipate with faith what lies ahead today. All experiences carry
me forward to fulfill my goal in life. I will be alert for the nudge.*

M Y   T H O U G H T S 🌺 F O R   T H E   D A Y

....

....

....

....

....

....

....

....

I do not want to die . . . until I have faithfully made the most of my talent and cultivated the seed that was placed in me until the last small twig has grown.
—KÄTHE KOLLWITZ

There's so much to do before we rest . . . so much to do. We each are gifted with talents, similar in some respects to others' talents, but unique in how we'll be able to use them. Do we realize our talents? We need only to dare to dream, and there they'll be.

It's so easy to fall into the trap of self-pity, thinking we have no purpose, fearing we'll take life nowhere, dreading others' expectations of us. But we can turn our thinking around at any moment. The choice is ours. We can simply decide to discover our talents, and nurture them and enrich the lives of others. The benefits will be many. So will the joys.

We have a very important part to play, today, in the lives we touch. We can expect adventure, and we'll find it. We can look for our purpose; it's at hand. We can remember, we aren't alone. We are in partnership every moment. Our talents are God-given, and guidance for their full use is part of the gift.

I will have a dream today. In my dream is my direction.

MY THOUGHTS ❀ FOR THE DAY

....

....

....

....

....

....

....

....

SEPTEMBER 10

It isn't for the moment you are struck that you need courage,
but for the long uphill climb back to sanity and faith and security.
—ANNE MORROW LINDBERGH

Most of us are on a long uphill climb at this moment. It is a climb we are making together, and yet a climb we can't do for each other. I can reach out my hand to you, and you can grasp my hand in return. But my steps are my own, just as you, too, can only take one step at a time.

For brief periods we skip, even run, along the uphill path. The rocks and the occasional boulder momentarily trip us up. We need patience and trust that the summit is still achievable. We can help one another have patience. We can remind one another to trust.

We look back at the periods that devastated us so long ago. And now we are here. We have climbed this far. We are stronger, saner, more secure. Each step makes easier the next step— each step puts us on more solid ground.

I may run into some rocks or even a boulder today.
I have stepped around them in the past. I will do so again.

MY THOUGHTS ❧ FOR THE DAY

....

....

....

....

....

....

....

....

SEPTEMBER 11

I used to think I'd never know the difference between serenity
and depression because depression subdued me.
—S.H.

Depression is familiar to us all, and less incapacitating than it used to be. We have made progress, we can be assured. "This too shall pass" is not an empty slogan.

Each of us can recall, with ease probably, a period we thought we'd never survive. Maybe our problem was family-related, or a tough on-the-job situation. Or maybe we felt inadequate and lacking in strength to cope with all situations. But we managed. Here we are today, taking charge of our lives and moving forward in search of serenity.

Serenity no doubt eludes us, again and again, throughout the day. But we can let our minds rest. We can give our thoughts to the wind, and serenity will find us. Serenity's peace nurtures us, strengthens us to withstand the turmoil ahead. There is always turmoil ahead. Life's lessons are found there. The irony is that a life with no problems doesn't offer the opportunities we must have if we are to grow.

I will let the serene moments wash over me. I will cherish them.
They soften me. And the blows of today's tumultuous storm will be lessened.

MY THOUGHTS FOR THE DAY

....

....

....

....

....

....

....

....

SEPTEMBER 12

No person is your enemy, no person is your friend,
every person is your teacher.
—FLORENCE SCOVEL SHINN

We can open ourselves to opportunities today. They abound in our lives. No circumstance we find ourselves in is detrimental to our progress. No relationship with someone at work or at home is superfluous to our development. Teachers are everywhere. And as we become ready for a new lesson, one will appear.

We can marvel at the wonder of our lives today. We can reflect on our yesterdays and be grateful for the lessons they taught. We can look with hopeful anticipation at the days ahead—gifts, all of them. We are on a special journey, serving a special purpose, uniquely our own. No baffler, no difficult person, no tumultuous time is designed to interrupt our progress. All experiences are simply to teach us what we have yet to learn.

Trusting in the goodness of all people, all situations, all paths to progress will release whatever our fears, freeing us to go forth with a quicker step and an assurance that eases all moments.

The Twelve Steps help us to recognize the teachers in our lives. They help us clear away the baggage of the past and free us to accept and trust the will of God, made known to us by the teachers as they appear.

I am a student of life. I can learn only if I open my mind to my teachers.

MY THOUGHTS FOR THE DAY

....

....

....

....

....

....

SEPTEMBER 13

Nobody told me how hard and lonely change is.
—JOAN GILBERTSON

Pain, repeatedly experienced, indicates a need for self-assessment, an inventory of our behavior. Honest self-appraisal may well call for change, a change in attitude perhaps, a change in specific behavior in some instances, or maybe a change in direction. We get off the right path occasionally, but go merrily on our way until bafflers surface, doors close, and experiences become painful.

Most of us willingly wallow in our pain a while, not because we like it, but because its familiarity offers security. We find some comfort in our pain because at least it holds no surprises.

When our trust in God is high, we are more willing to change. And we open ourselves to the indications for movement in a new direction. Each of us must find our own willingness. Each of us must develop attentiveness to the signs that repeatedly invite changes in our behavior. But most of all, each of us has to travel the road to change, singly. Changes we must find the courage to make will never be exactly like someone else's changes.

Courage to change accompanies faith. My fears are telling me to look within to the spiritual source of strength, ever present but often forgotten.

MY THOUGHTS ❦ FOR THE DAY

....

....

....

....

....

....

....

What a strange pattern the shuttle of life can weave.
—FRANCES MARION

How shortsighted is our judgment about today's experiences! We'll see with clarity where they may lead us only after we've reached our destination. Of one thing we can be certain: Today's experiences, in concert with yesterday's and all that's gone before, are combining to weave an intricate life design, unique, purposeful, and for our ultimate good.

We need not feel remorse over lost chances or unproductive behavior in the past. Our destination remains the same, and our arrival is guaranteed. Our actions and decisions are never wrong. We may veer off course for a time, but the design for our lives will pull us back on the track.

The program is part of the design for our lives. It's helping us to stay on course. In fact, when we're working the Steps, we're at ease with our direction, and we trust the outcome of our efforts to the power of the program. We will add to the richness of our design, today, just as we have every day of our lives. We can anticipate today's experiences with an excited heart.

There is something special going on in my life today.
I will give everybody and every event my full attention.

M Y   T H O U G H T S   F O R   T H E   D A Y

....

....

....

....

....

....

....

SEPTEMBER 15

When our myths, dreams, and ideals are shattered, our world topples.
—KATHLEEN CASEY THIESEN

The act of "becoming" topples our world, and rightly so. We outgrow yesterday's ideals, and we have begun realizing, in our unfolding, the dreams of last year. Now new dreams call us. Recovery has toppled our world. Hallelujah!

In our abstinence, each day offers us fresh opportunities to "create" new realities to replace the outworn, outgrown myths of the using days. But letting go of the old takes patience, persistence, and strength. The old comforted us when there was little else.

Perhaps we need reminding that were it not for the shattered myths of last year or last week, we'd not be progressing, unfolding, as the bigger picture calls us. We have a part to play in this life, as do our sisters, our friends, our children. New dreams and ideals will lead us on our way. Old dreams served us yesterday, and the past is gone. They can't direct our present.

I will look with excitement at my toppling world. It signifies growth—
intellectual, emotional and spiritual. Old ideals will bind me—I will
dare to dream new dreams and go where they lead with confidence.

MY THOUGHTS ❦ FOR THE DAY

....

....

....

....

....

....

....

....

*I long to speak out the intense inspiration that
comes to me from lives of strong women.*
—RUTH BENEDICT

Each day that we thoughtfully make choices about our behavior and our attitudes, we offer ourselves as examples to others—examples of strength.

As women on recovery paths, we find encouragement from one another's successes. No one of us met our experiences very successfully before discovering this program. In most cases we lacked the structure that comes with the Steps. Direction was missing from our lives. Too often we passively bounced from man to man, job to job, drunk to drunk.

When working the Steps, we are never in doubt about the manner for proceeding in any situation. The Steps provide the parameters that secure our growth. They help us to see where we've been and push us toward the goals which crowd our dreams.

We have changed. We will continue to grow. The past need haunt us no more. The future can be faced with confidence. Whatever strength is needed to fulfill our destinies will find us. And our forward steps will make the way easier for the women who follow.

*What a blessing these Steps are! They answer my every question.
They fulfill my every need.*

M Y   T H O U G H T S   ❧   F O R   T H E   D A Y

....

....

....

....

....

....

....

Desire and longing are the whips of God.
—ANNA WICKHAM

Our dreams and desires inspire us to reach beyond our present stopping-place. That which we can achieve will draw our attention, and with certainty, a partner is on hand to help us chart the steps for realizing the goal.

Before our introduction to the Twelve Steps, we experienced desires and set many goals. Some we attained. What we often lacked was confidence, and then our commitment wavered. The program is helping us realize that all pure desires are attainable when we invite the program's structure into our daily planning.

Our lives are purposeful. Each of us is fulfilling a necessary role. The longings that tug at us, longings that bring no harm to ourselves or others, push us to realize our full potential.

Courage and strength, ability and resourcefulness are never lacking when we follow the guidance within and trust in its direction. All the wisdom necessary for succeeding at any task, completing any goal, charting any desire, is as close as our attention is to God.

I will pay heed to my desires today. I will pray for the wisdom to fulfill them. All doors will open and my steps will be guided, when the desire is spiritually sound.

M Y   T H O U G H T S   F O R   T H E   D A Y

....

....

....

....

....

....

....

SEPTEMBER 18

The future is made of the same stuff as the present.
—SIMONE WEIL

The moment is eternal. It is unending. When we move with the moment, we experience all that life can offer. Being fully awake to right now guarantees rapture even when there's pain, because we know we are evolving, and we thrill with the knowledge. We are one with all that's going on around us. Our existence is purposeful and part of the whole of creation, and we can sense our purpose.

Nothing is—but now. And when we dwell on what was, or what may be, we are cut off from life—essentially dead. The only reality is the present, and it's only in the present that we are invited to make our special contribution to life; perhaps at this moment our special contribution is to reach out to another person, an act that will change two lives, ours and hers.

We must cling to the present or we'll miss its invitation to grow, to help a friend perhaps, to be part of the only reality there is. The present holds all we need and all we'll ever need to fulfill our lives. It provides every opportunity for our happiness—the only happiness there is.

Abstinence offers me the gift of the present. I will cherish it, be grateful, relish it.

MY THOUGHTS FOR THE DAY

. . . concern should drive us into action and not into depression.
—KAREN HORNEY

The role of victim is all too familiar to many of us. Life *did* us injustices—we thought. And we passively waited for circumstances to change. With the bottle we waited, or maybe the little white pills. Nothing was our fault. That we were willing participants to victimization is an awareness not easily accepted, but true nonetheless.

Victims no more, we are actors, now. And since committing ourselves to this program, we have readily available a willing and very able director for our role in life. Every event invites an action, and we have opted for the responsible life.

Depression may be on the fringes of our consciousness today. But it need not become our state of mind. The antidote is and always will be action, responsible action. Every concern, every experience wants our attention, our active attention.

Today stretches before me, an unknown quantity. Concerns will crowd upon me,
but guidance regarding the best action to take is always available to me.

M Y   T H O U G H T S   FOR   T H E   D A Y

....

....

....

....

....

....

....

....

SEPTEMBER 20

What difference does it make how I am treated by life? My real life is within.
—ANGELA L. WOZNIAK

It is said that we teach people how to treat us. How we treat others invites similar treatment. Our response to the external conditions of our lives can be greatly altered by our perceptions of those conditions. And we have control of that perception. No experience has to demoralize us. Each situation can be appreciated for its long-term contribution to our growth as happy, secure women.

No outside circumstances will offer us full time and forever the security we all long for. And in like manner, none will adversely interfere with our well-being, except briefly and on occasion.

The program offers us the awareness that our security, happiness, and well-being reside within. The uplifting moments of our lives may enhance our security, but they can't guarantee that it will last. Only the relationship we have with ourselves and God within can promise the gift of security.

The ripples in my day are reminders to me to go within.

MY THOUGHTS FOR THE DAY

....

....

....

....

....

....

....

....

SEPTEMBER 21

Praise and an attitude of gratitude are unbeatable
stimulators . . . we increase whatever we extol.
—SYLVIA STITT EDWARDS

What outlook are we carrying forth into the day ahead? Are we feeling fearful about the circumstances confronting us? Do we dread a planned meeting? Are we worried about the welfare of a friend or lover? Whatever our present outlook, its power over the outcome of our day is profound. Our attitude in regard to any situation attracting our attention influences the outcome. Sometimes to our favor, often to our disfavor if our attitude is negative.

Thankfulness toward life guarantees the rewards we desire, the rewards we seek too often from an ungrateful stance. The feeling of gratitude is foreign to many of us. We came to this program feeling worthless, sometimes rejected, frequently depressed. It seemed life had heaped problems in our laps, and so it had. The more we lamented what life "gave us," the more reasons we were given to lament. We got just what we expected. We still get just what we expect. The difference is that the program has offered us the key to higher expectations. Gratitude for the good in our lives increases the good.

I have the personal power to influence my day; I will make it a good one.

MY THOUGHTS ❀ FOR THE DAY

Anger conquers when unresolved.
—ANONYMOUS

Emotions need recognition. But not only attention; they also need acceptance as powerful dimensions of who we are. Their influence over who we are capable of becoming is mighty.

Respectful attention to and willing acceptance of our emotions, whether fear or anger or hateful jealousy, take away their sting. We can prevent them from growing larger than they are. Like a child who screams and misbehaves more and more fiercely until attention is won, our emotions grow larger and more intense the longer we deny their existence.

Our emotions bless us, in reality. They enrich our experiences. They serve as guideposts on the road we're traveling. How we "feel" at any single moment flags the level of our security, how close we are to our higher power, the level of our commitment to the program. Our emotions serve us well when they are acknowledged. On the other hand, when ignored or denied, they can immobilize us, even defeat us.

My feelings frequent my being, always. They steer my behavior.
They reflect my attitudes. They hint at my closeness to God.

M Y   T H O U G H T S   F O R   T H E   D A Y

....

....

....

....

....

....

....

....

Who will I be today? The "Cosmopolitan" woman, the little girl,
the scholar, the mother? Who will I be to answer the needs of others,
and yet answer the needs of me?
—DEIDRA SARAULT

We wear many hats. One aspect of our maturity is our ability to balance our roles. It's often quite difficult to do so; however, the program offers us many tools for balancing our lives.

Fulfilling some of the needs of significant others in our lives brings us joy. Our own needs must be given priority, though. We cannot give away what we don't have, and we have nothing unless we give sincere attention and love to ourselves.

In years gone by, we may have taken too little care of others, or we overdid it. In either case, we probably neglected ourselves. Most of us starved ourselves spiritually, many of us emotionally, a few physically. We were all too often "all-or-nothing" women.

Today we're aware of our choices. We've been making a number of good ones lately: We're abstinent. We're living the Steps. And we're choosing how to spend our time, and what to do with our lives. But no choice will turn out very well if we haven't taken care of ourselves.

I will center on myself. I will nurture the maturing
woman within and then reach out.

M Y   T H O U G H T S   ❧   F O R   T H E   D A Y

....

....

....

....

....

....

Woman must not be awed by that which has been built up around her; she
must reverence that woman in her which struggles for expression.
—MARGARET SANGER

Let us not stifle ourselves any longer. Let us dare to dream and realize those dreams. Let us dare to take risks, having faith that to advance in any respect implies taking risks. Fortunately, we have the support of the program and one another to cushion the fall, if it should come. But more important, we have one another's example to inspire us as we contemplate our own agenda for self-expression.

Many of us for far too long passively watched others move forward. No longer need we be passive observers, but the familiarity of no action, no choice-making, and irresponsibility, makes passivity attractive at times. We must remember responsible choices, for only those make possible our very special contributions.

Not every day do we awaken with the strength needed to "do our part." But the strength will be available just as quickly as we call for it. Alone, we are strugglers; however, we have a ready partnership, and it guarantees us guidance, wisdom, and strength when we ask for it.

I have so much to offer other women. And I need another's example.
Every expression of my strength will boost another woman's strength. I will give.

M Y   T H O U G H T S   ❀   F O R   T H E   D A Y

....

....

....

....

....

....

....

S E P T E M B E R 2 5

. . . we do not always like what is good for us in this world.
—ELEANOR ROOSEVELT

Most of us can look back and recall how we fought a particular change. How certain we were that we wouldn't survive the upheaval! Perhaps we lost a love or were forced to leave a home or a job. Retrospect allows us to see the good of the change, and we can see the necessary part each change has played in our development as recovering women. We've had to change to cover the distances we've traveled. And we'll have to continue changing.

The program and its structure, and our faith in that structure, can ease the harsh consequences of change. Our higher power wants only the best for us, of that we can be sure. However, the best may not always "fit" when first we try it. Patience, trust, and prayer are a winning combination when the time comes for us to accept a change. We'll know when it's coming. Our present circumstances will begin to pinch.

*Change means growth. It's a time for celebration, not dread. It means
I am ready to move ahead—that I have "passed" the current test.*

M Y T H O U G H T S F O R T H E D A Y

....

....

....

....

....

....

....

....

SEPTEMBER 26

Why is life so tragic, so like a little strip of pavement over an abyss?
I look down; I feel giddy; I wonder how I am ever to walk to the end.
—VIRGINIA WOOLF

As we look toward the hours ahead, we can be thankful that we need be concerned with only a single day's worth of hours. No more. What may come tomorrow, a decision that might be necessary next week, a big change in our lives coming next year, all will be handled with ease, when the time is right.

How fortunate we are, those of us who share this program for living! Our worries about the future are over, if we want them to be. We need to take only one step at a time. One day at a time. And always in the care of God. Relief from our lives of worry is immediate when we live the axiom, "Let go and let God."

Life does present us with tragedies, and we learn from them. They need not detour us, however. In fact, they strengthen us and encourage personal growth. And no experience will ever be more than we and our higher power can handle.

I will turn to the program and everything it offers today.
Just today, and no more, is my concern.

MY THOUGHTS 🌸 FOR THE DAY

....

....

....

....

....

....

....

....

The wisdom of all ages and cultures emphasizes the tremendous power our thoughts have over our character and circumstances.
—LIANE CORDES

As we think, so we are." We are gifted with the personal power to make thoughtful choices and thus decide who we are. Our actions and choices combine to create our character, and our character influences the circumstances of our lives.

Our personal mind power will work to our advantage when we think positively, or it will contribute to our disadvantage. Imagining our good fortunes will prepare us for them. Imagining the successful completion of a task heightens and strengthens the commitment we must make daily to it. Imagining the steps necessary to the successful accomplishment of any goal directs our efforts so we don't falter along the way. Our minds work powerfully for our good. And just as powerfully to our detriment, when fears intrude on all our thoughts.

The program has given me positive personal power; it lies in the relationship I have with my higher power. My outlook and attitude toward life reveal the strength of my connection to God. I will work with God and imagine my good fortune today.

M Y   T H O U G H T S   ❀   F O R   T H E   D A Y

....

....

....

....

....

....

....

I can honestly say that I was never affected by the question of the
success of an undertaking. If I felt it was the right thing to do,
I was for it regardless of the possible outcome.
—GOLDA MEIR

Living a principled life is what the inner self desires. It's what God desires. And it's what the healthier ego desires. Living the program's principles is giving each of us practice in living a principled life, one that is free of guilt for our shortcomings.

Having principles assures direction. We need not ponder long how to proceed in any situation, what decision to make regarding any matter, when we are guided by principles. They offer us completeness. They help us define who we are and who we will be, in any turn of events.

As women, particularly as recovering women, we have struggled with self-definition. Often we were as others defined us, or we merely imitated those close by. Sometimes we may slip into old behavior and lose sight of who we are and how we want to live. It's then that the program's principles come immediately to our aid.

There is no doubt about how today should be lived.
I will do it with confidence and joy.

M Y   T H O U G H T S   ❧   F O R   T H E   D A Y

....

....

....

....

....

....

....

Female friendships that work are relationships in which
women help each other to belong to themselves.
—LOUISE BERNIKOW

To have anything worth giving to a friend, we must belong to ourselves. Are we someone we like? Does our behavior agree with our beliefs? Do our friends share our values, and when we are together do we support one another?

If we don't like our own company, we will try to hide our real selves. The more we hide, the further we are running from wholeness and health. We can assess ourselves, calmly and lovingly, so that we can keep on becoming the women we want to be. The more congruent are our behavior and our beliefs, the more we belong to ourselves. The better we like ourselves, the better friends we can be.

The love and sympathy of my women friends can help me in my spiritual
journey toward serenity, and I can help theirs. Today, I will accompany
others on their journey, and thus find company for my own.

M Y   T H O U G H T S   F O R   T H E   D A Y

....

....

....

....

....

....

....

....

SEPTEMBER 30

Birds sing after a storm; why shouldn't people feel as free
to delight in whatever remains to them?
—ROSE FITZGERALD KENNEDY

We choose the lives we lead. We choose sadness or happiness; success or failure; dread or excited anticipation. Whether or not we are conscious of our choices, we are making them every moment.

Accepting full responsibility for our actions is one of the requirements of maturity. Not always the easiest thing to do, but necessary to our further development. An unexpected benefit of accepting our responsibility is that it heightens our awareness of personal power. Our well-being is within our power. Happiness is within our power. Our attitude about any condition, present or future, is within our power, if we take it.

Life is "doing unto us" only what we allow. And it will favor us with whatever we choose. If we look for excitement, we'll find it. We can search out the positive in any experience. All situations present seeds of new understanding, if we are open to them. Our responses to the events around us determine whatever meaning life offers. We are in control of our outlook. And our outlook decides our future.

This day is mine fully, to delight in—or to dread. The decision is always mine.

MY THOUGHTS ❧ FOR THE DAY

October

OCTOBER 1

Women are often caught between conforming to existing standards or role definitions and exploring the promise of new alternatives.
—STANLEE PHELPS AND NANCY AUSTIN

This is a time of exploring for many of us. Recovery means change in habits, change in behavior, change in attitudes. And change is seldom easy. But change we must, if we want to recover successfully.

We do have support for trying our new alternatives. We have support from our groups and our higher power. Perhaps we want a career or more education. Perhaps we want to develop a hobby or try a sport. Sharing that desire and then looking for support guarantees some guidance. This program has given us a chance to start fresh—to become our inner desire.

We are only caught in an old pattern if we assent to it. The going won't always be easy, but support and guidance are available and free if we but look for them.

Today I will consider my alternatives. Do I want to make a change?

M Y   T H O U G H T S   ❦   F O R   T H E   D A Y

....

....

....

....

....

....

....

....

OCTOBER 2

Fortunate are the people whose roots are deep.
—AGNES MEYER

Deep roots offer strength and stability to an organism. They nourish it plentifully. They anchor it when the fierce winds blow. We each are offered the gifts of roots when we give ourselves fully to the program.

We are never going to face, alone, any difficult situation after discovering recovery. Never again need we make any decision in isolation. Help is constant. Guidance through companionship with others and our contacts with God will always be as close as our requests. The program anchors us; every prayer we make, every step we take, nourishes the roots we are developing.

Becoming rooted in the program, with daily attention to the nourishment we need, offers us sanity and hope. We discover that all things can be handled; no situation is too much for us. Strength, confidence, freedom from fear are the benefits of our deepening roots. We will be anchored if we do what needs to be done by us. The program's gifts are ours, only if we work the program.

I won't neglect my roots today. I will nourish them so they in turn can fill me up with confidence when my need is there.

MY THOUGHTS FOR THE DAY

....

....

....

....

....

....

....

*Ambiguity means admitting more than one response to a situation and allowing
yourself to be aware of those contradictory responses. You may want something
and fear it at the same time. You may find it both beautiful and ugly.*
—TRISTINE RAINER

Flexibility is a goal worth the striving. It eases our relations with others, and it stretches
our realm of awareness. Letting go of rigid adherence to what our perceptions were yesterday assures us of heightened understanding of life's variables and lessons.

Being torn between two decisions, feeling ambivalent about them, need not create consternation, though it often does. Hopefully, it will encourage us to pray for direction, and
then to be responsive to the guidance. And we must keep in mind that no decision is ever
wrong. It may lead us astray for a time, but it will also introduce us to uncharted territories
which offer many opportunities for flexibility.

Our contradictory responses, which we may express to others or to ourselves, keep us on
our toes, lend an element of excitement to our lives, and push us to think creatively about
our perceptions. Growth and change are guaranteed.

I will be in tune with myself today. I will let my perceptions guide me.

M Y   T H O U G H T S   ❀   F O R   T H E   D A Y

....

....

....

....

....

....

....

....

OCTOBER 4

If I love with my Spirit, I don't have to think so hard with my head.
—PEGGY CAHN

Love smooths all ruffles. All situations are calmed, all tension is eased. The expression of love is a balm on all wounds, particularly our own. Feeling love toward the people in our lives today will boost our spirits; our personal difficulties will lessen. We'll discover resolution. The answers we've been searching for become known to us when we concentrate less on our problems and more on the gift of love we can give to the travelers we encounter today.

The solutions to our problems are seldom found in our heads. They burst forth from our hearts. We suddenly seem to know what to do. Perhaps someone else's words or behavior will trigger the inspiration we've longed for. We can let our concern today be on the moment and the experience. We can let its power wash over us, and in the wake we'll find the answers we search for.

When we're brittle, cold to others, we close off whatever messages are being directed to us. Our love for others softens us, making it possible for the words and ideas we await to permeate us.

If I am in need today, if I have a problem that wants a solution,
I will reach out to others with love. They'll hand me my answer in return.

MY THOUGHTS FOR THE DAY

OCTOBER 5

Sometimes I think I'm the luckiest person in the world. There's nothing better than having work you really care about. Sometimes I think my greatest problem is lack of confidence. I'm scared, and I think that's healthy.
—JANE FONDA

We each vacillate between feeling confident on some days, lucky on others, and yet frequently scared on others. It's very human to vacillate. We need not be anxious because our emotions refuse to stand still.

Changing emotions are part of the process of normal living. And changing emotions reflect an involvement with the moment. Situations do touch us, as they should. They do invite responses, as they should. And our responses will reveal our emotional involvement, as they should. We can cherish the variety of our emotions. They enrich us. But they may also create problems, if they go unchecked.

We need to maintain a balance. Confidence, certainly desirable, can become overconfidence and thus complacency. Confidence needs humility to temper it. Fear makes us cautious, and that's good; but too much can immobilize us. Being in charge of our emotions makes them work for us.

Emotions can energize me and keep me involved with the moment.
They can also control me. It's my decision to be in charge.

M Y   T H O U G H T S   *FOR*   T H E   D A Y

OCTOBER 6

Many people are living in an emotional jail without recognizing it.
—Virginia Satir

Each of us is blessed with an internal guide, a source able to direct our actions if we but acknowledge it. Never are we in doubt for long about what path to take. The courage to take it might not be immediately forthcoming; however, it, too, is one of the gifts with which we've been blessed. Courage is ours for the asking. Right direction is ours for the taking.

Trusting our inner selves takes practice, followed by attention to the results of our risks. Before recovery, many of us passively waited for others to orchestrate our behavior, our feelings, our attitudes. Stepping forward as the leading lady, with our own script in hand, is quite a change, but one we are being coached, daily, to make.

The Steps help us to know who we are. More importantly, they help us become the women we long to be. But most important, they offer us the spiritual strength to risk listening to the message within and the strength to go forth as directed.

Right results, again and again, are elicited by right action.
And my knowledge of the right action is always, and forever, as close as myself.

MY THOUGHTS 🌿 FOR THE DAY

....

....

....

....

....

....

....

....

There is a divine plan of good at work in my life. I will let go and let it unfold.
—RUTH P. FREEDMAN

We are never certain of the full importance or the eventual impact of any single event in our lives. But of one thing we can be sure: Each experience offers something valuable to our overall development. We must not discount the experiences that are long gone. They contributed to all we've achieved at the present. And wherever today takes us will influence what tomorrow will bring.

Perhaps our greatest difficulty as recovering women is not trusting that life is a process and one that promises goodness. That growth and change are guaranteed. That our lives have design, and we're blessed therein. Trusting isn't easy. But we can learn, and we'll discover freedom.

Letting go of the outcome of every experience, focusing instead on our efforts, making them as good as possible, validates our trust in the ultimate goodness of life. Our frustrations diminish when our efforts, only, are our concern. How much easier our days go when we do our work and leave the outcome where it belongs.

I will know a new freedom when I let go and trust that "my plan"
is unfolding as it must. I will do my part, and no more.

MY THOUGHTS FOR THE DAY

....

....

....

....

....

....

....

The great creative power is everything. If you leave out one whole chunk of it,
by making God only masculine, you have to redress the balance.
—MARTHA BOESING

What a blessing, to be part of God! For many of us, invoking God with a male pronoun put an obstacle in the path of our spiritual growth. We felt left out. Worship of something called "He" or "Him" didn't jibe with our spirituality. When we pray, we pray to a spiritual source that includes everything, that leaves nothing out: both sexes, all races, all ages and conditions.

Some of us had no trouble understanding that God is everything, no matter how God is invoked. But whatever our path to spirituality, the Twelve Step program has enriched our understanding. Before we practiced the Twelve Steps, we had allowed ourselves to forget the strength and nurture that are always at hand, and now we are grateful to be reminded that God is with us, within us, and all is well.

One woman says, "When I feel far from God, I ask myself "Who moved?"
God is always there. Today I will pray for the wisdom to
stay close to my spiritual source, the Creator Spirit.

M Y   T H O U G H T S   F O R   T H E   D A Y

OCTOBER 9

When all of the remedies and all of the rhetorical armor have been dropped, the absence of love in our lives is what makes them seem raw and unfinished.
—INGRID BENGIS

Love soothes, encourages, inspires. It enhances our wholeness, both when we give it and when we receive it. Without the expression of love we are severed from our family and friends. It's the bond that strengthens each of us, giving us the courage to tackle what's lying ahead.

We need not wait for someone else's expression of love before giving it. Loving must be unconditional. And when it is, it will be returned tenfold. Loving attracts itself, and it will heal us, soften the hard edges of our lives, and open us up to receive the blessings that others' gratitude will foster.

It's such a simple thing asked of us—to love one another. Unconditional love of our sisters, our lovers, our children breaks down the barriers to our achievements and theirs. Loving frees us to enjoy life. It energizes us and makes all goals attainable. We carry God's message through our love of one another.

I am charged with only one responsibility today:
to love someone dearly and wholly.

MY THOUGHTS ❧ FOR THE DAY

OCTOBER 10

Sometimes it's worse to win a fight than to lose.
—BILLIE HOLIDAY

Our struggles with other people always take their toll on us. They often push us to behavior we're not proud of. They may result in irreparable rifts. They frequently trigger an emotional relapse. No battle is worth the damage to the psyche that nearly any battle can cause. Nonresistance is the safer way to chart our daily course.

Bowing with the wind, flowing with the tide, eases the steps we need to take, the steps that will carry us to our personal fulfillment. Part of the process of our growth is learning to slide past the negative situations that confront us, coming to understand that we are in this life to fulfill a unique purpose. The many barriers that get in our way can strengthen our reliance on God if we'll let them. We need never be thwarted by people or situations. We will profit from taking all experiences in our stride. The course we travel is the one we chart. The progress we make toward our life goals is proportionate to the smoothness of our steps.

I will flow with the tide. It will assuredly move me closer to my destination.

MY THOUGHTS FOR THE DAY

....

....

....

....

....

....

....

....

OCTOBER 11

Be still and listen to the stillness within.
—DARLENE LARSON JENKS

No answer eludes us if we turn to the source of all answers—the stillness within. Prayer accompanied by meditation will always provide the answers we need for the situations facing us. The answers we want are not guaranteed, however. We must trust that we will be directed to take the right steps. Our well-being is assured if we let go of being the one in control and turn our wills over to the care of God, our messenger within.

How comforting to know that all answers are as close as our quiet moments. God never chooses to keep the answers from us. We simply fail to quiet our thoughts long enough to heed them. Our minds race, obsessively, all too often. We jump from one scenario to another, one fear to another, one emotion to another. And each time our thoughts capture a new focus, we push the answer we seek further into the background.

The process is simple, if I want to follow it. The answers await me
if I truly want them. I need only sit quietly and ask God to
offer the guidance I need. And then I will sit quietly some more.

MY THOUGHTS ❧ FOR THE DAY

....

....

....

....

....

....

....

....

OCTOBER 12

. . . there are two entirely opposite attitudes possible in facing the
problems of one's life. One, to try and change the external world,
the other, to try and change oneself.
—JOANNA FIELD

God grant us the courage to change what we can—ourselves. How difficult it is to let go of our struggles to control and change someone else. How frequently we assume that everything would be fine if only someone else would change. All that needs to change is an attitude, our own.

Taking responsibility for improving one's own life is an important step toward emotional health. Blaming another for our circumstances keeps us stuck and offers no hope for improved conditions. Personal power is as available as our decision to use it. And it is bolstered by all the strength we'll ever need. The decision to take our lives in hand will exhilarate us. The decision each day to be thoughtful, prayerful, and wholly responsible for all that we do will nourish our developing selves. Each responsible choice moves us toward our wholeness, strengthening our sense of self, our well-being.

I will change only who I can today: myself.

MY THOUGHTS ❦ FOR THE DAY

....

....

....

....

....

....

....

....

OCTOBER 13

Never turn down a job because you think it's too small;
you don't know where it can lead.
—Julia Morgan

How short is our vision of where an invitation might take us! Any invitation. Of one thing we can be certain, it offers an opportunity for making a choice, which means taking responsibility for who we're becoming. Choice-making is growth-enhancing because it strengthens our awareness of personal power.

Our lives unfold in small measures, just as small as they need to be for our personal comfort. It's doubtful that we could handle everything the future has in store, today; however, we will be prepared for it, measure by measure, choice by choice, day by day. We need not fear; what is meted out to us in the invitations offered is for our benefit. We are on a pathway to goodness.

The thrill of making choices is new to many of us when we enter this program. We'd opted for the passive life, all too often, and we became increasingly aware of, and often depressed by, our self-imposed powerlessness. Free at last! We are free at last to fully participate in our lives.

I will be grateful for the many options to act tugging at me today.
Every choice I make strengthens my womanhood.

MY THOUGHTS ❧ FOR THE DAY

OCTOBER 14

The balance between mind and spirit comes hard for me. The eternal split.
Two entities, perfectly aware and yet perfectly unwilling to cooperate.
—MARY CASEY

The program directs our spiritual growth, a human aspect that had atrophied, if ever it had existed, for most of us before abstinence. And the process of developing our spiritual nature is painstaking. Living by our wits, or the fervent application of "situational analysis," had been our survival tools for months or years.

To return repeatedly to the old tools for quick solutions to serious situations is second nature. Learning to rely on spiritual guidance for solutions and to use it to sharpen our analytical focus takes patience and continual effort.

Within our spiritual realm we find our connection to God. We have been given the wisdom; all the knowledge we need is at our fingertips. The confidence to move ahead and offer our special talent to others comes from our Spirit. We are all that we need to be. Our mind and our Spirits, in concert, can tackle any challenge and succeed.

My mind and my Spirit can become compatible entities with the
development of my trust in each. Knowledge plus courage
can move mountains. I have been given both.

MY THOUGHTS ❧ FOR THE DAY

OCTOBER 15

Character contributes to beauty. It fortifies a woman as her youth fades.
—JACQUELINE BISSET

How common it is for us to be overly concerned with our looks. The culture encourages it through our families, our friends, the media. Many of us anguished over our looks in years past, and the pain of fading youth haunts some even now.

Perhaps it's time for us to take special note of the women we admire for their achievements. We should emulate them, honor them, and celebrate their particular beauty—a beauty generally enhanced by dignity, perseverance, courage.

We can cultivate our special interests. They'll contribute to our achievements, which will add depth to our soul—the home of true beauty. Mature persons who acknowledge this true beauty are those we wish to attract into our lives. How fickle is the beautiful face! And even more fickle is the one who can see no deeper.

Youth and its beauty are fleeting. Not so the beauty of the developing character; time strengthens it. The program makes character development not only possible but simple. Each of the Twelve Steps, any Step, offers us an opportunity to take charge of our lives, right now.

I will remember, it's who I am inside that truly counts in the lives of others.

MY THOUGHTS ❧ FOR THE DAY

....

....

....

....

....

....

....

OCTOBER 16

History provides abundant examples of . . . women whose greatest gift was in redeeming, inspiring, liberating, and nurturing the gifts of others.
—SONYA RUDIKOFF

Part of our calling as members of the human community is to unconditionally love and support the people emotionally close to us. We have been drawn together for purposes wonderful but seldom readily apparent. We need one another's gifts, compassion, and inspiration in order to contribute our individual parts to the whole.

Not only do we need to nurture and to inspire others, but our personal development, emotionally and spiritually, demands that we honor ourselves in like fashion. Self-love, full self-acceptance, is necessary before we can give anything of lasting value to someone else. We must selflessly give to others if, indeed, our love and support are meant to serve, and giving anything selflessly is evidence of healthy self-love.

Selfless love liberates the giver and the recipient. Giving selflessly reveals our personal contentment, and it means we are free to nurture our own gifts.

It's good and right that I should encourage someone else today.
I will pay the same respect to myself, too.

MY THOUGHTS ❧ FOR THE DAY

....

....

....

....

....

....

....

....

OCTOBER 17

Pride, we are told, my children, "goeth before a fall" and oh,
the pride was there, and so the fall was not far away.
—WILHELMINA KEMP JOHNSTONE

Requesting help. Admitting we are wrong. Owning our mistake in either a big or small matter. Asking for another chance or someone's love. All very difficult to do, and yet necessary if we are to grow. The difficulty is our pride, the big ego. We think we need to always be right. If we're wrong, then others may think less of us, look down on us, question our worth. "Perfectionism" versus "worthlessness."

If we are not perfect (and of course we never are), then we must be worthless. In between these two points on the scale is "being human." Our emotional growth, as women, is equal to how readily we accept our humanness, how able we are to be wrong. With humility comes a softness that smooths our every experience, our every relationship. Pride makes us hard, keeps us hard, keeps others away, and sets us up for the fall.

I will let myself be human today. It will soften my vision of life.

MY THOUGHTS FOR THE DAY

....

....

....

....

....

....

....

....

OCTOBER 18

When people bother you in any way, it is because their souls are
trying to get your divine attention and your blessing.
—CATHERINE PONDER

We are in constant communication with one another and, in the spiritual realm, with God. No matter how singular our particular course may appear, our path is running parallel to many paths. And all paths will intersect when the need is present. The point of intersection is the moment when another soul seeks our attention. We can be attentive and loving to the people seeking our attention. Their growth and ours is at stake.

We can be grateful for our involvement with other lives. We can be mindful that our particular blessing is like no one else's and that we all need input from the many significant persons in our lives. There is no insignificant encounter in our passage through life. Each juncture with someone else is part of the destiny of both participants.

I will look carefully and lovingly at the people around me today and bless them,
one and all. They are in my life because they need to be. I, likewise, need them.

MY THOUGHTS ❧ FOR THE DAY

....

....

....

....

....

....

....

....

OCTOBER 19

One of the conclusions I have come to in my old age is the importance of living in the ever-present now. In the past, too often I indulged in the belief that somehow or other tomorrow would be brighter or happier or richer.
—RUTH CASEY

How easily our minds jump from the present to the foibles of the past or our fears about the future. How seldom are our minds on this moment, and only this moment.

Before we picked up this book, where were our thoughts? We need to practice, with diligence, returning our minds to whatever the experience is at hand. A truly creative response to any situation can only be made when we are giving it our undivided attention. And each creative response initiates an even more exciting follow-up experience.

All we have of life, all that it can offer us is here, now. If we close our minds to the present, this present, we'll only continue to do so when the tomorrow we dream of now becomes the present. There are no tomorrows.

I will let go of the past and the future. My only reality is here, now. God's gifts are here, today, right now.

MY THOUGHTS ❧ FOR THE DAY

....

....

....

....

....

....

....

....

. . . You don't get to choose how you're going to die. Or when.
You can only decide how you're going to live. Now.
—JOAN BAEZ

How thrilling to contemplate that we can choose every attitude we have and every action we take. We have been gifted with full responsibility for our development. What will we try today? It's our personal choice. How will we decide on a particular issue? Our options are only limited by our vision.

Every situation in life offers us a significant opportunity for making a decision that will, of necessity, influence the remaining situations we encounter. Just as we are interdependent, needing and influencing one another in all instances that bring us together, likewise our decisions are never inviolate. Each is singly important; however, its impact is multiplied by the variety of other decisions triggered.

The choice is ours for living fully today, for taking advantage of all the opportunities that present themselves. Our personal growth, our emotional and spiritual development, are in our hands. God will provide us with the guidance, and the program offers us the tools. The decision to act is ours, alone.

I will exercise my personal power. My choices determine my development.

M Y   T H O U G H T S   ❧   F O R   T H E   D A Y

....

....

....

....

....

....

....

The strength of the drive determines the force required to suppress it.
—MARY JANE SHERFEY

We are all struggling to succeed. And each day of our lives we'll be confronted with major or minor adversities that might well interfere with our success. Adversities don't have to hinder us, however. They can strengthen us, if we incorporate them as opportunities for growth.

For many of us, the ability to handle adversity is a fairly recent phenomenon. And not always can we do it securely and with ease. But we are coming to believe that a power greater than ourselves is at hand and will guarantee us all the strength we'll ever need. Knowing that action is always possible, that passive acceptance of any condition need never be necessary are unconditional gifts of living the Twelve Step program.

Our path forward is as certain as our commitment to it, our belief in the strength of the program, and our faith that all is well even when times are troubled. No one ever promised that our new way of life would be always easy. But we have been promised that we'll arrive at our proper destination if we do the footwork and let God do the navigating.

Success is at hand. I will apply what I'm learning, and I'll meet it.

M Y   T H O U G H T S ❀ F O R   T H E   D A Y

OCTOBER 22

Children awaken your own sense of self when you see them hurting,
struggling, testing; when you watch their eyes and listen to their hearts.
Children are gifts, if we accept them.
—KATHLEEN TIERNEY CRILLY

Children look to us and their world with fresh eyes, uncynical attitudes, open hearts. They react spontaneously to the events in their lives; what they feel is who they are.

Close observation of children can help us. See how complex we have made our lives! Their simple honesty can serve us well. To look at the world, once again, with wonder, is a by-product offered us when we live the principles of this program.

So many gifts await us when we accept the program and its principles. We dispense with the baggage of the past. We learn to live this day only. And we come to believe that there is a power greater than ourselves that has us and everything in our lives under control. Children instinctively trust those who take care of them. We can learn to trust, once again, when we apply the Steps of this program to our lives.

I will look to this day with wonder and trust. Everything is okay.
I am in the care of a power greater than myself.

MY THOUGHTS ❧ FOR THE DAY

O C T O B E R   2 3

*. . . words are more powerful than perhaps anyone suspects, and once deeply
engraved in a child's mind, they are not easily eradicated.*
—MAY SARTON

How burdened we became, as little girls, with the labels applied by parents, teachers, even school chums. We believe about ourselves what others teach us to believe. The messages aren't always overt. But even the very subtle ones are etched in our minds, and they remind us of our "shortcomings" long into adulthood.

Try as we might to forget the criticisms, the names, they linger in our memories and influence our self-perceptions as adults. The intervening years have done little to erase whatever emotional scars we acquired as children.

Our partnership with God will help us understand that we are spiritual beings with a wonderful purpose in this life. And we are as lovely, as capable, as successful as we perceive ourselves to be. Our own thoughts and words, our own labels can become as powerful as those of our youth. It takes practice to believe in ourselves. But we can break the past's hold on us.

*My higher power will help me know the real me. I am all that I ever needed to be;
I am special, and I will come to believe that.*

M Y   T H O U G H T S   F O R   T H E   D A Y

OCTOBER 24

The universal human yearning [is] for something permanent,
enduring, without shadow of change.
—WILLA CATHER

The specter of change builds dread in most of us. We fear the effects on our personal lives. We lack faith that the impending change will benefit us. Only time can assure us of that. And it will, just as every change we've survived up to now has done.

Changes are gifts, really. They come as hallmarks to our present attainments. They signify successful growth. And they announce our readiness for more growth. How we struggle to understand this, and how quickly we forget it once we have adapted to the change. The struggle is then repeated the next time change visits us.

We long for permanence, believing it guarantees security, not realizing the only real security available to us comes with our trust in God, from whom all change comes as a blessing on the growth we've attained. If we were to experience total lack of change, we'd find death. Life is challenge, continued change, always endurable and growth-enhancing. We can reflect on what's gone before, and trust that which faces us now.

Change means I am progressing, on course.

M Y   T H O U G H T S   &   F O R   T H E   D A Y

....

....

....

....

....

....

....

....

OCTOBER 25

Love has the quality of informing almost everything—even one's work.
—SYLVIA ASHTON-WARNER

We are changed through loving and being loved. Our attitudes are profoundly and positively affected by the presence of love in our lives. Each time we offer a loving response to a friend, co-worker, even a stranger, we powerfully influence the dynamics of the interaction between us.

Every response we make to someone changes us while it informs them. When we treat others with disdain, we invite the same. When we express only criticism of others, our self-assessment is equally negative. The beauty of a loving posture is that it calls forth love in response. The more love we give away, the more we receive.

Any task before us is lessened when we carry love in our hearts. Love is more powerful than fear. Love helps to open the channel to God, assuring us of the strength, the understanding, the patience needed to complete any assignment confronting us.

*I am loved, unconditionally, by God. And I will experience the reality of that
love the more I give it away. Love wants to change me—and it can.*

M Y   T H O U G H T S   *   F O R   T H E   D A Y

....

....

....

....

....

....

....

....

My life has been a tapestry of rich and royal hue,
An everlasting vision of the ever-changing view.
—CAROLE KING

Every event of our lives is contributing a rich thread to our personal tapestry. Each of us is weaving one unique to ourselves, but all of our tapestries are complementary. We need others' rich designs in order to create our own.

We seldom have the foresight to understand the worth, the ultimate value of a particular circumstance at its beginning. But hindsight offers us clarity. It's good to reflect on the many circumstances that failed to thrill us; in all cases we can now see why we needed them. As our trust in God and the goodness of all experiences grow, we'll more quickly respond with gladness when situations are fresh. No experience is meant for harm. We are coming to understand that, even though on occasion we forget.

Practicing gratitude will help us more fully appreciate what has been offered us. Being grateful influences our attitude; it softens our harsh exterior and takes the threat out of most new situations.

If I greet the day, glad to be alive, I will be gladdened by all the experiences in
store for me. Each is making a necessary contribution to my wholeness.

MY THOUGHTS ❧ FOR THE DAY

....

....

....

....

....

....

....

OCTOBER 27

Problems have only the size and the power that you give them.
—S.H.

We will not be free from all difficulties today, or during any period of our lives. But we have the personal power to eliminate the threat, the sting of any challenge. But it's our vision of circumstances that gives them their interpretation.

At this moment, we are defining our experience. We are labeling events good or bad, valuable or meaningless. And our growth, particularly this day, is greatly influenced by the value judgments we attach to our experiences.

As we grow stronger emotionally and spiritually, we learn that all difficulties are truly opportunities for exceptional growth and increased awareness of the truth of existence. All experiences can be taken in stride if we are trustful of their intended blessing.

We are sharing this life, every moment of it, with a power greater than ourselves. We need not worry about any circumstance. Always we are watched over. We never need struggle alone.

We can let go of our problems. It's ourselves and the attitude we have cultivated that make any situation a problem. We can turn it loose and therein discover the solution.

I will not make mountains out of the molehills of my life.

MY   THOUGHTS   FOR   THE   DAY

....

....

....

....

....

....

....

OCTOBER 28

The most elusive knowledge of all is self-knowledge.
—MIRRA KOMAROVSKY

Discovering who we are is an adventure, one that will thrill and sometimes trouble us and will frequently occupy our thoughtful reflections. We are growing and changing as a result of our commitment to the program. And it's that process of commitment that heightens our self-awareness.

We learn who we are by listening to others, by sensing their perceptions of us, by taking an honest, careful inventory of our own behavior. The inner conversations that haunt us while we're interacting with others are poignant guidelines to self-knowledge, self-definition. Just when we think we've figured out who we are and how to handle our flaws, a new challenge will enter our realm of experiences, shaking up all the understandings that have given us guidance heretofore.

It is not an easy task to discover who we really are. It's an even harder job to love and accept the woman we discover. But too many years went by while we avoided or denied or, worse yet, denounced the only person we knew how to be. The program offers us the way to learn about and love fully the person within. Nor will we find the way easy every day. But there's time enough to let the process ease our investigation.

I will be soft and deliberate today as I listen to myself and others.

MY THOUGHTS FOR THE DAY

....

....

....

....

....

....

....

OCTOBER 29

Let your tears come. Let them water your soul.
—EILEEN MAYHEW

Letting down our guard, releasing the tension that keeps us taut, often invites our tears, tears that soften us, melt our resistance, reveal our vulnerability, which reminds us that we are only human. So often we need reminding that we are only human.

Perfectionism may be our bane, as it is for so many of us in this program. We've learned to push, push harder, and even harder yet, not only ourselves but those around us. We must be better, we think, and we tighten our hold on life. The program can teach us to loosen our grip, if we'll let it. The magic is that when we loosen our grip on this day, this activity, this person, we get carried gently along and find that which we struggled to control happening smoothly and naturally. Life is a series of ironies.

We should not hide from our tears. We can trust their need to be present. Perhaps they need to be present for someone else, as well as ourselves. Tears encourage compassion; maybe our assignment in life, today, is to help someone else experience compassion.

My tears will heal. And the wounded are everywhere.

MY THOUGHTS ❀ FOR THE DAY

....

....

....

....

....

....

....

....

OCTOBER 30

Intuition is a spiritual faculty and does not explain, but simply points the way.
—FLORENCE SCOVEL SHINN

Should we make this move? Should we change jobs? Should we talk to others about our feelings? We are seldom short on prayers when we're filled with fear and indecision. We are, however, short on answers. Our worries block them out.

No prayer ever goes unanswered. Of this we can be certain. On the other hand, the answer may not be what we'd hoped for. In fact, we may not recognize it as the answer because we are expecting something quite different. It takes a willingness on our part to be free of our preconceptions—free to accept whatever answers are offered.

Our answers come unexpectedly, a chance meeting on the street, a passage in a book or newspaper, a nagging feeling within. God speaks to each of us throughout the day. Our prayers are answered, our problems find solutions, our worries are eased, if we but attune ourselves to the messages. They are all around.

I will be attentive to all the signs from God today.
Whatever answer I seek is finding its way to me.

MY THOUGHTS FOR THE DAY

OCTOBER 31

It's a simple formula; do your best and somebody might like it.
—DOROTHY BAKER

We're never guaranteed success by others' standards. However, if we do our best according to the standards we think God has in mind, we'll be successful. And from God we'll always receive unconditional love and acceptance.

In the past many of us were haunted by fears that our best wasn't good enough. And not infrequently those fears hindered our performance, thus validating our fears. We can slip back into those immobilizing fears if we don't attend, with vigilance, to the program and its suggestions.

Our higher power will help us do whatever task lies before us. And no task will be ours except those for which we've been readied. Our job is simply to go forth, taking God as our partner, and set about completing the task. We will not falter if we remember where our strength rests, where the guidance lies.

Self-esteem is one of the by-products of a job done with God's help. An additional by-product is that we learn more quickly to rely on God's direction and strength the next time, thus reducing the time we give to fear.

I can be successful today, in every endeavor, if I let God manage my moves.

MY THOUGHTS ❀ FOR THE DAY

....

....

....

....

....

....

....

November

NOVEMBER 1

*For to be a woman is to have interests and duties, raying out in all directions
from the central mother-core, like spokes from the hub of a wheel.*
—ANNE MORROW LINDBERGH

It is sometimes easy to get overwhelmed by our duties, forgetting that our interests fit the scheme of our lives. They are inspired by our lives and flow from them. Our interests round us out; they beckon us to become our better selves.

Our duties have their places as well. In our careers, with our families and friends, we have responsibilities. People need to be able to count on us for our part in completing their particular scheme for life.

Finding the right balance between our duties and our interests takes daily attention. It is perhaps our greatest struggle. Feeling duty-bound is common among women; putting a low value on our interests is a familiar trick we play on ourselves.

We need reminding that our interests will cull out our better, inner selves. We must stretch to become all we are meant to be. Our interests entice us to live up to God's expectations.

*Each day I need to pay heed to interests as well as duties.
I will let no day go by without heeding an interest.*

MY THOUGHTS FOR THE DAY

....

....

....

....

....

....

....

....

NOVEMBER 2

Love and the hope of it are not things one can learn;
they are a part of life's heritage.
—Maria Montessori

Love is a gift we've been given by our Creator. The fact of our existence guarantees that we deserve it. As our recognition of this grows, so does our self-love and our ability to love others.

High self-esteem, stable self-worth were not our legacies before finding this program. We sought both through means which led nowhere. These Steps and our present relationships are providing the substance and direction needed in our lives to discover our worthiness.

Had we understood that we were loved, in all the years of our youth, perhaps we'd not have struggled so in the pain of alienation. We were always at the right hand of God, never apart, loved and watched over. But we didn't recognize the signs. The signs are everywhere present now. Each Step is a constant reminder. Every human contact is a message from God. Any desire we are eager to make manifest is a beckoning from God for growth.

I will look for the signs of my benefactor today. They're present everywhere.

MY THOUGHTS 🌿 FOR THE DAY

NOVEMBER 3

It is the calm after the storm. I feel a rainbow where there once were clouds,
and while my Spirit dances in gratitude,
my mind speculates on the next disaster. Duality.
—MARY CASEY

Our growth as women is contingent on our ability to flow with the dualities, the contradictions inherent in one's lifetime, not only to flow with them but to capitalize on them.

We are not offered a painless existence, but we are offered opportunities for gathering perspective from the painful moments. And our perspectives are cushioned by the principles of the program. The rough edges of life, the storms that whip our very being, are gifts in disguise. We see life anew, when the storm has subsided.

We can enjoy the calm, if that surrounds us today. We deserve the resting periods. They give us a chance to contemplate and make fully our own that which the recent storm brought so forcefully to our attention. We are powerless over the storm's onslaught. But we can gain from it and be assured that the storm gives all the meaning there is in the calm.

I will be glad today for the clouds or the rainbows.
Both are meant for my good. And without both, neither has meaning.

MY THOUGHTS ❧ FOR THE DAY

NOVEMBER 4

Beginnings are apt to be shadowy.
—RACHEL CARSON

When we embark on a new career, open an unfamiliar door, begin a loving relationship, we can seldom see nor can we even anticipate where the experience may take us. At best we can see only what this day brings. We can trust with certainty that we will be safely led through the "shadows."

To make gains in this life we must venture forth to new places, contact new people, chance new experiences. Even though we may be fearful of the new, we must go forward. It's comforting to remember that we never take any step alone. It is our destiny to experience many new beginnings. And a dimension of the growth process is to develop trust that each of these experiences will in time comfort us and offer us the knowledge our inner self awaits. Without the new beginnings we are unable to fulfill the purpose for which we've been created.

No new beginning is more than we can handle. Every new beginning is needed by our developing selves, and we are ready for whatever comes.

I will look to my new beginnings gladly.
They are special to the growth I am now ready for.

M Y T H O U G H T S ❧ F O R T H E D A Y

NOVEMBER 5

Perhaps this very instant is your time . . .
—LOUISE BOGAN

The only lessons that matter for our lives at this time will come to us today. Just as what we needed and were ready for yesterday came yesterday, tomorrow ensures more of the same. Concerning ourselves with any other moment but the present prevents us from responding when "the teacher appears."

In years gone by, we perhaps hung on to yesterday's problems. We may still struggle to hang on to them. Or perhaps we try to see too far ahead. But we are learning that there is a right time for all growth. A right time for all experiences. And the right time may not fit our timetable. What doesn't come our way today, will come when the time is right. Each day we are granted just what is needed. We need not worry about the future. It will offer us whatever rightly comes next, but it can't do so until we have experienced these 24 hours before us.

There is wonder and joy awaiting me, each day. The growth I experience is just what is needed at this time. I am a student, and the teacher will appear.

MY THOUGHTS ❧ FOR THE DAY

NOVEMBER 6

Of course fortune has its part in human affairs,
but conduct is really much more important.
—JEANNE DETOURBEY

Behaving the way we honestly and sincerely believe God wants us to behave eliminates our confusion. When we contribute in a loving manner to the circumstances involving us, we carry God's message; and that's all that's expected of us in this life.

This recovery program has involved us in the affairs of many other people. We are needed to listen, to guide, to sponsor, to suggest. Each time we have an opportunity to make an impact on another person, it's to our benefit, and hers too, to let God direct our conduct.

Too often God's message is missed due to our selfish concerns, but it's never too late to begin listening for it. God is forever at hand, awaiting our recognition. We can be mindful that the ease of our lives is directly proportional to the recognition we offer.

Right conduct is never a mystery to us. We may not always choose to do it, but we never fail to know what should be done.

I will trust my conscience to be my guide every moment.

MY THOUGHTS FOR THE DAY

NOVEMBER 7

. . . we will be victorious if we have not forgotten how to learn.
—Rosa Luxemburg

For most of us the struggle was long, painful and lonely to the place where we are now. But survive we have, and survive we will. The times we thought we could go no further are only dimly recalled. The experiences we were certain would destroy us fit ever so neatly into our book of memories.

We have survived, and the program is offering us the means for continued survival. Step by Step we are learning to handle our problems, build relationships based on honesty, and choose responsible behavior. We are promised serenity if we follow the Steps.

Gratitude for our survival is best expressed by working the program, setting an example for others, helping those women who haven't yet attained victory. We must give away what we have learned to make way for our own new growth. There are many victories in our future if we keep pressing forward, opening new doors, and trusting in the process of the program and its promises.

I am still willing to learn or I wouldn't be here, now.
There are victories in my future. I will look for a victory today.
It's certain to accompany responsible action on my part.

MY THOUGHTS ❦ FOR THE DAY

....

....

....

....

....

....

....

NOVEMBER 8

As in the physical world, so in the spiritual world, pain does not "last forever."
—KATHERINE MANSFIELD

Each of us struggles with pain and its repercussions; some of us more than others. At times pain seems unending. Sometimes we hang on to the pain in our lives, maybe because we fear even more what's on the other side. The unknown so easily controls us. Right at this moment, each of us can look back on other painful times and feel thankful for what they taught us. The puzzle pieces take on a deeper meaning when we enjoy the gift of perspective. The pain at this moment fits, too, in the bigger picture of our lives. And it will pass. It is passing.

The wisdom of the past tells us that pain enriches us, prepares us to better serve others. We come to know who we are and the specialness of our gifts through the despair that at times encumbers us. An old, wise saying is, "We are never given more than we can handle."

My pain today is bringing me closer to the woman I'm meant to be.
With each breath I'll remember that.

MY THOUGHTS ❀ FOR THE DAY

....

....

....

....

....

....

....

....

On any journey, we must find out where we are before we can plan the first step.
—KATHY BOEVINK

Our lives in all aspects are a journey toward a destination, one fitting to our purpose, our special gifts, our particular needs as women. Each day contributes to our journey, carrying us closer to our destination. However, we often take a circuitous route. We get stranded or waylaid by our selfish desires, by the intrusion of our controlling ego.

We can reflect on the progress we've made toward our destination, the steps we've taken that have unknowingly contributed to our journey. Our easiest steps have been the ones we took in partnership with God. It's in God's mind that our path is well marked.

We are just where we need to be today. The experiences that we meet are like points on the map of our journey. Some of them are rest stops. Others resemble high-speed straightaways. The journey to our destination is not always smooth, but the more we let God sit in the driver's seat, the easier will be our ride.

I will plan my journey today with God's help, and my ride will be smooth.

M Y   T H O U G H T S   ❀   F O R   T H E   D A Y

....

....

....

....

....

....

....

....

....

Because society would rather we always wore a pretty face,
women have been trained to cut off anger.
—NANCY FRIDAY

Anger is an emotion. Not a bad one, nor a good one; it simply exists when particular conditions in our lives are not met as we'd hoped.

We can get free of our anger if we choose to take action appropriate to it. Anger can be a healthy prompter of action. But when no action is taken, anger turns inward, negatively influencing our perceptions of all experiences, all human interaction.

We need to befriend all of our emotions. We need to trust that they all can serve us when we befriend them, learn from them, act in healthy concert with them. Our emotions reveal the many faces of our soul. And all are valid, deserving respect and acceptance. They are all representative of the inner self.

Because we are less at home with anger, it becomes more powerful. When we deny it, it doesn't disappear. It surfaces in unrelated circumstances, complicating our lives in unnecessary ways. We can learn to enjoy our anger by celebrating the positive action it prompts. We can cherish the growth that accompanies it, when we take the steps we need to.

It's okay for me to be angry today. It's growthful, if I use it for good.

MY THOUGHTS FOR THE DAY

....

....

....

....

....

....

....

*Life has got to be lived—that's all there is to it. At 70 I would say the advantage
is that you take life more calmly. You know that, "This, too, shall pass!"*
—ELEANOR ROOSEVELT

Wisdom comes with age, but also with maturity. It is knowing that all is well in the midst of a storm. And as our faith grows, as we trust more that there is a power greater than ourselves which will see us through, we can relax, secure that a better time awaits us.

We will come to understand the part a difficult circumstance has played in our lives. Hindsight makes so much clear. The broken marriage, the lost job, the loneliness have all contributed to who we are becoming. The joy of the wisdom we are acquiring is that hindsight comes more quickly. We can, on occasion, begin to accept a difficult situation's contribution to our wholeness while caught in the turmoil.

How far we have come! So seldom do we stay caught, really trapped, in the fear of misunderstanding. Life must teach us all we need to know. We can make the way easier by stretching our trust—by knowing fully that the pain of the present will open the way to the serenity of the future.

I know that this too shall pass.

M Y T H O U G H T S FOR T H E D A Y

....

....

....

....

....

....

....

....

NOVEMBER 12

Fantasies are more than substitutes for unpleasant reality; they are also dress rehearsals, plans. All acts performed in the world begin in the imagination.
—Barbara Grizzuti Harrison

Our minds mold who we become. Our thoughts not only contribute to our achievements, they determine the posture of our lives. How very powerful they are. Fortunately, we have the power to think the thoughts we choose, which means our lives will unfold much as we expect.

The seeds we plant in our minds indicate the directions we'll explore in our development. And we won't explore areas we've never given attention to in our reflective moments. We must dare to dream extravagant, improbable dreams if we intend to find a new direction, and the steps necessary to it.

We will not achieve, we will not master that which goes unplanned in our dream world. We imagine first, and then we conceive the execution of a plan. Our minds prepare us for success. They can also prepare us for failure if we let our thoughts become negative.

I can succeed with my fondest hopes. But I must believe in my potential for success. I will ponder the positive today.

MY THOUGHTS ❀ FOR THE DAY

NOVEMBER 13

My Declaration of Self-Esteem:
I am me. In all the world there is no one else exactly like me. There are persons
who have some parts like me, but no one adds up exactly like me. Therefore,
everything that comes out of me is authentically mine because I alone chose it.
—Virginia Satir

Feeling special, feeling worthy and unique in the contribution we make to our surroundings is perhaps not a very familiar feeling to many of us in this recovery program. We may have recognized our differences from others, but not in a positive way. We may well have figured that to be our problem. "If only I were more like her . . ." To celebrate our specialness, the unique contribution we make to every situation we experience, is one of the gifts of recovery.

It's spiritually moving to realize the truth of our authenticity. To realize that no other choice will ever be just like our choice—to realize that no other contribution will be just like our contribution. Our gift to life is ourselves. Life's gift to us is the opportunity to realize our value.

Today, I will be aware of my gifts, I will offer them and receive them thankfully.

M Y   T H O U G H T S   F O R   T H E   D A Y

NOVEMBER 14

Pain is inevitable. Suffering is optional.
—Kathleen Casey Theisen

How awesome is our power, personally, to choose our attitudes and our responses to any situation, to every situation. We will feel only how we choose to feel, no matter the circumstance. Happiness is as free an option as sorrow.

Perceiving our challenges as opportunities for positive growth rather than stumbling blocks in our path to success is a choice readily available. What is inevitable—a matter over which we have no choice—is that difficult times, painful experiences will visit us. We can, however, greet them like welcome guests, celebrating their blessings on us and the personal growth they inspire.

No circumstance demands suffering. Every circumstance has a silver lining. In one instance you may choose to feel self-pity; in the next, gladness.

We do not always feel confident about our choices, even when we accept the responsibility for making them. How lucky for us that the program offers a solution! Prayer and meditation, guidance from our higher power, can help us make the right choice every time.

I will relish my freedom to choose, to feel, to act. I and only I can take it away.

MY THOUGHTS ❧ FOR THE DAY

....

....

....

....

....

....

....

....

Zeal is the faculty igniting the other mind powers into the full flame of activity.
—SYLVIA STITT EDWARDS

When enthusiasm is absent in our lives, no activity appears inviting. In fact, most situations foster fear. We're ever so familiar with fear. The program we're committed to relieves us of all fear, when we work it. And it offers us the enthusiasm that will guarantee positive outcomes for our efforts, when we look to our higher power for the right attitude.

An open, trusting, sincere relationship with our higher power equals enthusiasm about life. But that relationship takes work on our part. When we've done our homework we discover that no lesson will baffle us. Prayer and meditation make all things understandable and guarantee that we will "pass the course" on life.

I will begin this day, and every day, looking to God for the gift of zeal to live fully every moment, to give fully what I have to give, and to glory fully in all that I receive. My attitude of gratitude will increase my happiness manyfold. I will look to this day with zeal.

MY THOUGHTS ❀ FOR THE DAY

....

....

....

....

....

....

....

....

....

NOVEMBER 16

Rigidity is prevented most of the time as love and
compassion mesh us into tolerant human beings.
—KAETHE S. CRAWFORD

Looking outward with love, offering it freely to our friends and family, makes fluid, flowing, and fertile our existence. Each expression of love engenders more love, keeping tender our ties to one another, encouraging more ties.

The more flexible our lives, the more easily we'll be attracted to an unexpected opportunity. And flexibility is fostered by a loving posture. As we approach the world, so it greets us. We are not mere recipients of life's trials and tribulations. We find what our eyes are wanting to see. When our focus is rigid and narrow, so are our opportunities.

The Steps are leading us to be freer with our love, more tolerant in our expectations. The level of our compassion, fully felt and fully expressed, is the measure of our emotional health. Rigid attitudes, rigid behavior, rigid expectations of others recede as the level of our emotional health rises. Our approach to life changes and so do the results we meet.

I will love others. It's my only assignment in life,
and it guarantees the security I crave.

MY THOUGHTS FOR THE DAY

I think happiness is like the effect on an audience (when acting), if you think of it all the time you will not get it, you must get lost in the part, lost in your purposes and let the effect be the criterion of your success.
—JOANNA FIELD

Happiness is a gift that accompanies every instance of our lives if we approach each situation with gratitude, knowing that what's offered to us is special to our particular needs. The experiences we meet day to day are honing our Spirit, tempering our hard edges. For these we should offer gratitude.

Our well-being is the gift. Deciding what will make us happy, in fact, what we must have to be happy, prevents us from grasping the unexpected pleasure of the "chance" events of the moment. When we intently look for what we think we need, we may well be blind to more beneficial opportunities God has chosen for us.

Our self-centeredness hinders every breath we take. It prejudices every encounter. It stifles our creative potential. And most of all, it blocks any chance for a spontaneous reaction to the moment. Spontaneity is the breeding ground for creative living. And happiness is the by-product.

Happiness is my decision, every moment.

M Y   T H O U G H T S   FOR   T H E   D A Y

....

....

....

....

....

....

....

NOVEMBER 18

Do not compare yourself with others, for you are a unique and
wonderful creation. Make your own beautiful footprints in the snow.
—BARBARA KIMBALL

Comparisons we make of ourselves to other women do destruction far greater than our conscious minds are aware of. Positioning ourselves or her on the "beloved pedestal" prevents the equality of sisterhood that offers each woman the freedom to be solely herself.

Comparisons in which we are the losers darken the moment, cut us off from the actual rhythms of that moment. The consequences can be grave. Within any moment might be the opportunity we've awaited, the opportunity to achieve a particular dream. We must not miss our opportunities.

Each life is symbolized by a particular set of footprints in the snow. How wonderful and how freeing to know that we each offer something uniquely our own. We need never compete to be noticed. Each of us is guaranteed recognition for what we contribute, because it is offered by us alone.

Envy eats at us; it interferes with all of our interactions. It possesses all of our thoughts, caging us, denying us the freedom to achieve that can be ours.

I will look with love on my sisters. I will free them
and myself to be all we are capable of becoming.

MY THOUGHTS ❧ FOR THE DAY

....

....

....

....

....

....

....

NOVEMBER 19

Experience is a good teacher, but she sends in terrific bills.
—MINNA ANTRIM

It is not by chance but by design that the sorrows we experience throughout our lives are countered by equal servings of joy. One offsets the other. And we are strengthened by their combination.

Our longing for only life's joys is human—also folly. Joy would become insipid if it were our steady diet. Joyful times serve us well as respites from the trying situations that push our growth and development as women.

Laughter softens the cutting edges of the lessons we seek or are cornered by. It offers perspective when the outlook is bleak. And for those of us who are recovering, wallowing in the bleaker times used to be acceptable behavior. But no more. The reality is that each day will present both occasions for anguish and ones inviting easy laughter. Both are valuable. Neither should dominate.

Joy and sorrow are analogous to the ebb and flow of the ocean tide. They are natural rhythms. And we are mellowed by their presence when we accept them as necessary to our very existence.

Any pain today guarantees an equal amount of pleasure,
if I willingly accept them both.

MY THOUGHTS FOR THE DAY

NOVEMBER 20

Continuous effort—not strength or intelligence—is the
key to unlocking our potential.
—LIANE CORDES

Perseverance may well be our greatest asset. As we forge ahead on a project, it loses its power over us. Our confidence and abilities grow in concert with our progress on the project, preparing us to tackle the next one too.

We have something special, uniquely our own to offer in this life. And we also have the potential to offer it successfully. However, we don't always realize our potential. Many of us stifled our development with fears of failure, low self-worth, assumed inadequacies. The past need plague us no longer.

Help is readily available for us to discover our capacities for success. Abilities stand ready to be tapped, goals and projects await our recognition. Any commitment we make to a task that draws our interest will be reinforced by God's commitment to our efforts. We have a partner. Our efforts are always doubled when we make them—truly make them.

I will not back away from a project today.
I will persevere and find completion. I'll feel completed.

M Y   T H O U G H T S   F O R   T H E   D A Y

....

....

....

....

....

....

....

....

NOVEMBER 21

. . . as awareness increases, the need for personal secrecy
almost proportionately decreases.
—CHARLOTTE PAINTER

We hang on to secrets when we're unsure of ourselves and the role we're asked to play—secrets about our inner thoughts, our dreams and aspirations, our feared inadequacies.

Because we strive for perfection, assume it's achievable, and settle for no less in all our activities, we are haunted by our secret fears of not measuring up. The more committed we become to this program, the greater is our understanding of the fallacy of this way of thinking. And as our awareness increases, the more accepting we become of our human frailty, and the less need we have to cover it up. Our mental health is measurable by the openness we offer to the world. Secrets belie good health and heighten the barriers to it.

The program's Fourth and Fifth Steps are the antidotes to being stuck in an unhealthy state of mind. They push us to let go of our secrets, freeing us from the power they wield. Practicing the principles of the program offers the remedy we need for the happiness we deserve.

I will share a secret today and be free of its power over my life.

MY THOUGHTS ❀ FOR THE DAY

NOVEMBER 22

*All of the fantasies in your life will never match those I once
tried to attain. Now older, it's more important reaching
the more realistic goals, and having them come true.*
—DEIDRA SARAULT

Simply knowing that we are important creatures of the universe offers too little security for most of us. We do have a role to play; our talents are special and unique to each of us. Using them in a well-planned manner will benefit us emotionally and spiritually. Others will profit from our talents as well.

Fantasies have their place in our lives, too. They often tempt us to even greater heights. We can't always collar our fantasies, but we can take the necessary steps to realize the goals that our fantasies have birthed.

Recovery is freeing us to achieve those goals we'd only dreamed of or perhaps feared tackling in the past. The defects that we hid behind before are, with patience, giving way to positive behavior. We can accomplish our heart's pure desires. We need not let the fear of failure trap us again as it did so many of us for so long.

*I will set my sights high and trust the program to coach my progress. My goals
are attainable. It only takes one small step at a time.*

MY THOUGHTS ❧ FOR THE DAY

When you send out real love, real love will return to you.
—FLORENCE SCOVEL SHINN

Real love is selfless love. It expects nothing in return. It is not conditional. It doesn't keep score. It is too seldom given. Many of us came into the program hurting, feeling unloved, looking desperately for love, unable to love selflessly. But we are learning.

We are climbing the same mountain, all of us. Our particular paths will cross the paths of many others before reaching the top, where we will find full enlightenment. And any path we cross has a special contribution to make to our own progress. We can be grateful for all intersecting paths, no matter how adverse they seem at the time. We can offer all our fellow travelers real love, and our own trip will benefit manyfold.

We need not be ashamed of our desire for love. Nor need we feel shame that we've bargained for it. But we do need to understand that the kind of love we seek can only be gained when we quit searching for it and simply offer it to all the people in our midst.

I will look into the hearts of all the people I encounter today and offer them love.
I'll receive that which I give.

M Y   T H O U G H T S   ❧   F O R   T H E   D A Y

....

....

....

....

....

....

....

....

NOVEMBER 24

"If onlys" are lonely.
—MORGAN JENNINGS

The circumstances of our lives seldom live up to our expectations or desires. However, in each circumstance we are offered an opportunity for growth or change, a chance for greater understanding of life's heights and pitfalls. Each time we choose to lament what isn't, we close the door on the invitation to a better existence.

We simply don't know just what's best for us. Our vision is limited. Less so today than yesterday, but limited still. The experiences we are offered will fail to satisfy our expectations because we expect so much less than God has planned for us in the days ahead.

We get what we need, in the way of relationships, adventures, joys and sorrows, today and every day. Celebrating what we get and knowing there is good in it eases whatever trial we are undergoing. We are cared for, right now. We need not lament what we think we need. We do have what we need. We will always get what we need, when we need it.

I will breathe deeply and relax. At this moment my every need is being attended to. My life is unfolding exactly as it should.

MY THOUGHTS ❧ FOR THE DAY

....

....

....

....

....

....

....

....

NOVEMBER 25

Change occurs when one becomes what she is,
not when she tries to become what she is not.
—RUTH P. FREEDMAN

Learning self-acceptance, and then loving the selves we are, present perhaps our two biggest hurdles to the attainment of emotional and spiritual health. Fortunately, they are not insurmountable hurdles. The program offers ready assistance.

Women everywhere are making great strides in self-love and self-acceptance. We are learning self-love. And we are changing. The support we can give our sisters, and the support we receive, multiplies many times the healthy energy created—healthy energy that touches us all.

Emotional and spiritual health are gifts promised by the program, when we work it. We must move beyond our perfectionism and relish our humanness, and the Steps are the way. We must learn humility and develop faith, and the Steps are the way. Learning to love all our parts, the qualities we like and the traits that discouragingly hang on, offers a new freedom. A freedom that invites change. A freedom that safeguards the emotional and spiritual well-being that we strive for.

Confidence will come with my healthy self-acceptance.

MY THOUGHTS 🌿 FOR THE DAY

....

....

....

....

....

....

....

We are all held in place by the pressure of the crowd around us.
We must all lean upon others. Let us see that we lean
gracefully and freely and acknowledge their support.
—MARGARET COLLIER GRAHAM

We did not come into this world alone. And our voyage through this life is in concert with many others: some who directly aid us, while others seem to hinder our paths. We don't have full knowledge, however. We can't determine the many ways we are being helped to take the right steps, even by those who block our way for the moment.

Likewise, our presence is helping to pave the way for both the friends and the strangers we will encounter today, at work, on the street, at the meeting perhaps. We have all been charged, in this life, with a similar responsibility—to help one another fulfill our destinies. Our impatience with one another, our wavering love and acceptance of each other, at times our disavowal of our brothers and sisters comes because we fail to understand the necessary part we each play in the drama of one another's life.

In my personal drama, I am sharing the stage with everyone else I encounter
today. I need a supporting cast. And I need applause. I will give it freely today.

M Y T H O U G H T S ❀ F O R T H E D A Y

NOVEMBER 27

Limited expectations yield only limited results.
—SUSAN LAURSON WILLIG

Schoolchildren perform according to the expectations their teachers have of them. Likewise, what we women achieve depends greatly on what we believe about ourselves, and too many of us have too little belief in ourselves. Perhaps we grew up in a negative household or had a nonsupportive marriage. But we contributed, too, in our negative self-assessment. The good news is that it no longer needs to control us.

We can boost our own performance by lifting our own expectations, even in the absence of support from others. It may not be easy, but each of us is capable of changing a negative self-image to a positive one. It takes commitment to the program, a serious relationship with our higher power, and the development of positive, healthy relationships with others.

It's true, we can't control other people in our lives. And we can't absolutely control the outcome of any particular situation. But we can control our own attitudes. Interestingly, when we've begun seeing ourselves as competent and capable, instead of inadequate, we find that other people and other situations become more to our liking, too.

I will be fair with myself. I can do what I need to do wherever I am today.
Only I can hold myself down.

MY THOUGHTS ❧ FOR THE DAY

....

....

....

....

....

....

....

NOVEMBER 28

The idea of God is different in every person.
The joy of my recovery was to find God within me.
—ANGELA L. WOZNIAK

The program promises peace. Day by day, step by step, we move closer to it. Each time we clearly are touched by someone else, and each time we touch another, carries us closer to a realization of God's presence, in others, in ourselves, in all experiences. The search for God is over, just as soon as we realize the Spirit is as close as our thoughts, our breath.

Coming to believe in a greater power brings such relief to us in our daily struggles. And on occasion we still fight for control to be all-powerful ourselves, only to realize that the barriers we confront are of our own making. We are on easy street, just as soon as we choose to let God be our guide in all decisions, large and small.

The program's greatest gift to us is relief from anxiety, the anxiety that so often turned us to booze, or pills, or candy. Relief is felt every time we let go of the problem that's entrapped us and wait for the comfort and guidance God guarantees.

God's help is mine just as quickly as I fully avail myself of it.
I will let go of today's problems.

MY THOUGHTS FOR THE DAY

Faith is like the air in a balloon. If you've got it you're filled.
If you don't, you're empty.
—PEGGY CAHN

Being faith-filled takes effort, not unlike becoming a good writer, tennis player, or pianist. Faith grows within our hearts, but we must devote time to foster this growth. Daily discussions with God are required, frequent quiet times to hear God's messages to us—just as practice on the court hitting balls or sitting for extended periods at the typewriter or a piano are necessary to attain these other goals.

Life's difficulties are eased when we have faith. The most frightening situation, a job interview, an evaluation with our boss, a showdown with a friend, can be handled confidently when we let our faith work for us. But, we must first work for it, work to attain it and work to keep it. Like any skill, it gets rusty with lack of use.

I will make sure to add to my reserves today. We never know when we may need
to let our faith direct our every action. I will make a friend of my higher power,
and that partnership will carry me over any troubled time.

M Y T H O U G H T S F O R T H E D A Y

....

....

....

....

....

....

....

....

NOVEMBER 30

Doubt indulged soon becomes doubt realized.
—FRANCES RIDLEY HAVERGAL

We are powerless over our addictions, whether liquor, pills, people, food. We are powerless over the outcome of all events involving us. And we are powerless over the lives of our friends and family members. We are not powerless, however, over our own attitudes, our own behavior, our own self-image, our own determination, our own commitment to life and this simple program.

Power aplenty we have, but we must exercise it in order to understand its breadth. We'll find all the day's activities, interactions, plans decidedly more exciting when we exercise control over our responses. We don't have to feel or respond except in the way that pleases us. We have total control and we'll find this realization exhilarating.

Our recovery is strengthened each time we determine the proper behavior, choose an action that feels right, take responsibility where it is clearly ours to take. The benefits will startle us and bring us joy.

I will take charge of my life today.

MY THOUGHTS 🌺 FOR THE DAY

....

....

....

....

....

....

....

....

December

DECEMBER 1

And it isn't the thing you do, dear,
It's the thing you leave undone
Which gives you a bit of a heartache
At the setting of the sun.
—MARGARET SANGSTER

A quality we all share, a very human quality, is to expect perfection from ourselves, to expect the impossible in all tasks done. We must rejoice for the good we do. Each time we pat ourselves on the back for a job well done, our confidence grows a little bit more. Recovery is best measured by our emotional and spiritual health, expressed in our apparent confidence and trust in "the process."

We need to recognize and celebrate our strong points, and they'll gain even more strength. Likewise, we need to practice prayer and listening to guidance first to develop our ties to God, but more importantly to be able to acknowledge when help is at hand. We can do all we need to do with God's help.

Having goals but keeping them realistic, for the day or the year, is a sign of emotional health. Not dwelling on those that can't be accomplished, at the moment, is another sign. A change of attitude is all most of us need to move from where we are to a better place emotionally.

There's never a better time than right now for rejoicing over what I've done.

MY THOUGHTS ❀ FOR THE DAY

....

....

....

....

....

....

DECEMBER 2

The old woman I shall become will be quite different from the woman I am now.
Another I is beginning . . .
—GEORGE SAND

Change is constant. And we are always becoming. Each chance, each feeling, each responsibility we commit ourselves to adds to the richness of our womanhood. We are not yesterday's woman, today. Our new awarenesses have brought us beyond her. And we can't go back without knowing, somehow, that she no longer meets the needs of today.

We can look forward to our changes, to the older woman we are becoming. She will have the wisdom that we still lack. She will have learned to live and let live. She will have acquired, through years of experiences, a perspective that lends sanity to all situations.

The lessons we are learning today, the pain that overwhelms us now and again, are nurturing the developing woman within each of us. If only we could accept the lessons and master them. If only we could trust the gift of change that accompanies the pain.

I am becoming. And with the becoming, comes peace. I can sense it today.
I know where I was yesterday.

MY THOUGHTS FOR THE DAY

DECEMBER 3

Sometimes, sisters have the same journey in their hearts. One may help the other or betray her. Will they cross over? Will the ship sail without them?
—LOUISE BERNIKOW

Other women share our struggle. When we treat our women friends as sisters and fellow pilgrims, we find great joy in our mutual help. We pray for the wisdom to let go our feelings of insecurity and rivalry with other women.

Rivalry is not good for us. It leads us to forget our own unique qualities. We each are the best person in the world at one thing: being ourselves. When we compete, we need to retain a balanced perspective and to think well of ourselves whether we win or lose. We run the best race we can; therefore, let us not regard other women as rivals. They are our sisters, and they, too, are doing the best they can.

Today, I will pray for the serenity that will let me see when my sisters have the same journey in their hearts as I.

MY THOUGHTS ❀ FOR THE DAY

....

....

....

....

....

....

....

....

DECEMBER 4

I want to feel myself part of things, of the great drift and swirl; not cut off,
missing things, like being sent to bed early as a child.
—JOANNA FIELD

Feeling apart from the action and always looking on; wanting attention, and yet afraid of being noticed; no doubt these are familiar memories to most of us. We may still struggle with our self-perception, but we can celebrate that we no longer drown our moods. Connecting with the people next to us, though difficult, is no longer impossible when we rely on the program.

There is a way to be a part of the action, a way that never fails. It takes only a small effort, really. We can simply look, with love, at someone nearby today and extend our hearts in honest attention. When we make someone else feel special, we'll become special too.

Recovery can help each of us move beyond the boundaries of our own ego. Trusting that our lives are in the loving care of God, however we understand God, relieves us of the need for self-centeredness. We can let go of ourselves now that God is in charge, and we'll discover that we have joined the action.

I will open my heart, and I'll be joined to all that's around me.

MY THOUGHTS 🌿 FOR THE DAY

....

....

....

....

....

....

....

....

DECEMBER 5

It is a long baptism into the seas of humankind, my daughter.
Better immersion than to live untouched.
—TILLIE OLSEN

We have each had days when we preferred hiding under the covers, avoiding life at all costs. And in times gone by, we did just that, sometimes too frequently. What we didn't always know, and what we still forget on occasion, is that we have a ready and willing partner who will join us in every pursuit.

The more fully we commit ourselves to one another and to all our experience, the closer we will come to the very serenity we long for. Serenity accompanies our increasing understanding of life's many mysteries. It's easy to cheat ourselves out of the prizes any day offers us. Fear fosters inertia, leaving us separate, alone, even more afraid. But we have an appointment with life. And our appointment will bring us to the place of full understanding, the place where we'll be certain, forever after, that all is well. And that life is good.

Today's appointments are part of the bigger plan for my life.
I will face them, enjoy them, and reap their rewards.

MY THOUGHTS FOR THE DAY

....

....

....

....

....

....

....

DECEMBER 6

Each day provides its own gifts.
—RUTH P. FREEDMAN

We are guaranteed experiences that are absolutely right for us today. We are progressing on schedule. Even when our personal hopes are unmet, we are given the necessary opportunities for achieving those goals that complement our unique destinies.

Today is full of special surprises, and we will be the recipient of the ones which are sent to help us grow—in all the ways necessary for our continued recovery. We might not consider every experience a gift at this time. But hindsight will offer the clarity lacking at the moment, just as it has done in many instances that have gone before.

We are only offered part of our personal drama each day. But we can trust our lives to have many scenes, many acts, points of climax, and a conclusion. Each of us tells a story with our lives, one different from all other stories and yet necessary to the telling of many other stories too. The days ahead will help us tell our story. Our interactions with others will influence our outcomes and theirs. We can trust the drama and give fully to our roles.

Every day is a gift exchange. I give, and I will receive.

MY THOUGHTS FOR THE DAY

....

....

....

....

....

....

....

....

*Promises that you make to yourself are often like the
Japanese plum tree—they bear no fruit.*
—FRANCES MARION

The resolve to fulfill commitments we make to ourselves and others may be lacking until we learn to rely on the wisdom and strength offered by our higher power—strength that will make us confident in any situation; wisdom that will ensure our right actions. What is difficult alone is always eased in partnership.

We promise ourselves changed behavior, new habits, perhaps, or a positive attitude. But then we proceed to focus on our liabilities, giving them even more power, a greater hold over us. We can practice our assets, and they'll foster the promises we want to keep.

No longer need we shame ourselves about unfulfilled promises. Whatever our desires, whatever our commitments, if for the good of others and ourselves, they will come to fruition. We can ask for direction. We can ask for resolve, and each worthy hope and unrealized promise will become reality.

*My assets, when strengthened through use, pave the way for God's help. Any
promise can bear fruit when I make it in partnership with God.*

MY THOUGHTS ❧ FOR THE DAY

....

....

....

....

....

....

....

DECEMBER 8

I have found that sitting in a place where you
have never sat before can be inspiring.
—DODIE SMITH

Repeatedly, today and every day, we will be in new situations, new settings with old friends, and old settings and situations with new friends. Each instance is fresh, unlike all the times before. And inspiration can accompany each moment, if we but recognize how special it is.

"We will never pass this way again," so the song says, which heightens the meaning of each encounter, every experience. Acknowledging that something can be gained each step along the way invites inspiration.

Inspiration moves us to new heights. We will be called to step beyond our present boundaries. Maybe today. Whenever the inspiration catches our attention, we can trust its invitation; we are ready for the challenge it offers. We need not let our narrow, personal expectations of an experience, a new situation perhaps, prevent us from being open to all the dynamic possibilities it offers.

I must be willing to let my whole self be moved, inspired. I must be willing to
let each moment I experience be the only moment getting my attention.

MY THOUGHTS 🌼 FOR THE DAY

....

....

....

....

....

....

....

DECEMBER 9

*To do nothing is failure. To try, and in the trying you make
some mistakes and then you make some positive changes as
a result of those mistakes, is to learn and to grow and to blossom.*
—DARLENE LARSON JENKS

Life is a process, one that is continuously changing. And with each change, we are offered unexpected opportunities for growth. Change is what fosters our development as women. It encourages us to risk new behavior and may even result in some mistakes. Fortunately, no mistakes can seriously hinder us. In fact, most mistakes give us an additional opportunity to learn.

Where we stand today is far removed from our position last year, or even last week. Each and every moment offers us new input that influences any decision from this moment forward. The process that we're participating in guarantees our growth as long as we remain conscious of our opportunities and willingly respond to them. We can be glad that the life process is, in fact, never static, always moving, always inviting us to participate fully.

I will have the courage to make a mistake today. It's a promise of growth.

MY THOUGHTS ❧ FOR THE DAY

....

....

....

....

....

....

....

....

DECEMBER 10

*The forgiving state of mind is a magnetic power for attracting good. No good
thing can be withheld from the forgiving state of mind.*
—CATHERINE PONDER

Forgiveness fosters humility, which invites gratitude. And gratitude blesses us; it makes manifest greater happiness. The more grateful we feel for all aspects of our lives, the greater will be our rewards. We don't recognize the goodness of our lives until we practice gratitude. And gratitude comes easiest when we're in a forgiving state of mind.

Forgiveness should be an ongoing process. Attention to it daily will ease our relationships with others and encourage greater self-love. First on our list for forgiveness should be ourselves. Daily, we heap recriminations upon ourselves. And our lack of self-love hinders our ability to love others, which in turn affects our treatment of them. We've come full circle—and forgiveness is in order. It can free us. It will change our perceptions of life's events, and it promises greater happiness.

*The forgiving heart is magical. My whole life will undergo
a dynamic change when I develop a forgiving heart.*

MY THOUGHTS FOR THE DAY

....

....

....

....

....

....

....

....

DECEMBER 11

Occupation is essential.
—VIRGINIA WOOLF

Having desires, setting goals, and achieving them are necessary to our fulfillment. There is purpose to our lives, even when we can't clearly see our direction, even when we doubt our abilities to contribute. Let us continue to respond to our opportunities.

Many of us experienced the clouds of inaction in earlier periods . . . waiting, waiting, waiting, hoping our circumstances would change, even praying they would, but taking no responsibility for changing what was in our power. Inaction caged us. Stripped of power, life held little or no meaning. However, we've been given another chance. The program has changed our lives. We have a reason for living, each day, even the days we feel hopeless and worthless.

Maybe we are without a goal at this time. Perhaps the guidance is not catching our attention. We can become quiet with ourselves and let our daydreams act as indicators. We have something essential to do, and we are being given all the chances we'll need to fulfill our purpose. We can trust in our worth, our necessity to others.

I will remember, the program came to me. I must have a part to play.
I will look and listen for my opportunities today.

MY THOUGHTS ❧ FOR THE DAY

....

....

....

....

....

....

....

DECEMBER 12

If I am to be remembered, I hope it is for the honesty I try to demonstrate, the patience I try to live by, and the compassion I feel for others.
—JoAnn Reed

Each of us hopes we are leaving a lasting, positive impression on those we befriend and maybe even those we encounter by chance. Having others speak well of us provides the strokes that are often necessary to our "keeping on" when difficulties surface. What we sometimes forget is that we are responsible for whatever lasting impression we leave. Our behavior does influence what another person carries away from our mutual experience.

We may have left unfavorable impressions during our using days. On occasion, we do yet. However, it's progress, not perfection, we're after. And each day we begin anew, with a clear slate and fresh opportunities to spread good cheer, to treat others with love and respect, to face head-on and with full honesty all situations drawing our attention and participation.

As I look forward to the hours ahead, I will remember that I control my actions toward others. If I want to be remembered fondly, I must treat each person so.

MY THOUGHTS ✿ FOR THE DAY

DECEMBER 13

Across the fields I can see the radiance of your smile and
I know in my heart you are there. But the anguish
I am feeling makes the distance so very far to cross.
—DEIDRA SARAULT

Looking down the hallway of our lives, we sense many uncomfortable corners. And they are there. But through the discomfort comes the ease of understanding. The security that we long for, we discover has been ours all along. All we needed to do was move into the corner—with trust.

As we stand before any problems, any new task, any unfamiliar environment, dread may overwhelm us. We stand there alone. But the choice available to us now and always is to invite the spirit of God to share the space we're in. In concert with God's Spirit, no problem or task can be greater than our combined abilities to handle it.

Our lives will be eased in direct proportion to our faith that God is there, caring for our every concern, putting before us the experiences we need to grow on. We can let go of our anguish, our doubts and fears. Eternal triumph is ours for the asking.

The smiling faces I encounter today—I will let them assure me that all is well.

MY THOUGHTS FOR THE DAY

....

....

....

....

....

....

....

....

DECEMBER 14

A theme may seem to have been put aside, but it keeps returning—the same thing modulated, somewhat changed in form.
—MURIEL RUKEYSER

No struggle we have is really new. It's another shade of the struggle that plagued us last week or perhaps last year. And we'll stumble again and again until we learn to quit struggling. The trying situations at work, or the personality type that irritates us, will always exist. But when we've come to accept as good and growth-enhancing all situations and all persons, we'll sense the subtle absence of struggle. We'll realize that the person we couldn't tolerate has become a friend. The situation we couldn't handle is resolved, forever.

The lessons we need to learn keep presenting themselves, until we've finished the homework. If we sense a struggle today, we can look at it as an assignment, one that is meant for our growth. We can remember that our struggles represent our opportunities to grow. Fortunately, the program has given us a tutor. We have a willing teacher to help us. We need to move on, to be open to other assignments. No problem will be too much for us to handle.

I will enjoy my role as student today. I will be grateful for all opportunities to grow. They make possible my very special contribution in this life.

MY THOUGHTS 🌺 FOR THE DAY

....

....

....

....

....

....

....

....

DECEMBER 15

Happiness is a form of freedom, and of all people I should be the freest.
I've earned this happiness and this freedom.
—ANGELA L. WOZNIAK

Life is a process, and we are progressing beautifully. We are no longer abusing our bodies and minds with drugs. We are taking special time, daily, to look for guidance. We are working the Steps of the program, better and better as the abstinent days add up. We are free from past behaviors. And we can be free from our negative attitudes too.

Making a decision to look for the good in our experiences and in our friends and acquaintances frees us from so much frustration. It ushers in happiness, not only for us but for the others we are treating agreeably. Happiness is a by-product of living the right kind of life.

We can take a moment today, each time an action is called for, to consider our response. The one that squares with our inner selves and feels good is the right one. Happiness will accompany it.

Happiness is always within my power. My attitude is at the helm.

MY THOUGHTS 🌿 FOR THE DAY

....

....

....

....

....

....

....

....

....

DECEMBER 16

To have someone who brings out the colors of life and whose
very presence offers tranquility and contentment enriches my
being and makes me grateful for the opportunity to share.
—KATHLEEN TIERNEY CRILLY

Loneliness and isolation are familiar states to most of us. We often protected our insecurities by hiding out, believing that we'd survive if others didn't know who we really were. But we discovered that our insecurities multiplied. The remedy is people—talking to people, exposing our insecurities to them, risking, risking, risking.

Sharing our mutual vulnerabilities helps us see how fully alike we are. Our most hated shortcoming is not unique, and that brings relief. It's so easy to feel utterly shamed in isolation. Hearing another woman say "I understand. I struggle with jealousy too," lifts the shame, the dread, the burden of silence. The program has taught us that secrets make us sick, and the longer we protect them, the greater are our struggles.

The program promises fulfillment, serenity, achievement when we willingly share our lives. Each day we can lighten our burdens and help another lighten hers, too.

I will be alert today to the needs of others.
I will risk sharing. I will be a purveyor of tranquility.

MY THOUGHTS ❧ FOR THE DAY

DECEMBER 17

Give to the world the best you have, and the best will come back to you.
—MADELINE BRIDGE

We do reap, in some measure, at some time, what we sow. Our respect for others will result in kind. Our love expressed will return tenfold. The kindness we greet others with will ease their relations with us. We get from others what we give, if not at this time and place, at another. We can be certain that our best efforts toward others do not go unnoticed. And we can measure our due by what we give.

A major element of our recovery is the focus we place on our behavior, the seriousness with which we tackle our inventories. We can look at ourselves and how we reach out and act toward others; it is a far cry from where we were before entering this program. Most of us obsessed on "What he did to me," or "What she said." And then returned their actions in kind.

How thrilling is the knowledge that we can invite loving behavior by giving it! We have a great deal of control over the ebb and flow of our lives. In every instance we can control our behavior. Thus never should we be surprised about the conditions of our lives.

What goes around comes around.
I will look for the opportunities to be kind and feel the results.

MY THOUGHTS ✿ FOR THE DAY

....

....

....

....

....

....

....

Destruction. Crashing realities exploding in imperfect landings. Ouch. It's my heart that's breaking, for these have been my fantasies and my world.
—MARY CASEY

We frequently aren't given what we want—whether it's a particular job, a certain relationship, a special talent. But we are always given exactly what we need at the moment. None of us can see what tomorrow is designed to bring, and our fantasies are always tied to a future moment. Our fantasies seldom correlate with the real conditions that are necessary to our continued spiritual growth.

Fantasies are purposeful. They give us goals to strive for, directions to move in. They are never as farsighted as the goals our higher power has in store for us, though. We have far greater gifts than we are aware of, and we are being pushed to develop them at the very times when it seems our world is crashing down.

We can cherish our fantasies—but let them go. Our real purpose in life far exceeds our fondest dreams. The Steps have given us the tools to make God's plan for us a reality.

How limited is my vision, my dreams. If one of mine is dashed today,
I will rest assured that an even better one will present itself, if I but let it.

M Y   T H O U G H T S   ❦   F O R   T H E   D A Y

....

....

....

....

....

....

....

....

DECEMBER 19

My singing is very therapeutic. For three hours I have
no troubles—I know how it's all going to come out.
—BEVERLY SILLS

Have we each found an activity that takes us outside of ourselves? An activity that gives us a place to focus our attention? Being self-centered and focused on ourselves accompanies the illness we're struggling to recover from. The decision to quit being preoccupied with ourselves, our own struggles with life, is not easy to maintain. But when we have an activity that excites us, on which we periodically concentrate our attention, we are strengthened. And the more we get outside of ourselves, the more aware we become that all is well.

It seems our struggles are intensified as women. So often we face difficult situations at work and with children, alone. The preoccupation with our problems exaggerates them. And the vicious cycle entraps us. However, we don't have to stay trapped. We can pursue a hobby. We can take a class, join a health club. We can dare to follow whatever our desire— to try something new. We need to experience freedom from the inner turmoil in order to know that we deserve even more freedom.

Emotional health is just around the corner.
I will turn my attention to the world outside myself.

MY THOUGHTS FOR THE DAY

....

....

....

....

....

....

....

DECEMBER 20

Somewhere along the line of development we discover what we really are,
and then we make our real decision for which we are responsible.
Make that decision primarily for yourself because you can never really
live anyone else's life, not even your own child's. The influence you
exert is through your own life and what you become yourself.
—ELEANOR ROOSEVELT

Taking full responsibility for who we are, choosing friends, making plans for personal achievement, consciously deciding day by day where we want to go with our lives, ushers in adventure such as we've never known. For many of us, months and years were wasted while we passively hid from life in alcohol, drugs, food, other people. But we are breathing new life today.

Recovery offers us, daily, the opportunity to participate in the adventure of life. It offers us the opportunity to share our talents, our special gifts with those with whom we share moments of time.

We are becoming, every moment of time. As are our friends. Discovering who and what we really are, alone and with one another within our experiences, is worthy of celebration.

I will congratulate myself and others today.

MY THOUGHTS ✿ FOR THE DAY

....

....

....

....

....

....

....

DECEMBER 21

Every person is responsible for all the good within the
scope of her abilities, and no more . . .
—GAIL HAMILTON

We have been given the gift of life. Our recovery validates that fact. Our pleasure with that gift is best expressed by the fullness with which we greet and live life. We need not back off from the invitations our experiences offer. Each one of them gives us a chance, a bit different from all other chances, to fulfill part of our purpose in the lives of others.

It has been said that the most prayerful life is the one most actively lived. Full encounter with each moment is evidence of our trust in the now and thus our trust in our higher power. When we fear what may come or worry over what has gone before, we're not trusting in God. Growth in the program will help us remember that fact, thus releasing us to participate more actively in the special circumstances of our lives.

When we look around us today, we know that the persons in our midst need our best, and they're not there by accident but by Divine appointment. We can offer them the best we have—acceptance, love, support, our prayers, and we can know that is God's plan for our lives and theirs.

I will celebrate my opportunities for goodness today. They'll bless me in turn.

MY THOUGHTS FOR THE DAY

DECEMBER 22

When action grows unprofitable, gather information;
when information grows unprofitable, sleep.
—URSULA K. LEGUIN

Sometimes we need to turn away from what's troubling us. Turn it over, says the Third Step. Hanging onto a situation for which no solution is immediately apparent only exaggerates the situation. It is often said the solution to any problem lies within it. However, turning the problem over and over in our minds keeps our attention on the outer appearance, not the inner solution.

Rest, meditation, quiet attention to other matters, other persons, opens the way for God to reveal the solution. Every problem can be resolved. And no answer is ever withheld for long. We need to be open to it, though. We need to step away from our ego, outside of the problem and then listen fully to the words of friends, to the words that rise from our own hearts. Too much thinking, incessant analyzing, will keep any problem a problem.

I will rest from my thoughts. I will give my attention wholly to the present.
Therein will come the solution, and when least expected.

MY THOUGHTS FOR THE DAY

DECEMBER 23

. . . The present enshrines the past.
—SIMONE DE BEAUVOIR

Each of our lives is a multitude of interconnecting pieces, not unlike a mosaic. What has gone before, what will come today, are at once and always entwined. The past has done its part, never to be erased. The present is always a composite.

In months and years gone by, perhaps we anticipated the days with dread. Fearing the worst, often we found it; we generally find that which we fear. But we can influence the mosaic our experiences create. The contribution today makes to our mosaic can lighten its shade, can heighten its contrast, can make bold its design.

What faces us today? A job we enjoy or one we fear? Growing pains of our children? Loneliness? How we move through the minutes, the hours, influences our perception of future minutes and hours.

No moment is inviolate. Every moment is part of the whole that we are creating. We are artists. We create our present from influences of our past.

I will go forth today; I will anticipate goodness.
I will create the kind of moments that will add beauty to my mosaic.

MY THOUGHTS FOR THE DAY

....

....

....

....

....

....

....

....

DECEMBER 24

Follow your dream . . .
if you stumble, don't stop
and lose sight of your goal,
press on to the top.
For only on top
Can we see the whole view
—AMANDA BRADLEY

Today, we can, each of us, look back on our lives and get a glimmering of why something happened and how it fit into the larger mosaic of our lives. And this will continue to be true for us. We have stumbled. We will stumble. And we learn about ourselves, about what makes us stumble and about the methods of picking ourselves up.

Life is a process, a learning process that needs those stumbles to increase our awareness of the steps we need to take to find our dream at the top. None of us could realize the part our stumbling played in the past. But now we see. When we fall, we need to trust that, as before, our falls are "up," not down.

I will see the whole view in time. I see part of it daily.
My mosaic is right and good and needs my stumbles.

MY THOUGHTS ✿ FOR THE DAY

DECEMBER 25

What we suffer, what we endure . . . is done by us, as individuals, in private.
—LOUISE BOGAN

Empathy we can give. Empathy we can find, and it comforts. But our pain, the depth of it, can never be wholly shared, fully understood, actually realized by anyone other than ourselves. Alone, each of us comes to terms with our grief, our despair, even our guilt.

Knowing that we are not alone in what we suffer makes the difficulties each of us must face easier. We haven't been singled out, of that we're certain. Remembering that our challenges offer us the lessons we need in the school of life makes them more acceptable. In time, as our recovery progresses, we'll even look eagerly to our challenges as the real exciting opportunities for which we've been created.

Suffering prompts the changes necessary for spiritual growth. It pushes us like no other experience to God—for understanding, for relief, for unwavering security. It's not easy to look upon suffering as a gift. And we need not fully understand it; however, in time, its value in our lives will become clear.

I will not be wary of the challenges today. I will celebrate their part of my growth.

MY THOUGHTS FOR THE DAY

....

....

....

....

....

....

....

....

DECEMBER 26

It is only framed in space that beauty blooms; only in space are events,
and objects and people unique and significant and therefore beautiful.
—ANNE MORROW LINDBERGH

We must look closely, focus intently on the subjects of our attention. Within these subjects is the explanation of life's mysteries. To observe anything closely means we must pull it aside with our minds and fondle it, perhaps. We must let the richness of the object, the person, the event wash over us and savor its memory.

Many of us only now are able to look around ourselves slowly, with care, noting the detail, the brilliant color of life. Each day is an opportunity to observe and absorb the beauty while it blooms.

I will look for beauty today, in myself, and in a friend, and I will find it.

MY THOUGHTS FOR THE DAY

....

....

....

....

....

....

....

....

....

....

DECEMBER 27

One needs something to believe in, something for
which one can have wholehearted enthusiasm.
—HANNAH SENESH

Life offers little, if we sit passively in the midst of activity. Involvement is a prerequisite if we are to grow. For our lives' purposes we need enthusiasm; we need enthusiasm in order to greet the day expectantly. When we look toward the day with anticipation, we are open to all the possibilities for action.

We must respond to our possibilities if we are to mature emotionally and recover spiritually. Idly observing life from the sidelines guarantees no development beyond our present level. We begin to change once we start living up to our commitment to the program, its possibilities and our purpose, and it's that change, many days over, that moves us beyond the negative, passive outlook of days gone by.

The program has offered us something to believe in. We are no longer the women we were. So much more have we become! Each day's worth of recovery carries us closer to fulfilling our purpose in life.

I believe in recovery, my own; when I believe in success, I'll find it.
There is magic in believing.

MY THOUGHTS FOR THE DAY

....

....

....

....

....

....

....

The human heart dares not stay away too long from that which hurt it most.
There is a return journey to anguish that few of us are released from making.
—LILLIAN SMITH

As the sore tooth draws our tongue, so do rejections, affronts, and painful criticisms, both past and present, draw our minds. We court self-pity, both loving and hating it. But we can change this pattern. First we must decide we are ready to do so. The program tells us we must become "entirely ready." And then we must ask to have this shortcoming removed.

The desire to dwell on the injustices of our lives becomes habitual. It takes hours of our time. It influences our perceptions of all other experiences. We have to be willing to replace that time-consuming activity with one that's good and healthy.

We must be prepared for all of life to change. Our overriding self-pity has so tarnished our perceptions that we may never have sensed all the good that life daily offers. How often we see the glass as half-empty rather than half-full!

A new set of experiences awaits me today. And I can perceive them
unfettered by the memories of the painful past. Self-pity need not cage me today.

MY THOUGHTS 🌹 FOR THE DAY

....

....

....

....

....

....

....

....

Kindness and intelligence don't always deliver us from the pitfalls and traps.
There is no way to take the danger out of human relationships.
—BARBARA GRIZZUTI HARRISON

Relationships with other people are necessary to escape loneliness; however, relationships do not guarantee freedom from pain. Nurturing a meaningful relationship with another human being takes patience, even when we don't have any. It takes tolerance, even if we don't feel it. It takes selflessness, at those very moments our own ego is crying for attention.

Yet, we need relationships with others; they inspire us. We learn who we are and who we can become through relationships. They precipitate our accomplishments. Our creativity is encouraged by them, and so is our emotional and spiritual development.

We can look around us, attentively. We can feel blessed, even when it's a negative situation. Every situation is capable of inspiring a positive step forward. Every situation is meant for our good.

There's risk in human relationships, and it's often accompanied by pain.
But I am guaranteed growth, and I will find the happiness
I seek. I will reach out to someone today.

M Y   T H O U G H T S   F O R   T H E   D A Y

And what a delight it is to make friends with someone you have despised!
—COLETTE

What does it mean to say we "despise" someone? Usually it means that we have invested a lot of energy in negative feelings; it means that we have let ourselves care deeply about someone. We would never say we "despised" someone who wasn't important to us. Why have we chosen to let negative feelings occupy so much of our hearts?

Sometimes, in the past, that negative energy became almost an obsession, consuming our time, gnawing at our self-esteem. But in recovery there comes a moment of lightning change; a moment of release from the bonds of obsession. The other person is, after all, just another person—a seeker, like ourselves. And, since we cared enough to devote our time and energies to disliking her, she is probably someone who would be rewarding to know.

Recovery has given us the opportunity to turn over many negative feelings, to discover that "friend" and "enemy" can be two sides of the same person.

Today, I will look into my heart and see whether I am clinging to
obsessive concerns with other people. I will resolve to let them go.

MY THOUGHTS FOR THE DAY

DECEMBER 31

*In the process of growing to spiritual maturity,
we all go through many adolescent stages.*
—MIKI L. BOWEN

Progress, not perfection, is our goal in this recovery program. And many days we'll be haunted by the feeling that we've regressed. We will display old behavior. We will feel unable to change, to go on, to make gains once again. But these periods will pass, and soon progress will be evident again.

We must be wary of our need for perfection. It's this need that makes normal progress seem not good enough. And yet, that's all we're capable of—and all we'll ever need to be capable of. The program, its Steps and the promises offered, provide the tools we have lacked, yet need to use in order to accept ourselves wholly and imperfectly.

Daily attention to our spiritual side will foster the spiritual and emotional health we long for. Prayer and meditation, combined with honest inventory taking, can show us the personal progress needed, the personal progress made. However, we will falter on occasion. We will neglect our program some days. But it won't ever be beyond our reach. *And each day is a new beginning.*

*Today is before me, and I can make progress.
I will begin with a quiet prayer and a moment of meditation.*

MY THOUGHTS 🌿 FOR THE DAY

....

....

....

....

....

....

....

THE TWELVE STEPS OF ALCOHOLICS ANONYMOUS*

1. We admitted we were powerless over alcohol—that our lives
had become unmanageable.

2. Came to believe that a Power greater than ourselves could
restore us to sanity.

3. Made a decision to turn our will and our lives over
to the care of God *as we understood Him.*

4. Made a searching and fearless moral inventory of ourselves.

5. Admitted to God, to ourselves, and to another human being
the exact nature of our wrongs.

6. Were entirely ready to have God remove all these
defects of character.

7. Humbly asked Him to remove our shortcomings.

8. Made a list of all persons we had harmed, and became willing
to make amends to them all.

9. Made direct amends to such people wherever possible,
except when to do so would injure them or others.

10. Continued to take personal inventory and when
we were wrong promptly admitted it.

11. Sought through prayer and meditation to improve our conscious
contact with God *as we understood Him*, praying only for knowledge of
His will for us and the power to carry that out.

12. Having had a spiritual awakening as the result of these steps,
we tried to carry this message to alcoholics, and to
practice these principles in all our affairs.

*The Twelve Steps of AA are taken from *Alcoholics Anonymous*, 3d ed., published by AA World Services, Inc., New York, N.Y., 59–60. Reprinted with permission of AA World Services, Inc. (See editor's note on copyright page.)

INDEX

Hazelden Information and Educational Services is a division of the Hazelden Foundation, a not-for-profit organization. Since 1949, Hazelden has been a leader in promoting the dignity and treatment of people afflicted with the disease of chemical dependency.

The mission of the foundation is to improve the quality of life for individuals, families, and communities by providing a national continuum of information, education, and recovery services that are widely accessible; to advance the field through research and training; and to improve our quality and effectiveness through continuous improvement and innovation.

Stemming from that, the mission of this division is to provide quality information and support to people wherever they may be in their personal journey—from education and early intervention, through treatment and recovery, to personal and spiritual growth.

Although our treatment programs do not necessarily use everything Hazelden publishes, our bibliotherapeutic materials support our mission and the Twelve Step philosophy upon which it is based. We encourage your comments and feedback.

The headquarters of the Hazelden Foundation are in Center City, Minnesota. Additional treatment facilities are located in Chicago, Illinois; New York, New York; Plymouth, Minnesota; St. Paul, Minnesota; and West Palm Beach, Florida. At these sites, we provide a continuum of care for men and women of all ages. Our Plymouth facility is designed specifically for youth and families.

For more information on Hazelden, please call **1-800-257-7800**. Or you may access our World Wide Web site on the Internet at **www.hazelden.org**.